CAPITALIST FAMILY VALUES

CAPITALIST FAMILY VALUES

GENDER, WORK, AND CORPORATE CULTURE AT BOEING

Polly Reed Myers

UNIVERSITY OF NEBRASKA PRESS | LINCOLN AND LONDON

Portions of chapter 2 appeared in "Boeing Aircraft
Company's 'Manpower Campaign' during World
War II," *Pacific Northwest Quarterly* 98, no. 4 (Fall
2007): 183–95. Portions of chapter 4 appeared in
"*Jane Doe v. Boeing Company*: Transsexuality and
Compulsory Gendering in Corporate Capitalism,"
Feminist Studies 36, no. 3 (Fall 2010): 493–517.

Library of Congress
Cataloging-in-Publication Data

Myers, Polly Reed.
Capitalist family values: gender, work, and
corporate culture at Boeing / Polly Reed Myers.
pages   cm
Includes bibliographical references and index.
ISBN 978-0-8032-7869-1 (hardback: alk. paper)
ISBN 978-0-8032-8080-9 (epub)
ISBN 978-0-8032-8081-6 (mobi)
ISBN 978-0-8032-8082-3 (pdf)
1. Boeing Company—History. 2. Corporate
culture—United States—History. 3. Work
environment—United States—History.
4. Capitalism—Social aspects—United
States—History. I. Title.
TL686.B65M84 2015
338.7'62910973—dc23
2015013917

Set in Lyon by L. Auten.
Designed by N. Putens.

For Agnes Elvebak Trulson,
Julia Olsen Elvebak,
and Regin Hanson Elvebak
Tusen Takk

CONTENTS

ILLUSTRATIONS

PREFACE

Finding Women at Boeing

This book began with a single box at the Boeing Historical Archives that was marked "Women at Boeing." In 2000 I had the truly wonderful opportunity to work for a year as an intern at the Boeing Historical Archives. Most visitors to the archives wanted to know about technology and airplane parts, but I was intrigued by the social and cultural history contained in that box, tucked away in other areas of the archives, and embedded in Boeing's history. At the time of my internship, my knowledge of women's employment at Boeing was limited to some rudimentary ideas about Rosie the Riveter, derived mostly from the popular poster and its attendant story. I assumed women had flocked to Boeing during World War II, had patriotically done their duty, and then retreated back to the home. But, as I read through the newspaper articles, company meeting minutes, and oral history interviews contained in the "Women at Boeing" box, this story became more complicated. I found that women had not simply retreated to the home at the war's end, and, rather than serving as a "stop-gap" labor force, women were integral to developments and shifts in company culture during and long after World War II. Yet, as the "Women at Boeing" box revealed, women's stories were not widely or deeply known or fully integrated into the company history contained in the thousands of other archival documents that have preserved company history. I wanted to know more about women's work lives at Boeing. What did it mean to be a woman at Boeing, a company known for male expertise and technology? This book is the rather unexpected result of my effort to answer that question.

Traditionally, women have been positioned apart from technology, both rhetorically and structurally. The historian David Noble argues that technology was "defined from the outset as masculine" and that "the idea of technology became the modern measure of elite masculine identity."[1] Women have been described in both popular culture and in engineering and scientific workforces as "the antithesis of the scientist." Noble describes an ethos of "masculine millenarianism" that was "all at once militaristic, misogynist, monkish, apocalyptic, and transcendent."[2] Certainly Boeing's identity is tied in with images of masculinity and technology. The company's name is synonymous with airplanes, aerospace and military technology, male Boeing CEOs, and Seattle. My focus, however, is on the role of gender in workplace culture at Boeing: the people, work rules, and negotiated and imposed expectations that have shaped both men's and women's experiences. In aviation and aerospace histories corporate culture is regularly defined as the business decisions of CEOs while technology is posited as the driving force behind company decisions. However, that perspective often conflates corporate culture with the leadership of a few select men and leaves out the experiences of women and the role of gender.[3] Scholars have shown how corporate cultures are a negotiated process that involves more than just technology.[4] Studies of gender and sexuality in particular have shown how social and cultural considerations order the workplace.[5] My archival sources have shown me that Boeing's history has as much to reveal about gender and workplace culture as it does economic currents and technological developments. In this book I seek to show how all these things are linked.

When we place women at the center of Boeing's history, it becomes clear how concerns over gender shaped the company's culture and history, as well as the experiences of the employees. Women's history as a field has flourished in recent decades, and recovering women's stories from the archives has revealed how gender has shaped power relations, politics, and work. Yet, as Susan Armitage notes, "The topic of women's work in the Pacific Northwest has yet to be investigated in a systemic way."[6] The Pacific Northwest is a vastly understudied region that deserves more attention than scholars have paid to it, particularly in women's and business history.[7] Similarly, scholars will need to examine the region more fully to gain a better understanding of how gender has shaped women's work in the West. As Susan Lee Johnson notes, after the wave of scholarship on women's and gender history in recent decades, gender should be fully integrated into western history but is not.[8] While this book does not comprehensively address women's work in the West, I take seriously Johnson's call to western historians to "get with the program" and take gender history into full account.[9] Margaret Jacobs concurs and argues that "the field of western women's and gender history has made little impact on the larger field of western history."[10] It is my hope that this work contributes to the larger conversations going on about women's place in the history of work in the West.[11] Beyond the American West, I also seek to engage labor history and studies of workplace organization more broadly.

Studying Boeing's corporate culture, as well as women's and gender history, opened up new questions for me about the relationship between gender and sexuality in corporate capitalism. Boeing's corporate culture relied on heteronormativity, whereby heterosexual norms are assumed to be "normal" and thus taken for granted, which has enforced social hierarchies and an unwritten code of conduct. As Michael Warner notes, heterosexism is so deeply embedded in social institutions and relations that it is rendered invisible: "So much privilege lies in heterosexual culture's exclusive ability to interpret itself as society."[12] Jonathan Ned Katz similarly points out that studying heterosexuality challenges the dominance of heterosexual norms: "We discover that the heterosexual, the normal, and the natural have a history of changing definitions. Studying the history of the term challenges its power."[13] While the concept of heteronormativity has influenced scholars to examine the social, cultural, and political constructions of sexuality, its links to capitalism are less clear. Rosemary Hennessy critiques this "well established convention of segregating the history of sexuality from the history of capitalism."[14] Chrys Ingraham calls on scholars to think more carefully about the ways in which heterosexuality is constructed and empowered and to analyze links between heteronormativity, gender, and capitalist relations; as Ingraham argues, "institutionalized heterosexuality" needs to be understood in connection with the "gender division of labor and the patriarchal relations of production." Ingraham also argues that the "material conditions of capitalist patriarchal societies are more centrally linked to institutionalized heterosexuality than to gender and, moreover, that gender (under the patriarchal arrangements prevailing now) is inextricably bound up with heterosexuality."[15] At Boeing, as at many corporate workplaces, the power of heterosexuality was tied directly to ideas of the patriarchal family, with assumptions that primarily white heterosexual men would assume the status of "head of household," with women assuming lower-paid and supportive roles, much like the assumptions of private family roles.[16]

Although others, particularly those with ties to or investments in Boeing, might disagree, this study is not an effort to portray Boeing, Boeing leaders, or Boeing workers in a negative light or to vilify anyone. I am trying, rather, to understand the larger social processes at play in how ideas about workers' identities shaped workplace relations. Boeing stands as an example of the ways in which corporate cultures can inhibit the opening of workplace opportunities and the complex, and often hidden, factors that shape workplace organization and experiences and employment discrimination. As the work of scholars such as Noble and Hennessy suggest, technology and business, particularly engineering, have long been gendered male and associated with heterosexual privilege within corporate capitalism. A recent study by Anthony Greenwald and Thomas Pettigrew suggests that most employment discrimination operates in implicit ways through "ingroup favoritism" rather than through explicit displays of hostility.[17] Work spaces across the United States are marked by a history of gendered conditions of labor that enable employment discrimination. While Boeing's history is not unique, the archival sources that form the foundation of this book *are* unique. They provide a rare opportunity to delve into the everyday workings of a corporation to see how ordinary interactions both reflected and shaped ideas about gender. As a major American corporation located within the city of Seattle, the Pacific Northwest region, the American West, and the global aerospace industry, Boeing provides an intriguing case for examining workplace culture across many different levels and for enhancing our understanding of how the workplace evolved over the course of the twentieth century. I seek to use Boeing as a means to glean insight into the large-scale capitalist processes that have come to define postwar corporations, especially government contractors.

Although Boeing provides insight into broader business patterns, very little is known about the company, other than the celebratory accounts released by the company or the technological histories written by engineers and those interested in aircraft and aerospace technology.[18] The limited public knowledge about Boeing reflects the challenges of studying postwar corporations. Many studies of business culture are concentrated at the beginning of the twentieth century through the 1930s and chronicle the rise of big business.[19] Post–World War II corporations were very different from their predecessors and are difficult to study because they are larger, have more direct ties to the federal government, and are greater bureaucracies. The aviation industry in particular presents enormous obstacles to scholarship because it relies very heavily on subsidiary manufacturing facilities and government contracts and regulation.[20] In the postwar years the aviation and aerospace industry became increasingly bureaucratic and dependent on national defense spending, thus becoming the "military-industrial complex," to use the term popularized in the postwar era.[21] While there is extensive work on the corporate cultures of aircraft manufacturers and defense industries during World War II, and especially the maintenance of a sexual division of labor, what happened after the war in aviation and aerospace firms remains less clear.[22] While this book provides insight into the operations of one powerful and influential firm, more broadly it offers a path to a better understanding of postwar American business history and the role that gendered expectations play in workplace culture.

It is vital to understand the power of corporate culture if we are to make progress in creating work environments that promote, rather than discourage, equal employment opportunity, equal pay, and a sense of respect and value for all workers. The economist Nancy Folbre points out that, for many, equal opportunity is defined as "the absence of unfair discrimination." She argues that this definition presents equality as a "buoyant cork that, left to itself, would always surface."[23] Equal opportunity, she points out, takes work, commitment, and a sense of collaborative focus. As Estelle Freedman points out, "Even small, unconscious biases can accumulate over time to create major inequalities."[24] It is my hope that this book contributes to a historical documentation of past experiences of inequality, as well as consideration of how workplaces can be organized equitably.

ACKNOWLEDGMENTS

I relied on many people over the years as I worked on this project. I am grateful to Michael Lombardi and Thomas Lubbesmeyer of the Boeing Historical Archives for providing me with an introduction to archival research and Boeing's rich history. Kelby Fletcher, Mary Monschein, and Cindy Lin of the Peterson, Young, and Putra law firm provided vital documentation on the Jane Doe case. I'm grateful to Marilynn Laird for her time and for sharing her experiences. I also want to thank the archivists, librarians, and staff at the University of Washington Libraries Special Collections and the Labor Archives of Washington. I'd also like to thank the Smithsonian National Air and Space Museum Archives, Paul E. Garber Facility; National Archives, Pacific Alaska Region; and Seattle Municipal Archives for their help. The final research for the book was supported by the James W. Scott Research Fellowship Award in 2012–13 from Western Washington University's Heritage Resources, and I'm grateful for the research assistance provided by the Heritage Resources and Center for Pacific Northwest Studies staff, in particular Ruth Steele, Elizabeth Joffrion, Rozlind Koester, Eric Mastor, and Tony Kurtz.

This project began under the guidance of Kathleen Kennedy and Kevin Leonard at Western Washington University. I am grateful to both for the thoughtful mentoring and continuing support and guidance. I also want to thank Tracey Deutsch, Sara Evans, and Kevin Murphy for their mentorship at the University of Minnesota and for having long remained a source of support and guidance. This project is far better for it. Others at the University of Minnesota also influenced this project, so I add thanks to Elaine Tyler May, Barbara Welke, Jennifer Pierce, and David Chang.

I'm grateful to all those who offered their time and patience in reading and commenting on drafts or portions of the manuscript. The Western Association of Women Historians and the Berkshire Conference on the History of Women have been especially welcoming and productive spaces, and I appreciate the helpful commentary I received when presenting at these conferences. Lisa Blee has been a patient and attentive friend and writing partner since graduate school. She read multiple drafts of every chapter, pushed me to clarify and refine my argument and analysis, and offered much-needed support for my career choices. I am lucky to have a writing partner whose research covers the Pacific Northwest and yet who also pushes the boundaries of her research to think beyond the confines of region and discipline. I am grateful also for the friendship of Aeleah Soine and Tovah Bender, who have been constant sources of advice and encouragement.

At the University of Nebraska Press, I am indebted to the two readers of this project. They improved the manuscript considerably and pushed my analysis into new and productive areas. Alicia Christianson has been a wonderful editor; her enthusiasm for this project has been a motivating factor in completing the manuscript. Maggie Boyle, Joeth Zucco, and Maureen Bemko have patiently helped me navigate the final manuscript process.

As I embark on a new position in Integrated Social Sciences and History at the University of Washington, I am grateful to Matthew Sparke, Mel Wensel, Aimee Kelly, Ryan Adams, Stefano Bettani, Frances McCue, Judith Howard, and the Department of History for their collegiality. The chance to be part of this new interdisciplinary project has encouraged me to think more broadly about the wider implications of my research.

Publishing a monograph while raising small children and working at several institutions has not been easy, and I'd like to thank the people who made those conditions easier. The photographs and final preparation of the manuscript were supported by a research grant from Western Washington University, and I'd like to thank Kathleen Kennedy and Tracey Finch for making this grant possible. Several colleagues offered various pieces of advice and encouragement that have helped get this book to the finish line:

Acknowledgments

Kevin Leonard, Amanda Eurich, Andrew Denning, Ricardo Lopez, Sarah Zimmerman, and Johann Neem. At the University of Washington, Hanauer Discretionary Funds from the Department of History made it possible to fund the indexing of the book. I'm grateful for the support of family and friends. I'd like to thank especially my mother, Susan Reed; my sister and brother-in-law, Rachel and Chris Franulovich; and my in-laws, Mona and Terry Myers. I'm grateful to Crissy Floe, Tom Savage, and Sarah Rael for their energy and patience. Matt and Jessica Coleman, Trista Sakuma, Kate Metcalf, Lisa Thomas, Sam and Mattilyn Fraser, and Brenda, Sean, Chase, and Caden Cornett have motivated and supported me in a variety of ways.

Kathleen Kennedy deserves special recognition. At a critical point in this project I considered stopping, but she motivated me to keep going. I hope that I can achieve the generosity in my mentorship and friendship that she has shown me. My spouse, Jason Myers, also deserves accolades. His encouragement, and sense of humor, have been critical. He and our two children, Reed and Rowan, have, above all else, helped me to keep things in perspective.

CAPITALIST FAMILY VALUES

Introduction

The Boeing Family

In November 2013 Boeing leaders presented a labor contract to the International Association of Machinists (IAM) that would have guaranteed that the 777X would be built in the Puget Sound region but that would also have frozen pension benefits, increased health care costs, and cut back on wage increases for new employees. Jeffrey Johnson, president of the Washington State Labor Council, called on Boeing's history of exemplifying a corporate culture based on conceptions of family to explain why union members rejected the proposal. He spoke of "machinist families" with "three generations of workers employed by Boeing" and recalled the power of Boeing's past to shape both present and future expectations: "While Boeing is no longer a family company, the workforce has strong family traditions." Although it seemed company leaders had disentangled themselves from the responsibilities that a familial ordering implied, workers had not. While membership in the Boeing family sometimes meant conflict between workers and managers, and even among workers themselves, it also entailed loyalty and obligation: "It would have been unthinkable for grandparents or parents to sell out younger workers and future workers, many of whom are sons and daughters or nieces and nephews, and prevent them from earning a secure retirement future."[1] Johnson also argued that the vote symbolized workers' efforts to preserve middle-class families, a comment that exposes the economic vulnerability industrial workers feel in the twenty-first century amid the shift to neoliberal capitalist policies. As David Harvey notes, neoliberalism "proposes that human well-being can best be advanced by liberating individual entrepreneurial freedoms and skills within an institutional framework characterized by strong private property rights, free markets, and free trade."[2] In practice this concept has meant loosened corporate regulations and the decline of social and state services and benefits. In this economic environment, job opportunities have declined and workers struggle to retain long-term employment and stable pay and benefits. As this introduction explains, workers' views of recent shifts at Boeing have been shaped by expectations of familialism. The brief company history offered here concludes with an overview of the remaining chapters, which all seek to explain how ideas of a workplace family have shaped the work environment and been challenged over time by social and economic pressures.

Johnson's comments about "family traditions" underscore the weight of familialism as an organizing principle at Boeing. Familialism, or the Boeing "family," encompassed a sense of empowerment and stability, sometimes real and sometimes perceived, derived from a sense of belonging. It is the goal of this book to examine how ideas of a company family were intertwined with the expectations and goals of workers and corporate managers over the course of the twentieth century, with a particular focus on how ideas of gender shaped workplace culture. Boeing's need for a sense of employment stability to combat the unstable cycles of the aerospace industry, and capitalism more broadly, motivated company leaders and managers to search for stability through a corporate culture based on the ideology of familialism. The construction of the Boeing "family" sustained a sense of belonging and stability for some workers, though it also gendered workplace opportunities and expectations in ways that excluded other workers and, in some cases, exacerbated inequalities. Beginning in the 1930s, the focus on familialism led to company traditions that emphasized fraternal relations between white heterosexual men. These traditions faced contradictions and challenges during and after World War II from social rights movements, economic shifts, and changes in labor conditions, especially the increasing number of women entering the paid labor market. For most of the twentieth century, however, Boeing leaders, and some workers, utilized familialism, and in particular the loyalty to company and concern for its welfare that familialism implied, to navigate the unpredictability of

2

the market and workforce structures and the challenges of changing social orders based on race, gender, and sexuality.

Boeing was not unique in shaping corporate culture around ideas of family. References to family and "familial corporate rhetoric" were enormously popular in U.S. businesses and corporations beginning in the early twentieth century.[3] Corporate managers and leaders, and even workers, embraced familial metaphors to describe workplace relations.[4] Familialism was especially linked to industrial labor as corporations grew larger and employers acted to curb the influence of unions and bridge the sudden distance between workers and management.[5] The idea of a corporate family reinforced the idea that workers should have close-knit connections with their coworkers as well as with company managers and leaders and also feel a familial sense of obligation and cooperation. The family metaphor became more prevalent; it was another tool in a series of corporate efforts to provide services and benefits to employees in order to maintain a stable workforce, protect profits, and avoid conflicts with employees, unions, and the federal government.[6] As the authors of the landmark study *Like a Family* note, the family metaphor also offered a way for industrial workers to make sense of their environment and develop strategies for building camaraderie and ethics of care and well-being among workers, even while creating opportunities for "conflict as well as reciprocity."[7]

Family metaphors in all kinds of settings have much to reveal about how labor politics have been negotiated within capitalism. While the home has traditionally been linked with morality, and business and the market with rationality, the family metaphor reflects how home and business are linked.[8] It is the home, and reproductive labor, which (invisibly) upholds capitalist accumulation through patriarchal relations.[9] As Rosemary Hennessy notes, patriarchy "has been necessary to most socioeconomic systems in the world and has been fundamental to capitalism's exploitive human relations." She provides a useful definition of patriarchy as "the structuring of social life—labor, state, and consciousness—such that more social resources and value accrue to men as a group at the expense of women as a group."[10] Evoking traditional family roles can be a way to exert patriarchal power and establish rights that exclude people in significant ways.[11] A number of historians have pointed out that traditional ideas of family suggest an artificial split between public and private worlds.[12] The patriarchal family upholds capitalist power because it retains men's power over women in the home and in the family, undermines worker solidarity by making women and minority men compete for jobs, and does not recognize women's contributions to men's successes and economic advantages in the workplace.[13] Nancy Folbre argues that the wage labor system began to disadvantage women as early as the seventeenth century: "As long as women were assigned primary responsibility for reproductive work, their productive contributions and their collective bargaining power would remain quite limited."[14] Kathi Weeks similarly argues that "the family and its ideology help to obscure the costs of productive labor by privatizing, feminizing, and naturalizing much of the work involved in its reproduction."[15] Since the 1930s, and the origination of Social Security in particular, the breadwinner family model has been upheld in public policy as well as corporate design.[16] As Hennessy points out, patriarchal capitalism is upheld through heterosexuality, which "helps guarantee patriarchal regulation of women's bodies, labor, and desires."[17] At Boeing, a familial sense of belonging was tied to an established hierarchy based on the assumptions and norms of patriarchal capitalism.[18] The Boeing "family" protected a vision of the "ideal worker" as white, male, and heterosexual, even while workers themselves contradicted this identity and social rights movements pursued change and increased rights and recognition for nonmale and nonwhite workers.

The construction of a workplace family at Boeing was a process, cultivated over the course of the twentieth century, in which leaders, managers, and workers negotiated how the company would organize work and the characteristics that would define that work while maintaining the company's stability. As the company grew, the corporate culture changed as new relationships among corporate leaders, managers, unions, and workers were negotiated and sometimes contested. The family metaphor was particularly important at Boeing because the shop-floor "home" was not stable. Federal and commercial contracts were cyclical, which led to volatile employment conditions. The family metaphor at Boeing was a way to try to conceptualize and manage the company's relationship with the federal government. In the mythology of the American family, as the historian Stephanie Coontz demonstrates, the family is seen as a bulwark against the supposed "intrusion" of the federal government. As she argues, however, this image is false because the nuclear family, as celebrated by the image of a mother, father, and children as a solid and independent unit, has never existed: "The strong nuclear family is in large measure a creation of the strong state."[19] Boeing leaders, as well as employees, readily embraced identification with the nuclear family model as a source of comfort and protection against economic and social changes. Company leaders and employees also viewed themselves as an independent company family, a solitary unit that acted with the state but was not determined by it. Ironically, however, it was the state, through federal contracts, that allowed Boeing to develop an identity as a private, independent family company. Boeing, then, like romanticized images of the nuclear family, developed an image of self-reliance, despite being reliant on the region, the state, and the federal government.[20]

The company's corporate culture upheld the Boeing "family." Boeing's corporate culture is best defined as the expectations (both written and unwritten) for workplace relations and the ways in which employees responded to those expectations. It encompasses the day-to-day operations, the regulatory policies of management, and the unspoken assumptions of employees. As Clark Davis notes in his study of the growth of the white-collar workforce in the early twentieth century, corporate cultures went beyond the inner workings of any single firm and pulled in broader societal values and norms: "Corporate cultures, both formal and informal, functioned only when congruent with prevailing middle-class practices and mores, or when designed to subtly reshape rather than contradict these norms."[21] Gary Alan Fine points out how the power of organizational cultures is localized: "Each workplace operates within a cultural context in which local features of interaction influence how employees conceptualize their workplace self."[22] Fine's concept of an "idioculture," in which workers share customs, beliefs, routines, and traditions, provides insight into the organizing power of workplace cultures: "Members recognize that they share experiences, and these experiences can be referred to with the expectation that they will be understood by other members."[23] Anthony Greenwald and Thomas Pettigrew's recent study of employment discrimination proves the power of shared expectations and identities among employees. As they argue,

"Ingroup-directed favoritism is, in the United States, a more potent engine for discriminatory impact than is outgroup-directed hostility." Discrimination is often subtly blended into workplace culture or "hidden even from those who practice it."[24]

In corporate settings like Boeing, the family metaphor helped reinforce the "idioculture" that Fine observes, and it obscured the practice of gendered employment discrimination. Coontz notes that the "language of private relations and family values" results in both a "contraction" and a "deformation of the public realm," with corrupting influences on diversity and equality. The language of family can lead to "suspicion of people who are different and attempts to exclude them from 'the family circle.'"[25] Dana Cloud also argues that the familial metaphor has a "domesticating rhetorical effect" in that it "encourages cross-class identification between workers and their employers."[26] But while both men and women have lost power as workers as corporations have gained more power, women remain disadvantaged by being concentrated in the lowest-paying positions. Estelle Freedman points out that, "in a sense, women workers are at a disadvantage because they do not have wives."[27] Boeing's "family traditions" emphasized opportunities for white male workers to have steady employment with access to mobility, fraternal networks, and a long-term career. Boeing workers were used to periods of unemployment, but the familial ordering offered a sense of normalcy and stability amid the capitalist chaos, at least for some workers. As David Harvey points out, capitalist economies routinely experience crises, and within the capitalist system there are "innumerable possibilities for crisis to occur." Periods of crisis, in fact, "enforce some kind of order and rationality" in the capitalist system, even while exacting "tragic human consequences" such as unemployment and financial ruin.[28] The Boeing "family" served the regulatory function that Harvey defines and "normalized" periods of crisis by creating an "idioculture" of "ingroup favoritism" whereby some workers, especially white heterosexual men, could expect company leaders, managers, and coworkers to look after their best interests.

Familialism stabilized the workforce, as well as the expectations of workers, in ways that the company's product line could not. It offered a way to govern employees and check the power of unions, and for male employees it offered a sense of stability that higher wages and the uncertainties of the airline market could not. As the authors of *Like a Family* note, the family metaphor worked to encourage norms defined by "a broad network of obligation, responsibility, and concern" in which workers provided social welfare benefits for one another and also built a sense of community.[29]

The family metaphor has remained popular within organizations striving for loyalty as well as a competitive edge; as Folbre observes, organizations use references to "symbolic kin" because "emotional connections to other people reinforce reciprocity and trust" as well as build solidarity.[30] Boeing leaders engineered company culture with the hope of creating a workforce family that would hold people in place. They adhered to white, heterosexual family norms in an attempt to stabilize the labor force during enormous political, social, and economic disruptions. The family metaphor offered common ground upon which the terms and expectations of the workplace were negotiated, though it was also dynamic and offered a number of ways for workers and managers to articulate and understand change. As the rest of this book will show, workers did not always uphold the tenets of the Boeing family or maintain the loyalty to company policies and procedures that the familial metaphor suggested, though the expectations of family loomed large in workplace culture for most of the twentieth century and its legacies carried into the twenty-first century.

Boeing provides a case study for understanding how social and cultural relations fundamentally shape business enterprises and vice versa. The case of Boeing helps us better understand the capitalist gender division of labor and employment discrimination. As scholars such as Ruth Milkman, Rosemary Hennessy, Karen Ramsay, and Martin Parker have pointed out, capitalism does not require a gender division of labor but has historically used a division of labor built on sex and gender norms. Capitalist economic structures and ideals rely on unequal employment opportunities that are upheld through gender and sexual norms.[31] As Weeks suggests, in the neoliberal context of recent decades, the lines between production and reproduction have been blurred so that, amid the flexible wages of neoliberalism, "productive and reproductive labor increasingly overlap," which has empowered corporations at the expense of workers.[32] Work has expanded while wages and equality of opportunity have not. In what

Hennessy terms "postmodern patriarchy," late capitalism is characterized by dual wage–earning families, consumption, increased power of the
welfare state and decreased power of husbands, and increasing numbers
of alternative families and households headed by single mothers.[33] Amid
these capitalist shifts, the family metaphor allows business and corporate
leaders to assume less responsibility for the social and economic well-
being of their workers, while shifting the caretaking burdens to workers
themselves.[34] Opportunities have opened for women as patriarchal notions
of the family and work have declined somewhat (or perhaps more accu-
rately, have been hidden and repackaged and repurposed in new ways) in
government and corporate policies, but women remain disadvantaged,
especially as notions of earned economic citizenship have become tied to
paid work, for which women continue to make less.[35] As feminist theorists
have argued, corporations, and capitalism more broadly, often mistakenly
get represented as invasive powers that exert total controlling force.[36]

Materialist feminism offers a useful lens through which to view the
ways in which cultures of labor hide the processes of gendering and discrimination as "natural" outcomes of capitalism. As Chrys Ingraham points
out, "Materialist feminism argues that the nexus of social arrangements
and institutions which form social totalities—patriarchy, capitalism, and
racism—regulates our everyday lives. They are not monolithic, but con-
sist of unstable patterns of interrelations and reciprocal determinations
which, when viewed together, provide a useful way of theorizing power
and domination."[37] This study seeks to expose those "unstable patterns of
interrelations and reciprocal determinations" of capitalism to show how
patriarchal labor relations have been negotiated on a daily basis among
workers, managers, and corporate leaders in ways that maintain patriarchal
capitalist power.

An examination of daily workplace relations reveals the larger patterns of gender employment discrimination that disempower women. To
understand how corporate capitalism enforces gender norms and creates
an appearance of stability and equality at the macro level, it is imperative
to examine the construction of gender norms and inequality on a micro
level. As Gary Fine notes, organizational cultures can disempower people
in small but significant ways: "While culture is often conceptualized as

a social good, situations occur in which idiocultures have destructive ramifications for morale or work outcomes."[38] An examination of Boeing's corporate culture shows how corporate capitalist power at the micro level is composed of day-to-day negotiations based on compulsory gender binarism and unwritten and assumed norms. As Estelle Freedman points out, "Structural discrimination operates through the everyday practices of individuals."[39] Ramsay and Parker similarly note that, "if we look at organizations as cultures, they begin to appear as webs of meaning that are constructed through the everyday practices of actors. Dress, language, symbolism and so on become the unrecognized material out of which the organization is built."[40] The case studies in this book expose this "unrecognized material" to provide insight into how corporate bureaucracies have functioned in recent decades. At Boeing, it was the unspoken and unwritten role of convention that allowed the workplace to function, though in ways that maintained inequality. More broadly, the Boeing case reveals the corporate investment in enforcing gendered norms in the workplace. Weeks notes the "gendering of work" results not only from the practice of enforcing and adhering to the gender division of labor but also because of "the ways that workers are often expected to do gender at work."[41] This study offers a unique opportunity to learn from the everyday encounters among company leaders, managers, and workers to understand how Boeing's workplace norms and the gendered expectations of postwar corporate capitalism were formed.

To understand Boeing's corporate culture, the power relations that supported that culture, and how it changed over time, it is necessary to understand the economic and social shifts Boeing underwent from the 1930s to the present day. The next section provides a brief overview of Boeing's history of corporate growth in order to contextualize the case studies that follow.

How Boeing "Grew Up"

To understand the debates and anxieties over the union contract with the 777X guarantee, one must look to Boeing's past. While a complete institutional or economic history of Boeing would take volumes, a brief history of the company's growth provides the necessary background for

FIG. 1. The wing room at Boeing, 1922. Courtesy Library of Congress, Prints and Photographs Division, LC-USZC2-6344.

understanding how its image and workplace culture have been shaped by economic considerations as well as changing demographics within the workforce, such as the employment of more women. The growth of Boeing from a small "family" company in which workers all knew one another to a global corporation by the twenty-first century challenged the family metaphor and eventually made the metaphor impossible to maintain, even while the historical memory of "family traditions" still looms large.

Despite the dominant position Boeing would eventually occupy in the aerospace industry, the company's beginnings were humble. As the *Boeing News* reported, the company started "with a one-room shop on Lake Union and only a handful of employees" in 1915, when William Boeing constructed twin-float seaplanes with navy engineer George Westervelt.[42] The founding headquarters were a far cry from the high-rise the company headquarters would eventually occupy. One resident born and raised in the Green Lake area of Seattle recalled Boeing's early plant and described streetcars that circled Lake Union and went past "Boeing's little old plant" but also noted that the area still had "cow paths and wooded areas, old rickety sidewalks."[43] During World War I Boeing received some military contracts, which boosted both production and payroll. At the time of the U.S. entry into World War I, in 1917, Boeing employed 28 people; by May

1918 the company employed 337 people. When the war ended, however, so did the company's growth, and by 1919 Boeing employed only 67 people. In order to survive the decline, the company began to build furniture.[44]

Although women began helping to build airplanes at Boeing during World War I, they were not employed in large numbers and worked mostly as seamstresses, sewing the fabric covering on the wings.[45] The few women who worked elsewhere in the company tended to be in positions that adhered to the traditional sexual division of labor, such as stenographer, bookkeeper, and telephone operator. Helen Holcombe was a notable exception; she was the company's first woman engineer, hired in 1917.[46] In October 1918 the Boeing workforce totaled 190 employees, including 30 women (15.8 percent).[47] The engineering department grew to 20 by 1920, with Holcombe still the only woman. In the 1920s government orders picked up with the introduction of new military aircraft, and by 1933 the company had expanded from a "one-room shop" to comprise thirteen buildings, fourteen shops, and an average yearly staff of 1,500 men. By January 1939 the company employed 3,000 workers.[48]

World War II ushered in the company's most dramatic growth. As a top defense contractor Boeing grew to an unprecedented degree. By February 9, 1945, employment at the Seattle plants and other plants together totaled 45,008.[49] The company hired women in substantial numbers for the first time during World War II; by the war's end women made up nearly half

FIG. 2. Male workers preparing patterns for the B-17F bomber in 1942. Courtesy Library of Congress, Prints and Photographs Division, FSA/OWI Collection, LC-USE6-D-008366.

of Boeing's workforce. The postwar years, however, were less certain and brought periodic layoffs. From a wartime peak of 31,750 on February 9, 1945, total employment at the Seattle Boeing plant had dropped to 17,722 by February 1948.[50]

Some recovery took place amid Cold War spending in the 1950s and 1960s as Boeing moved into aerospace research and design. Postwar policies such as the GI Bill, whose benefits flowed overwhelmingly to men, along with the masculinist imperatives of the burgeoning field of aerospace research and development, led to the dramatic growth of engineering as a skilled, white-collar professional occupation for men.[51] David Noble points out that in the "enchanted enclave of space enthusiasts" there was a "preponderantly male domain equally marked by imagery of exclusively patriarchal procreation."[52] Structurally, as well as rhetorically, engineering technology was coded male, with support services rendered female. In the

1960s and 1970s women made up only 2 to 3 percent of the scientific and engineering workforce but constituted 92 percent of clerical employees.[53]

Cold War federal spending changed the economy and the landscape throughout the American West, and Seattle was no exception.[54] Boeing, and Seattle, began to rely on federal spending, especially given the vast fluctuations in the commercial market. In 1985 Boeing CEO Frank Shrontz commented that one of the keys to Boeing's success was the company's "balance between government and commercial business." As he explained, "When commercial business has been down, government and defense has been good."[55] However, in reality the two divisions were not so easily separated. The huge influx of capital that was necessary to make advancements in commercial aircraft manufacturing came from Boeing's reliance on military spending and federal contracts.[56] The Supersonic Transport (SST) program is one example of these links. The program was both a military and a commercial endeavor and illustrates the blurred lines between military and commercial that the Cold War produced; although the SST program was funded by a federal contract awarded in 1966, it was run by Boeing's commercial aircraft division until the program's cancellation in 1971.[57] Cold War spending could not stave off all economic downturns.

In the late 1960s the company began a series of massive layoffs in what came to be termed the "Boeing Bust." In 1967 employment at Boeing reached a peak of nearly 150,000 workers, with more than 100,000 of those employed in the Seattle area.[58] Shortly thereafter, however, the market for commercial airliners deteriorated, and from 1967 to 1971 Boeing laid off three-fourths of those employed in the commercial aircraft division.[59] The situation was so dire that, in an effort to save money, the company stopped weeding the flowerbeds, mowing the lawn, cleaning some washrooms and toilets, and watering plants.[60] Between early 1970 and October 1971, the size of Boeing's workforce shrank from 107,962 to 61,826.[61] At its lowest point, in October 1971, total employment was 53,300, with 37,200 employed in the Seattle area. By July 1974 employment had risen to 74,000, with 53,500 employed in Seattle—still nowhere near the 1967 peak of 150,000 workers, 100,000 of them in Seattle.[62] The morale of former Boeing employees and Seattle residents deteriorated so badly that two local real estate agents put up a now infamous billboard that read, "Will the last person leaving Seattle turn out the lights?"[63] One Boeing leader characterized such "violent swings" as part of the "economic realities" of the aircraft industry, where there are "few winners and many losers."[64] As a result of the downturn, some workers began to take early retirement.[65] Things did not look up until 1983.[66]

Economic uncertainty in the 1970s changed the relationship between Boeing workers and company leaders. During the massive layoffs of that decade more than seventy-nine hundred engineers lost their jobs. At the end of the layoffs in 1972, slightly more than seventy-four hundred engineers remained at Boeing.[67] In the face of an uncertain job market, the image of engineering began to change, even at Boeing, where cyclical employment was common.[68] One 1972 study indicated that some engineers believed it was "Boeing policy" to retain engineers only as a way to gain competitive advantage on government contract bids.[69] Some of them thought that employment at Boeing could mark one for life: "Engineers seeking employment in the Seattle area and elsewhere soon find their aerospace background a handicap, the industry having a reputation for waste of manpower."[70]

To ease the economic downturn, company leaders pursued new areas of business, such as computer production, and opened new divisions, including Boeing Computer Services (BCS). In the 1970s company leaders decided to change the name from Boeing Aircraft Company to the Boeing Company in an effort to reflect their diversification into new areas, such as telecommunications. As Boeing reorganized its operations and added new divisions, the ranks of management swelled and the firm became more bureaucratic.[71] Despite an upswing in the commercial market, Boeing began to lose ground in the 1980s to a rival company, Airbus, and thus began to strategize new ways of organizing the company.[72]

Amid these disruptive employment cycles women were slow to move up the company ranks. They were concentrated in clerical and manufacturing positions, while their numbers in management and engineering, the highest-paid positions in the company next to the top managers, remained low. In 1974, for example, Boeing employed just 330 female engineers.[73] This figure decreased in 1979 to 227, which was just 2 percent of the total number of engineers Boeing employed. By 1989 only 1 in 15 Boeing engineers was a woman; out of 978 engineers total, only about 6.5 percent were women. Women's numbers were smaller in other occupations as well. By 1989 only 20 percent of Boeing production workers were women and only a handful of company executives were female.[74] The president of the Pacific Northwest branch of the Society of Women in Engineering, Suzanne Hakam, observed in 1989 that women were underrepresented within Boeing's ranks of management because "managers tend to come from technical backgrounds that traditionally have attracted few women."[75]

Boeing leaders recognized the shortage of women in positions of authority. In the 1980s the company began efforts to boost the number of women employees, especially in management. In 1988 the *Boeing News* observed, "Training and recruitment toward increasing the number of women and minorities in management and upper-level positions is the direction of the 1980s."[76] Boeing's corporate culture, however, could counteract such efforts at parity. As Dana Cloud notes, neoliberal downsizing and gender discrimination have gone hand in hand: "In the context of constantly threatened layoffs, there is pressure not to complain about being passed over for promotion."[77] Martha Gimenez also points out that the disappearance of the family-sustaining wage has been "exacerbated by the fact that employers, to cut labor costs, impose wage cuts at the time new contracts are negotiated and/or demand a lower starting salary for many blue and white collar jobs."[78] By the mid-1990s men still dominated the ranks of employees; in 1996 women made up 22 percent of Boeing's workforce and represented only 10 percent of managers (with most of that number concentrated in the lowest ranks of management) and just 5 percent of engineers.[79]

By the 1990s the company had diversified the workforce in a number of ways, though not necessarily in ways that empowered workers or sustained the family metaphor. Boeing began, for example, to reduce labor costs through downsizing and outsourcing. Some manufacturing work moved outside of the United States. For example, although the town of Everett remained the final assembly point for the Boeing 787, nearly 70 percent of the parts for the 787 were manufactured outside the United States and then shipped to the Puget Sound area for final assembly, which required only three days of work. One analyst notes the irony of this strategy: "In outsourcing, Boeing is really doing what once would have been unthinkable: copying the Airbus model."[80] Boeing was also following the lead of other large manufacturing and retail businesses in the United States: between 1990 and 1995 Sears cut 185,000 jobs, IBM cut 122,000 jobs, and General Electric cut 76,000 jobs. Boeing, in contrast, cut 57,000 jobs.[81] These numbers suggest the declining job opportunities afforded by the neoliberal context. Efforts to build and retain a loyal workforce and nurture familial relations between and among workers and corporate leadership are no longer paramount.

Beyond just Boeing, corporate America has shifted to embrace shareholder value as the central purpose of corporations. Karen Ho argues that, in this "shareholder value perspective," corporate leaders, managers, and employees alike view employment as "outside the concern of public corporations."[82] The political economists Bennett Harrison and Barry Bluestone point out how the economic restructuring of the 1980s affected wage levels and led to a "startling deterioration" in good jobs since the late 1970s and a "mushrooming" of low-wage and part-time work.[83] Nancy Folbre points out that the new normalization of the "footloose corporation," in which multinational corporations are less centralized and less tied to their home country, has further increased corporate power at the expense of workers: "The mere threat of job loss has enormous impact, discouraging both unionization and demands for higher wages."[84] Wall Street reconceptualized the corporation in the 1980s, transforming it from a "long-term social institution into an aggregation of stocks in individual portfolios."[85] Social welfare programs, in this process, seemed "inefficient" and at odds with corporate purpose; rather than addressing social inequalities or social welfare, corporate purposes shifted to vague and unbinding notions of a democracy based on ideas of shareholder value.[86] The increased leveraging of the rhetoric of "shareholder value" was evident in Boeing's communications with employees; in a 1986 memo to employees, for example, company president and CEO Frank Shrontz noted, "We have a paramount obligation to return top value for the funds entrusted to us by the government and by our stockholders. Our future success as a major aerospace contractor depends on it."[87] According to the neoliberal view, corporations are not responsible for maintaining jobs, which explains why

Boeing's decision to move more work outside of the Puget Sound region seems to make sense to some in the paradigm of neoliberal capitalism, but it is also profoundly painful to workers and union leaders who resist the devolution of the family norm and the job stability it seemed to promise.

As part of the shift to globalizing capital, Boeing leaders, in line with other corporate leaders, moved away from local and regional identifications. In March 2001 Boeing CEO Phil Condit shocked Seattle residents by announcing that Boeing corporate headquarters would move from Seattle to an as yet undetermined city. One news report called the announcement the "Boeing Bombshell."[88] Since its founding in 1916, Boeing had functioned as an integral part of the economy and image of the Seattle metropolitan area in both physical and emotional ways. Boeing was the top employer in the Pacific Northwest, and Washington State lawmakers went to great lengths to ensure that Boeing remained in Washington. Nevertheless, company leaders argued that moving Boeing's headquarters would transform the company into a modern diversified corporation. They viewed Boeing's strong history and relationship with the Pacific Northwest as a problem and wanted to separate the company from the major production spaces of the commercial plant headquarters in the Seattle area in order to facilitate global growth.[89] Company officials also argued that in order to conduct transnational business they needed a headquarters "within easier reach of [Boeing's] far-flung businesses."[90] The relocation of the headquarters was a move away from the family metaphor and was also consistent with the transition to globalizing capital since the 1990s. Boeing's corporate relocation is part of a broader trend of large corporations strategically shifting their headquarters. Companies such as Bank One and PepsiCo have recently moved their corporate headquarters in an effort to be closer to financial markets.[91] In May 2001 Condit announced that headquarters would move to Chicago, and he revealed that, for company leaders, Chicago's transportation infrastructure and "access to global markets" had tipped the balance in its favor.[92] Illinois state senator Lisa Madigan, a Democrat, observed that the neoliberal context provided room for corporate perks but no social welfare programs: "how disingenuous the argument is that it's a tight budget year, and we can't fund human services at the level they should be."[93]

Boeing's new office space overlooked the Chicago River, a very different view and setting than the low-rise industrial location in South Seattle.[94] Condit went so far as to refer to the company as the "new Boeing" and announced plans to lead it into its most extensive diversification efforts to date by focusing on financing, in-flight Internet services, airplane maintenance and overhaul, and satellite-based movie distribution. The "new" Boeing in fact spelled the end of the family metaphor and familialism and was rooted in the changes the company had experienced over the course of the twentieth century. By 2001 company leaders and workers had negotiated several large boom-and-bust cycles of employment, the growth of company unions, an increasingly diversified workforce, and new levels of management and corporate bureaucracy.[95]

Condit's ceremonious arrival on the runway at Midway International Airport in May 2001 signaled Boeing's official move to Chicago and the company's new global identity. *Chicago Sun-Times* writers David Roeder and Fran Spielman characterized Condit's "triumphant trip" to Chicago as an outlandish theatrical performance. Indeed, his arrival reveals much about the performance of global capitalism. Condit arrived on the runway, descended from the plane waving "like a victorious politician," and walked onto a red carpet to shake hands with state and local politicians and dignitaries, including Illinois governor George Ryan and Chicago mayor Richard M. Daley.[96] As his Boeing Business Jet loomed in the background, Condit praised Chicago's energetic image to members of the press who had gathered beside the runway: "The word I use a lot is vibrant. Things are going on. Things are happening in this city and that's important to me."[97] In the *Chicago Sun-Times* one editorial reported that Condit had ordered the "staging" and that company leaders wanted the plane in the background to highlight Boeing's product line. The editorial outlined the reactions of Chicagoans to Condit's arrival plan and to the Boeing move more broadly; they noted that some viewed Boeing's "attention to detail and secrecy" as "obsessive and controlling," while others chalked it up to "the orderliness of Boeing's engineer-dominated culture." Condit, however, dismissed the antics as "normal for any big corporate relocation."[98] Condit, as well as workers, recognized that the neoliberal context had empowered corporate leaders to ignore "family traditions" and move jobs to other locations.[99]

Boeing has a long history of partaking in various spectacles to debut company products and business decisions, though in the past such performances were tied to a regional identity. In June 1934, for example, the *Boeing News* described the scene of "Indians in colorful headdresses, war paint and full regalia; cowpunchers in ten-gallon hats, scarlet shirts and chaps; creaking stagecoaches and galloping Pony Express riders" that greeted a Boeing 247 transport from United Air Lines when that company opened service into "the famed Round-up town of Pendleton, Oregon." The stunt aimed to draw a "contrast between the old and new in western transportation methods." As part of the exhibition, the 247 took "two loads of Indian passengers" for a flight, "their feathers and beads making an odd picture inside the cabin of the 247."[100] Company leaders in 1934 embraced a regional identity and traditions based on popular assumptions embedded in the American West, including the assumption that Indians represent the opposite of modernity, and they worked to emphasize the modern technology of airplanes manufactured in the West. As Philip Deloria observes, in white American culture, Native Americans have been portrayed as embodying, among other things, a "technological incapacity" and an "inability to engage a modern capitalist market economy."[101] Boeing's promotion was certainly tied into this colonial history of assumptions of white racial and technical superiority. In contrast to the 1934 image, however, by 2001 company leaders wanted to cultivate an image of a global corporation on the cutting edge of technology in a manner that did not emphasize Boeing's links to the Pacific Northwest or the American West. Both images, however, belie a sense of economic vulnerability; leaders, even while they touted the technical superiority of the company, were in fact suspicious of the idea that the company's setting was a liability.

The company has long battled public perceptions of the Pacific Northwest, though this shared history helped workers develop a common identity and shared history. Seattle, along with much of the Pacific Northwest, has often been characterized as an unusual location for a prosperous industry like Boeing. Best known for resource extraction, it did not seem like a place that would facilitate industrial manufacturing. As Eugene Bauer characterizes it, "Seattle was an unlikely site for an airplane factory. Tucked away in the remote northwest corner of the country, the area was a vast ocean of timber, lakes, rivers, mountains, and islands."[102] Even as the company expanded it was still imagined as being in a frontier far removed from the nation's industrial heart.[103] A 1950 history of Washington State described Boeing as a "Western pioneer," underscoring the company's postwar significance and the surprising rise of a big business on the western frontier.[104] To many, it seemed unusual to have both manufacturing and corporate headquarters in such a place. In the 1950s the Bureau of Business Research, a collaborative organization made up of corporate leaders and faculty at the University of Washington, noted, "By any standard of measure the Boeing Airplane Company is one of the few very large industrial firms with both headquarters and major manufacturing facilities located in the Pacific Northwest."[105] The company's move to Chicago, then, provided a way for company leaders to distance themselves from both the responsibility of dealing with day-to-day labor problems, as the family metaphor suggested they should, and from images of the company tied to popular perceptions of the Pacific Northwest.[106]

Although Boeing's move to Chicago was rhetorically powerful in disrupting the family metaphor and regional history, it did not significantly or immediately alter the company's Puget Sound workforce; it required only 400 to 500 workers to move, or roughly .02 percent of the company's worldwide workforce of 198,000, of which 78,000 were based in Seattle.[107] Yet, the effects of the move were far reaching. After hearing of the move, a strong sense of "mourning" developed among Washington residents and Boeing workers. Gov. Gary Locke pointed out that the move would leave a "void in our economic and cultural life."[108] Workers noticed that the move was at odds with the family metaphor; they expressed deep concern about what it meant for future Boeing work in the Pacific Northwest and questioned the company's respect for and loyalty to the workers. One technical-support employee at Boeing voiced doubt that Seattle lacked good business conditions or global opportunities and noted, "I think I understand the logic, but I don't think it's necessary."[109] Another worker, Rebecca Cranz, who had been with Boeing for ten years, expressed worry that her job was threatened and underscored how removed she felt from company leaders and their decisions: "I have no idea what's going to happen. It would have been nice if I had found out a little earlier."[110] To many workers and union members, Boeing's move seemed to violate a shared history of familialism, in which both the company and its workers weathered the ups and down of the aerospace industry together and displayed both loyalty and respect toward one another. Mark Blondin, president of Lodge 751 of the International Association of Machinists and Aerospace Workers, observed that the move went against the traditions of the company since its founding in 1916 by William Boeing: "This decision is a blow to our entire community. Bill Boeing must be turning over in his grave to learn his company is being ripped from its roots and moved cross country."[111]

Boeing leaders dismissed workers' concerns over the demise of the Boeing family as being out of touch with twenty-first-century business realities. In a comment that highlighted the growing chasm between Boeing workers and leaders, Boeing's chief administrative officer, John Warner, told the *Seattle Times*, "I don't expect, ever, the ordinary man on the street [in Seattle] to really understand this arcane language of corporate strategy." Similarly, when Condit traced the company's Seattle roots he characterized them, and workers' expectations of corporate loyalty, as simplistic and outdated: "That's the way [Boeing] grew up.... It's just a different company than it was five years ago." Staying in Seattle posed a problem because, according to Condit, people "almost naturally" linked Boeing to Seattle.[112] One management researcher, Jim O'Toole, observed that these reasons were somewhat out of the ordinary: "Most of the time when corporations move, they do it to get closer to their work force, or for tax reasons. I have never heard of a company changing its location to change its culture or its perspective. This could be a first."[113] Boeing's move certainly included economic considerations, but it also removed company leaders from the familial workplace culture and its attendant traditions. The emphasis on individuality and self-reliance the company had developed in earlier conceptions of family values also fit the developing neoliberal context, with its focus on combating "all forms of social solidarity that hindered competitive flexibility," such as trade unions.[114] Thus, the family metaphor was flexible and utilitarian.

In addition to moving company headquarters, Boeing began to hire CEOs and top executives from outside the Seattle area. Historically, Boeing had utilized the local "old-boy network," with CEOs and top executives who had come from the University of Washington's engineering department and risen through company ranks. As the company diversified, however, by outsourcing work, moving company headquarters to Chicago, and hiring more women and minorities, Boeing began to recruit workers from outside the Seattle area. Changes in leadership also partly explain the recent trend among large corporations to move their headquarters. CEOs and corporate executives now hail from all over the world as opposed to the location of the corporate headquarters. One relocation specialist noted, "When [leaders] had the old-boy network, they all lived in that town."[115] Karen Ho points out how corporations have aligned more closely with Wall Street since the 1990s and workers have less opportunity for upward mobility. Managers are less likely to be former shop-floor workers than "financially trained MBAs and ex-investment bankers."[116] In 2005 W. James McNerney, who was born and raised in Rhode Island and at the time worked at 3M in Minnesota, "became the first outsider to run the Boeing Company."[117]

Understanding Boeing's growth, and the place of workers within that process, is key to understanding the end of the family metaphor and the present-day tensions. Capital accumulation has grown at the expense of workers in recent decades, as industrial jobs in the 1970s and 1980s were replaced with service-sector jobs that pay less and offer less job security.[118] That Boeing no longer supports workers in the same way was evident in the November 2013 union vote on where the 777X would be built. After the vote, an article in *Time* called the International Association of Machinists an "old school union" filled with members who had "worked decades to build a solid middle class existence."[119] Boeing, meanwhile, began to take bids from all over the United States to see which city would give the corporation the biggest tax breaks and the most lucrative incentives. The activist Ralph Nader wrote a letter to McNerney calling the "squeeze" put on workers "unseemly" and arguing that "Boeing's systemic campaigns for corporate welfare are shameful. Your company is one of the major corporate welfare kings in America."[120] As Nader pointed out, neoliberal tenets have been increasingly common in empowering corporate leaders and profits at the expense of workers. Workers are acutely aware of this vulnerability, which helps explain why the IAM voted to accept a revised contract for building the 777X in the Pacific Northwest in January 2014.

One thirty-year-old mechanic noted, "I don't ever want to gamble. I've got a family to take care of." Another worker who had been at Boeing twenty-five years echoed these fears, showing the vulnerability that both older and younger workers feel: "At this stage in my career, I'm not willing to take that chance."[121] Similarly, Nancy Stapleton, a sixty-year-old worker, argued that her "yes" vote was a way to protect future workers: "I call this protecting our younger generation. There's a lot of jobs at stake."[122] Another worker from a "three-generation Boeing family," whom the *Los Angeles Times* described as looking "briefly stricken" when asked how he voted, noted the pain that his "yes" vote cost him: "I voted for it. I'm not proud of that."[123]

These quotes suggest the profound shifts the company has undergone in recent decades. Over the course of the twentieth century, Boeing grew from a small, fairly monolithic "family" company based in the Pacific Northwest to a diversified global corporation with workers all over the world and corporate leaders removed from the daily interactions on the shop floor. This book examines the power struggles Boeing workers and leaders have faced as the company became a powerful global corporation with a workplace culture organized around business principles like "shareholder value" rather than the idea of family or traditions.

Organization of the Book

This book is organized around case studies that analyze the tensions accompanying Boeing's growth and diversification, especially the employment of white women, racial minorities, transsexuals, and other nonmale and nonwhite workers. Each case study considers how the family metaphor operated in the context of negotiating workplace conditions. Although the negotiations varied according to context, in all cases the familial narrative worked to organize the workplace in unequal ways. I consider all Boeing workers, as all were included in descriptions of family, though not in equal ways. While this broad view to some degree obscures the historical development of particular kinds of occupational tracks, it also offers an opportunity to compare workers' experiences in a manner that exposes the dynamics of workplace inequalities.

To set the context for the case studies, chapter 1 traces the development of the family metaphor at Boeing in the 1930s, when the company's growth first picked up and when company leaders began to organize corporate culture around the concept of the Boeing "family." As both David Harvey and Dana Cloud point out, the family metaphor is not about sharing power but about retaining power and concentrating it in the hands of management and the upper classes. Harvey notes that strata that are "organized through family and kinship" have "managed to hang on to a consistent power base."[124] Cloud argues that the "family values ideograph—in concert with the ideographs 'responsibility' and 'opportunity'—ultimately encourages the dislocation of attention away from structural social problems and onto private life and personal responsibility."[125] Chapter 1 shows how, in general, corporate culture attempted to unify workers, unite the interests of employees with their employer, and build a monolithic workplace identity around white patriarchal heterosexual fraternal norms even as the company grew larger and labor organizing gained momentum. The subsequent chapters all examine different episodes in which Boeing's corporate culture and its self-image as a family were challenged by social, economic, and cultural changes. Chapter 2 details company leaders' resistance to hiring women and African Americans during World War II, despite labor shortages and lagging production rates. Boeing had to hire more women to keep up production rates but at the same time reconcile diversified employment policies with the familial culture that had set a workplace standard of fraternal relations between white heterosexual men. Chapter 3 looks at the "EEO era" and the frustrations of women managers who tried to work their way up through Boeing's "old-boy" network, which blocked equal employment opportunity mandates. The Boeing family had to become more flexible to incorporate affirmative action programs into workplace organization, though the gendered traditions of the company's past muted the possibilities for more radical change. Chapter 4 analyzes the case of *Jane Doe v. Boeing Company*, in which a male-to-female transsexual in the traditionally male engineering department was fired for dressing as a woman and subsequently sued on the basis of employment discrimination. The chapter examines the disruption to the family metaphor, as well as the heteronormative culture it promoted, that occurred as a result of the case. Chapter 5 looks at two remarkable events that both began in February

2000: a strike by Boeing engineers and a class-action lawsuit waged by women employed by Boeing in the Pacific Northwest. These events show how neoliberal capitalism was at odds with the family metaphor to such a degree that a metaphor of "teamwork" emerged as a way to manage Boeing's growth and its shift toward global capitalism. Workers, as this chapter shows, were resistant to these changes, even while women acknowledged a past that never offered equality of opportunity.

Collectively, these case studies reveal that Boeing's corporate culture attempted to uphold masculine heterosexual fraternalism as a vital corporate strategy for most of the twentieth century. While such policies generated inequality, they also helped company leaders and managers navigate the profound social, cultural, and economic anxieties of corporate capitalism in the postwar period. When that culture shifted, it caused new rifts between workers, managers, and company leaders and exposed the power that company leaders had over workers in new ways. The chapters that follow offer a view of how Boeing's corporate culture emerged as a key strategy for negotiating change and maintaining corporate power. Boeing leaders, and sometimes workers, attempted to construct and maintain the Boeing "family" because it was a way to try to hold together a company that was growing while creating uniformity. This uniformity made it easier for company leaders to manage a stable workforce, and it provided some workers with a sense of job security that came with monetary and cultural benefits. This study, then, provides an examination of how corporate culture, and capitalism more broadly, upholds gender and sexual norms that permit, and foster, employment discrimination.

CHAPTER 1

Fraternalism and the
Boeing News in the 1930s

The March 1932 issue of Boeing's company publication, the *Boeing News*, introduced a new feature that offered Boeing employees' "news of interest."[1] Titled "Shop Notes," the section focused on the various shop-floor departments that housed the growing blue-collar, mostly male, workforce. Employees were to report stories and announcements to their shop-floor supervisors, who would in turn report them to the "shop reporter." The newspaper described the section as a way to honor the linkages between the company leaders and managers and the rank-and-file workers: "BOEING NEWS is your paper and we want your news to be published in it."[2] Typical is the December 1937 feature, which reported, among other things, that Alton Reese's wife had given birth to a baby girl; Carl Fields, who was affectionately nicknamed "Grandpapa," had been promoted; and Wayne Thompson had recently purchased a new Ford V-8.[3] Publicly recognizing life experiences as honored "shop traditions" reinforced and celebrated men's role as husbands, fathers, and most of all, company workers. The language of "family" increasingly permeated the *Boeing News* as the company expanded in the 1930s, but in ways that assumed fraternal bonding between men. This chapter analyzes passages in the *Boeing News* to show the development of Boeing's corporate culture and the growing pains it experienced throughout the 1930s. Boeing employed the family metaphor to counter the increasing fragmentation of Boeing's workforce in the 1930s amid the challenges posed by the Great Depression, the company's growth, and unionization efforts.

In the 1930s the Boeing "family" became a version of fraternalism that upheld masculine solidarity. As Boeing grew larger and managers assumed greater power, company initiatives like the *Boeing News* tried to retain the feeling of a "shop-floor" company and to build a company "family" based on fraternal norms and assumptions of masculine solidarity, between workers and management and among workers themselves. Workers were not entirely accepting of the family metaphor and struggled against corporate culture even while adhering to some masculine norms and traditions, especially in union efforts. As Francine Moccio notes, "Fraternity is the very foundation upon which proto-trade unionism was built," and fraternal societies of the nineteenth and early twentieth centuries "served valuable familial and community functions in an unstable economic environment."[4] Because fraternal organizations were "overwhelmingly male" with "gender solidarity" as the "uniting factor," women have had a difficult time breaking into blue-collar professions and unions coded as male. Fraternalism since the early twentieth century in skilled blue-collar jobs has meant "wiring together formal and informal cultural forms of male bonding and gender solidarity for purposes of organizational efficiency and commercial expansion."[5]

At Boeing, fraternalism offered a way to talk about company and worker solidarity despite the boom-and-bust cycles of the aircraft industry. Unlike earlier forms of familialism, the Boeing "family" was not familial in the sense that Boeing was the father, though a certain degree of paternalism toward women and minority workers did exist. Whereas earlier models of corporate familialism were more focused on benefits and paternalism and corresponded more closely to the patriarchal family structure, disciplinary control at Boeing was exerted less by a paternal authority figure than by a rigid social hierarchy that was enforced daily on the shop floor through workers' interactions with their managers and coworkers. In the pages of newsletters, in hiring and promotion practices, in shop-floor relations, and in Boeing-sponsored social events it was assumed that Boeing workers should identify with one another in terms of race, gender, and sexuality and through a shared masculine work experience and history. Corporate discourse helped to solidify a masculinized work space. Although the Boeing "family" would change in reaction to social and economic challenges, the fraternal expectations that were set in the 1930s, both by the company and by union efforts, had a lasting impact on company culture throughout the twentieth century. Fraternalism helped to build and uphold workplace hierarchies that set the stage for a workplace dominated by white patriarchal heterosexual norms.

The Company Publication as Management Strategy

Company publications like the *Boeing News* became a routine part of corporate management strategy beginning in the early twentieth century. They emerged in conjunction with paternalistic company-sponsored programs designed to monitor and shape workers' characters. This was a shift from earlier times, when employers had left issues of employee motivation and identification with the company to shop-floor supervisors or to managers.[6] Company publications supported company welfare and personnel management programs by using the family metaphor to rhetorically assign workers an important place within increasingly large corporate bureaucracies. As Roland Marchand argues, "We may justifiably remain skeptical of the power of the family metaphor . . . to reshape worker consciousness. But this imagery often functioned in tandem with efforts to decrease worker alienation through humanizing systems of employee representation and paternalistic welfare programs."[7] Corporations also began to institute programs of personnel management beginning in the 1920s.[8]

Like other corporations, Boeing recognized that publicity and public relations were important parts of efforts to maintain a cohesive company "family" amid economic and labor tensions. The institution of the *Boeing News* was part of a larger company attempt to bolster employee identification and company image and to manage employees. Beginning in 1922 Boeing began publishing the *Joystick*, which later became the *Boeing News*.[9] In 1930 Boeing's newly established public relations department began to publish the *Boeing News*. In 1939 company president P. G. Johnson created the position of public relations manager and hired Harold Mansfield to fill it because he recognized "the increasing significance of public relations." The position was eventually elevated to "vice presidential status."[10] In the first issue of the *Boeing News*, Johnson noted that the company's growth necessitated a company publication: "It is my belief that the Boeing family has grown so rapidly, our activities are so varied, our personnel so separated, that the time has come when all of us should be kept informed, about what the other groups are doing. That explains the *Boeing News.*"[11] Many company publications emerged after periods of strained relations between labor and management, such as labor strikes.[12] The *Boeing News* grew alongside union efforts to organize workers. By 1934 the company was facing the challenges brought on by the Great Depression. Workers were ready for union organization and reportedly displayed an "overwhelming opinion in favor of some form of organization."[13]

The *Boeing News* had wide distribution; in addition to providing it to employees, company leaders gave it to the media, company customers, libraries, and top military personnel. Boeing's plants in Wichita and Canada had their own plant publications. Company leaders were in fact rigorous in making sure that workers received the publication. One former Boeing manager at the Seattle plant recalled, "On publication day stacks of the magazine were placed at the various exit gates where the guards passed them out as they carried on their routine inspection of employees' lunch buckets and parcels at shift change."[14] These distribution methods suggest the presence of some tensions in the Boeing "family" and the imposition of corporate culture on workers, but they also highlight the centrality of corporate culture in the workplace. The *Boeing News* devoted so much copy to emphasizing the camaraderie, fraternalism, and shared backgrounds of Boeing workers that it would be easy to forget that Boeing leaders were the ones who published and circulated the *Boeing News*. But the publication reflected the company's growth into a powerful corporation with an increasingly hierarchical structure. By the 1930s the ranks of management at corporations like Boeing began to increase. Corporations gave more power to managers, rather than workers. As Julia Ott points out, even while corporations rhetorically began to tout ideas of a "shareholders' democracy," with employees "owning" a part of the corporation, corporate leaders controlled the distribution of the shares and retained power over the company.[15]

The changes in the "Shop Notes" feature of the *Boeing News* mirror the growth of the company in the 1930s and increased company efforts to manage unity. Although initially a page in length, the "Shop Notes" feature soon took up several pages and editors changed the name of it to "Personal Notes about Our Personnel." By the early 1940s the feature sometimes ran five or more pages and included information on new plants, departments, and shops. As the company expanded, such sections were needed in order to maintain a sense of familiarity among workers. Company leaders were increasingly removed from the ever-growing shop-floor departments, and, as Boeing grew, it was less likely that employees would know one another or about the functions and dynamics of other shops. The *Boeing News* also published a small column called "From the Observer's Cockpit" in the early 1930s, but the column on company happenings was short and often focused on news of the military representatives and corporate leaders.[16] In contrast the employee-centered "Shop Notes" and "Personal Notes about Our Personnel" functioned as spaces where company leaders tried to integrate the lives of shop-floor supervisors and employees into corporate culture in a way that would otherwise not have been possible.

In the late 1930s *Boeing News* editors added "All in the Family," compiled by company leaders to share important company news. A 1939 installment asked workers to consider the link between the Boeing family of workers and the company's technological innovations, conjuring the sense of family to describe the pride workers felt after filling an order for Boeing 314 clippers purchased by Pan American Airways: "Whether or not we had thought of ourselves in exactly that light, undoubtedly it was the 'proud parent' feeling that welled up inside of us the moment the first Clipper said goodby [*sic*] to home and struck off to make a living in the South Pacific."[17] In addition to promoting high work standards, "All in the Family" messages reinforced a sense of belonging and promoted a vision of the company as stable, inclusionary, and supportive—many of the characteristics one might expect from a family member. Similarly, "Personal Notes" used the language of family and home to describe workplace relations. In 1934, for example, an assembly shop contribution to "Shop Notes" equated the shop floor with the familiarity of hearth and home: "Jack Finney has returned to the fold after an absence of several months. Welcome home!"[18] As discussed below, the language of fraternalism increasingly took center stage in the *Boeing News* as the company battled the challenges of the Great Depression and witnessed union organization of its workers for the first time.

Labor Tensions, Corporate Confidence, and the Great Depression

Fraternalism became especially important in the 1930s because the company's future seemed uncertain and stability seemed elusive because of the Great Depression. Although the decade started on an optimistic note, the turbulent 1930s affected Boeing's employment levels. Company leaders worked hard to minimize any sense of impending economic doom and to instill a sense of confidence in workers regarding the company's future. The end of the 1920s and beginning of the 1930s brought significant company-wide development, and Boeing continued to expand despite the Great Depression. In 1928 William Boeing declared that it was time to "build up" engineering and research, so expansion of the Seattle plant included an administration building to accommodate the growing engineering department.[19] Company leaders celebrated a purported stability in a time of economic crisis and stressed Boeing's capabilities in outmaneuvering the economic crisis. The front page of the November 1931 *Boeing News*, for example, defiantly declared, "Depression? Far from It!"[20]

Employment rose to twelve hundred in 1932 in order to meet army and navy orders (for P-12E pursuit planes and F4B-4 fighters).[21] Those numbers were a far cry from Boeing's employment levels just thirteen years earlier, when the company had employed only sixty-seven people and built furniture in an attempt to survive the downturn.[22] Harold Mansfield, public relations manager and editor of the *Boeing News*, noted, "Throughout the generally bad business year of 1932, the plant on Duwamish [River] was bustle and hum."[23] The plant did take some steps to try to maintain stable employment levels. In June 1933 the company standardized the work week to five days "as a means of providing maximum employment." Yet in 1931 the *Boeing News* declared Boeing to be exceptional in the generally bad business climate: "We've forced the depression to give our plant a mighty wide berth. . . . Depression? Far from it, indeed!"[24] The publication emphasized the significance of the company to the surrounding region, and in 1934 the *Boeing News* boasted, "With local expenditures aggregating almost $3,000,000 for the year, our company played an increasingly important part in the affairs of Seattle and the surrounding district during

1933." While most of this figure ($2.5 million) was in salaries and wages, the company also noted the significance of local purchases and expenses.[25]

That optimism, however, had faded considerably by the mid-1930s. Mansfield notes, "That spring of 1934 everything seemed to be going backward. Everything."[26] In 1934 Congress passed antitrust legislation that barred aircraft manufacturers from participating in airmail delivery and airline services. Boeing had been engaged in the airmail business, so after the new law went into effect the company had to reorganize its operations and focus solely on aircraft manufacturing. The forced restructuring had a significant impact on workforce levels. In 1934 Boeing employed 1,738 people, up about 500 from the 1932 total of 1,200. By January 1935, only 613 people were on the company payroll.[27] Out of that number, 73 were engineers, who worked long hours six or seven days per week while designing the Flying Fortress.[28] In 1936 business started picking up again when Boeing began to sell B-17 bombers to the army; employment levels once again rose, with more than 3,000 workers on the job by the beginning of 1939.[29] In the mid-1930s, however, the plant situation was, as Mansfield characterizes it, "critical. . . . The plant was operating in the red."[30]

William Boeing was so disgusted with the new federal regulation that he left Boeing and the aviation industry altogether and began to raise horses.[31] People in Seattle and employees alike mourned the departure of Bill Boeing and worried about the impact of the changes on the company and region. A 1934 editorial in the *Seattle Times* that was reprinted in the *Boeing News* paid tribute to W. E. Boeing as a pioneer in the aviation industry and a voice announcing displeasure at the intrusion of the federal government into Boeing's business. From the perspective of "Mr. and Mrs. Boeing," the editorial was in the form of an open letter that promised to inform the company's founder about what residents thought of recent events: "Seattle remembers 'Bill' Boeing as a daring experimenter in a new field at a time when men now prominent in government probably were uncertain whether a heavier-than-air machine really could be made to fly." The editorial went on to describe a history of shop-floor togetherness and the significance of the company to the local and regional identity and economy: "The Boeing Company started with three men in a building that wouldn't house one of its minor departments now. . . . Today, his is the biggest industry and the largest payroll in Seattle. . . . Seattle has reason to feel proud of 'Bill' Boeing; so has the United States."[32] In the absence of Bill Boeing, company leaders focused on trying to build a company that retained a sense of camaraderie and continued to grow despite the bad economic climate and the new rules of operation.

The departure of Bill Boeing meant that the paradigm of a company family could take root more firmly, though in a way that was different from how other companies were using the family metaphor from the turn of the century through the 1930s.[33] In the absence of its founding figure, the company began to organize around fraternalism, or ideas of commonality among male workers. Bill Boeing remained important to narratives of the company's progress and growth, but company leaders had to find new ways to talk about the significance of work at Boeing after he left. In the wake of Boeing's departure, and especially after the postwar period (as discussed in subsequent chapters), the company's familialism became more of an assumed identification on the part of workers and management. Conceptions of skill, advancement, authority, friendship, and camaraderie all relied on a fraternal social order that emphasized masculine heterosexual norms.

These fraternal norms emerged out of a search for stability in an unstable and shifting work environment. After the forced restructuring, Boeing had a shortage of cash, which made it difficult to pay workers and to keep employment levels steady. In his narrative of the changes at Boeing during this time period, Mansfield emphasizes the unity of the workforce and the willingness of employees to sacrifice for the greater good of the company, recounting how employees effectively worked out a plan for sharing jobs, with one group on for two weeks and then off while the other group worked: "Then, when the plan was put into effect, a lot of them came down on their time off and worked without pay."[34] Mansfield's romantic assessment, however, masks the very real strains that the instability of the mid-1930s caused and the toll it took on employees' faith in their employer. Even in the 1920s Boeing employees worked under tenuous conditions, with erratic paydays, wage rates, and work schedules.[35] The "Shop Notes" feature of the *Boeing News* often welcomed back employees who had been laid off. In

1933, for example, the machine shop reported that night shift had "reacquired" about 50 percent of its employees.[36] Similarly, in 1934 the finishing shop noted the layoff of a "shop clerk, timekeeper, nurse and assistant jack-of-all-trades" who had been with the company for eight years.[37] Also in 1934 the finishing shop noted "a few of the other boys have been laid off—only temporarily, we hope."[38] One labor relations expert has noted the sharp divisions between shop-floor and salaried workers at Boeing in 1933, describing the benefits salaried workers received that hourly workers did not, including regular working hours, sick leave, a better insurance program, vacations, and even hot water in the washroom. Hourly workers, on the other hand, "could be called to work whenever their services were needed and sent home when they were not needed. A union might help control the sometimes unequal, and, it seemed to many hourly workers, unfair distribution of wages."[39] By 1934 shop-floor workers were fed up with the uncertainties and began assembling the infrastructure for a union.[40] As John McCann notes, "By the mid-thirties, the choice was no longer 'no union' or 'union'—but *which* union."[41]

Much of the material in the *Boeing News* asserted the existence of unity between the Boeing workforce and management and stressed that, despite the economic hardships that placed labor and management in very different positions, they shared the same goals. The publication, however, was careful to distinguish between managers and company leaders and shop-floor workers in union efforts, noting, "Any steps toward organization should originate with employees themselves."[42] The "Personal Notes" submissions indicated that some workers were not identifying with the company but were beginning to display loyalty to the union. The machine shop, for example, commented on union solidarity in 1934 when it noted, "The boys in the heat treating room report 100 per cent organization—they all wear union suits."[43] Unions, for some, seemed to provide the stability that the corporate family metaphor could not. The *Boeing News* sought to wrest control of the workforce, and employee loyalty, away from the union.[44]

Divisions within the Boeing "family" were based on not only rank in the company hierarchy but also occupational divisions. When Boeing workers organized under union representation, they split along occupational lines. Beginning in 1936 shop-floor employees organized under Boeing's contract with Aeronautical Mechanics Union Lodge 751, a branch of the International Association of Machinists (IAM).[45] The labor historian Robert Rodden notes that the union organization effort was fairly easy and that union-management relations into the 1940s were good: "The IAM's first contract with Boeing, signed in 1936, was followed by more than a decade of good relationships with the company."[46] McCann notes, however, that "the company's relaxed attitude toward unionization and willingness to deal with 751" derived from two factors: that the business of aircraft manufacturing required stable access to a skilled workforce and that federal legislation such as the Wagner Act helped facilitate unionization more broadly.[47] The IAM's long history of barring women and people of color reinforced the power of white male employees.[48] As a result, the sense of fraternalism, stability, and authority thrived among the white male workers. When the National Labor Relations Board (NLRB) certified Local Lodge 751 in 1937, about one thousand Boeing workers were members. By May 1939 membership had risen to twenty-one hundred.[49] By December 1939 membership stood at more than four thousand.[50] In a relatively short period of time, then, Lodge 751 had positioned itself as a white fraternal organization with a distinctly separate identity and interest from company leaders and managers.

In 1939 Lodge 751 created a union newspaper, *Aero Mechanic*, which featured some of the same organizational language as the *Boeing News*, though in ways that sought to solidify fraternalism among shop-floor workers rather than between workers and company leaders. The first issue used the language of family to announce that the union newspaper had been "born" and was still in the process of working out logistics, "like a newborn babe." The newspaper offered ten dollars to the winner of a contest to name the new publication and issued only two guidelines for the contest: do not make the name long, and do not use the word *Boeing* in the title.[51] *Aero Mechanic* also included an employee "Shop News" section that was quickly renamed "Shop Dial," though the commentary was markedly more biting and included references to wages—something not mentioned in the employee sections of the *Boeing News*. In the first issue, for example, the bench shop reported, "So many of the boys have been leaving Boeing's to go to work at the Navy Yard for more money, that soon they'll be able to build planes instead of ships in Bremerton."[52] Also in the first issue was a column by the president of Lodge 751 that emphasized accessibility and fraternal bonding: "This, Brothers, is the first issue of YOUR PAPER, edited by your fellow workers and the news articles and criticism, we hope, will be furnished by all of you. Remember that this is your paper, like the Local, belongs to you and not any office, group of officers or any other click [*sic*] or group." The column went on to note that working-class identities and norms were to be celebrated in *Aero Mechanic*: "Don't think that you must have a brilliant education to express yourself here, we want your ideas in good homely language that you use every day on the job. Talk to all of us as if we were the fellow alongside on the job."[53]

Engineers fought for a separate organization based on their identities as professional workers. As one engineer, Richard Henning, recalls of his experience working at Boeing in the 1930s and 1940s, "We were petitioning the NLRB for a separate vote to have our own professional organization completely separate of the shop union. We could not accept the idea of professionals being told how much they could earn and how they were to work on the job by a shop union." Henning goes on to describe how Boeing engineers eventually got their own union, the Seattle Professional Engineering Employees Association (SPEEA), which was created in 1944 and was approved by final vote in 1946, "in spite of the shop union and in spite of an all-out effort by the Boeing Company Labor Management V.P. to convince the engineers that they had their best interests at heart, and that we really didn't need a union organization."[54] Despite this early disagreement, Henning notes, "relationships with the Company were cordial."[55]

The instabilities from the forced restructuring in 1934 and the Great Depression threatened to exacerbate a sense of helplessness and reliance on the whims of both the federal government and the economic context. The construction and promotion of fraternal norms, by both union and company leaders, helped alleviate some of the economic and social divisions and promoted a sense of fraternal stability and solidarity, even while divisions between ranks of workers and between workers and management remained and tensions sometimes surfaced.

Tensions in Reporting "Family" News

The evolution of the *Boeing News* makes it clear that workers did not always rise to the expectations set forth by company leaders and the family metaphor. The first "Shop Notes" feature mentioned a shortage of items to report, and the *Boeing News* editor chided departments for not providing news items and sought to encourage greater future cooperation: "Other departments certainly have more news than is published here. Next month Boeing News wants to see every department included and we would like to have plenty of news from each shop."[56] Yet, even when contributing, workers did not always display the enthusiasm that company leaders sought. The floor supervisor of the cable shop humorously pointed out the unpleasantness of submitting news for consideration and offered the following poem for one 1934 issue:

> I'm quite a brave man when danger is near,
> To run I never choose,
> But one task makes me shiver and sets me aquiver,
> That's writing for Boeing News.[57]

Similarly, the assembly shop reported, "The 'fatal day' arrives again and as usual the mind is blank, the pencil broken and the shop's reporter on night shift. Oh well—."[58] When the machine shop reported, "We were hoping our idea of a moratorium on shop notes would go over big this month but the boss vetoed the proposition," the *Boeing News* editor replied in an "Editor's Note" that "the press knows no holiday."[59]

While comical in tone, such excerpts also showcase the various ways that shop-floor workers sought, and exerted, a sense of ownership over their own departments and maintained a distance from corporate management. Submissions for "Shop Notes" sometimes seemed to mock the status of shop-floor news in the workplace while focusing on the significance of employees' labor and workplace demands for that labor. The finishing shop, for example, listed a few marriages, births, and parties for its December 1933 entry and then noted that building the newest airplane design was in fact their top priority: "That's all for now. We're so busy chasing new pursuit parts that we can't very well concentrate on news."[60] Similarly, in April

1933 the dope shop, where lacquer was applied to fabric skins, reported that "transports are keeping everyone so busy that there's little time for anything else, including our news column."[61] Another entry admitted that motivation was lacking when the regular reporter was away: "Our official Boeing News correspondent, Roy Andrews, now is on vacation and his pinch hitter isn't exactly inspired, it seems—thus the lack of more news."[62] Such sentiments belie both the comical nature of many of the entries and the level of negotiation that took place on the shop floor about the place of shop-floor employees in helping to shape workplace culture, even while the *Boeing News* was an instrument of corporate power.

In general, the *Boeing News* entries from the late 1930s and early 1940s were more polished and routine, while the entries from the early 1930s reflect some stress over reporting news items and a less-than-inspiring level of shop-floor cooperation, perhaps not surprising given the turbulent economic situation plaguing the company in the early 1930s. Even with the establishment of routine reporting, however, workers continued to display some resistance to management strategies. Company leaders and workers were beginning to feel their interests conflict and diverge even as the company sought to solidify a workplace "family." One 1939 report, for example, chided inspection department workers for a seeming lack of cooperation: "Your correspondent would like to point out that news is scarce because members of the Department have not contributed any items. He would appreciate any cooperation from the gang in turning in news items, pictures and cartoons of interest. Leave them in the Inspection Booth."[63] *Aero Mechanic*, too, sometimes reported difficulty in obtaining worker support and loyalty. One shop news report, for example, stated, "If it hadn't been for the new members being initiated on our last meeting night it would have been a pretty sorry looking meeting. What holds you guys back?" *Aero Mechanic*, like the *Boeing News*, found it necessary to remind workers to submit news items and to sign up and show up for member events. One shop noted that the time demands of the union could be difficult to navigate in concert with work duties: "Since this is our first issue and time is short, we won't have very much to say."[64] The economic context and the instability of the workforce no doubt made keeping up the pace of news submission difficult.

Growing Pains and the "Boeing Spirit"
during the Great Depression

Part of what kept the business of submitting news items difficult was the same reason that a company news medium was needed and instituted in the first place: the rapid expansion and contraction of the company during the 1930s amid the challenges presented by the Great Depression. As the company weathered the crisis of the Depression in the early 1930s, the company saw an upswing in growth in the late 1930s; this cycle made it imperative for company leaders to try to foster unity between workers and management and temper unionization efforts, which threatened to fragment corporate culture. The *Boeing News* was an effort to maintain stability and retain worker confidence in corporate management decisions. After the significant downturn in the mid-1930s, employment levels rose. By 1939 the company had more than three thousand workers, or more than double the number at the beginning of the 1930s.[65] Throughout the 1930s the "Personal Notes" and "Shop Notes" sections were often dedicated to welcoming new workers to the various shop departments at Boeing.[66] The wood shop observed the growth in both itself and the company, and its reporter noted that, at least from the perspective of its workers, the growth made the task of submitting newsworthy items easier: "Well, its Boeing News time again and with our crew increasing at the rate it has been for the past few weeks, in the future we should be able to fill several volumes."[67] The column then went on to welcome ten new workers to the wood shop. In 1940 the finishing shop similarly reported on the "fast-growing brotherhood of paint splashers."[68] New additions of shops, such as the material preparation shop and the factory manager's office, were also noted, and the column provided a space for these shops to introduce workers and departments to one another.[69]

The *Boeing News* functioned as a space where company leaders could address the volatility of aircraft manufacturing. The publication informed workers of the ups and downs of the aircraft industry and attempted to soften the blows of company downturns, as one "All in the Family" column from the late 1930s makes evident. A May 1938 issue included a piece on the difficulties of working on a contract basis, such as high overhead costs and high initial investment for labor and materials. The piece concluded that it was in the interest of both management and labor to produce the most competitive wage because "a continuous flow of new business must be secured."[70] Boeing workers were expected to shoulder part of the burden of the high manufacturing costs through loyalty to the company and acceptance of wages that might not increase on a yearly basis. A guest columnist for "All in the Family," Ben J. Pearson, who worked in the sales department, picked up on these themes when he urged workers to maintain productivity in order to ensure government contracts for Flying Fortresses as part of the national defense rearmament program: "The biggest thing that we can do toward getting this business, which would mean jobs for us all, is to meet our schedule and deliver two B-17B's in May."[71] A worker's response, titled "An Appeal to Ourselves," was printed in the *Boeing News* in April 1939. The response suggests that some workers identified with the responsibilities and expectations that company leaders had established: "Our opportunity is to achieve greater fame by proving to our customers that we can meet and even surpass their demands. To do this we must assume the responsibility of our individual jobs; we might realize the importance of assignments; we must cooperate with each other and the management, with faster production as our common objective."[72] Signed "An Hourly Employee," the letter suggests the possibility of tensions between managers and employees on the shop floor, as well as the significance of work culture for motivating workers—and that workers themselves were an important part of this process. And Boeing's status as a defense contractor meant that familial endeavors were about more than an effort to secure workers' loyalty; there was also an effort to discipline workers to be good citizens of the state. For workers, it was about trying to achieve status and stability through long-term employment in a volatile, often unpredictable industry.

Despite the tensions caused by the turbulent employment cycles, the union organization efforts, and the growing distance between company leaders and shop-floor workers, Boeing had constructed a sense of stability that helped company leaders and workers weather the Great Depression. A sense of optimism often permeated the pages of the "Personal Notes" reports and paid homage, often in comical ways, to the Depression. One

1932 item, for example, reflected a sense of removal from the economic instability and the social changes manifest during the Great Depression: "Bob Hamlin, one of the 'old faithfuls' in this department, still has a cheerful outlook on life in spite of the depression, for he is planning to be married shortly. Good luck to you, Bob."[73] Boeing seemed to offer a foundation for creating family stability at a time when the Depression was putting strains on male breadwinners and families. Talk of marriage in the "Shop Notes" feature was often framed not as a risky endeavor, even while marriages were often abandoned or put on hold during the economic instabilities of the Great Depression, but as a normal part of a worker's life, as seen in the engineering department's report that Phil Close was "shaping a little love nest, and will soon be splitting his pay check on a 95 to 5 basis, with Phil on the short end."[74] Another entry made note of a wave of marriages: "Among those who will be running up the middle aisle this month are Ralph Berg and Wayne Sheridan. Who started all this? We wish them the best of everything."[75] The passages reflect a sense that employment at Boeing could, ironically, insulate people from the effects of the Great Depression, despite the turbulent employment cycles, and provide a living wage to support more than just a single man.

Some passages did note the effects of the Great Depression on family life. A 1934 entry from the dope shop, for example, pointed out, "From observations in this shop, the depression must still be on. We're unable to report a single June bride or new arrival. The only thing June has produced thus far is a lot of nice weather for picnickers and fisherman [*sic*]."[76] The economic collapse did in fact cause people to delay marriages and birth rates to decline, though they had been declining prior to the Great Depression. To many, having children during a major downturn was an economic risk.[77] At Boeing, however, at least according to the *Boeing News*, it seemed more newsworthy to comment on a month *without* a birth or marriage, such as when the assembly shop ended a news report in 1932 by noting, "No new babies; no new marriages; no new divorces. Final score—even up."[78] More often than not, the "Personal Notes" entries displayed a humorous optimism about family changes, such as when one worker reportedly noted, "This depression's awful. Chuck Becvar gets a baby boy. Warren Mowery gets a boy also, and we get no cigars."[79]

As the 1930s wore on, the reporting of marriages and births came to dominate "Shop News." For the production planning department, births were so common that their entries referenced the "Production 'Proud Pappy' Club."[80] That department reported in 1939, "Our old 'one-a-month' club is still going strong. This time we report the birth of two bouncing baby boys. The proud daddies are George Choate and Don Joy."[81] Such excerpts reflect both the routine nature of family additions as well as the sheer growth in numbers at the company. Celebrations of births were conducted on the shop floor: "Joe Romoseth reports the glad news of a baby girl, Jo Ann, born week before last. The proud papa's chest expansion has increased about four inches, and we are looking for the cigars."[82] Such celebrations are explained not just by the structural changes of the company but also by its shifting culture.

Along with the increase in employment levels at the end of the 1930s, there was a sense of stability derived from the shop-floor "family." Its members included a growing cohort of men around the same age and in the same stage of life, and they came to dominate the shop floor at Boeing. Workers were increasingly like one another, as humorously observed in an entry submitted by assembly shop plant 2 in 1940: "That all airplane mechanics are screwy is a fact; that they may get pickled as a pastime is well known, that lots of them are building boats is a popular rumor, that all the rest are married, we know."[83] With unionization and with the growth of the company, employment at Boeing did not seem as risky as it otherwise might have seemed in an industry plagued by cyclical layoffs. As these men aged and advanced their careers at Boeing, they together celebrated the milestones of family norms such as getting married, welcoming babies, buying new cars and homes, and taking vacations. The "Shop Notes" in the *Boeing News* helped to build this sense of shop-floor camaraderie and institutionalized such events as the norms of worker identity. On the shop floor, and in the pages of the *Boeing News*, there was an assumed bonding over family norms. Boeing's corporate culture relied on heterosexual norms, which enforced social hierarchies and an unwritten code of conduct. Indeed, Boeing's corporate culture upheld heterosexual norms as the cornerstone of workplace order.

For white men, who constituted nearly all of the Boeing workforce until

World War II, a corporate culture built around family norms provided a sense of inclusion and recognition of men's importance as breadwinners for their families. They also gained fraternal networks of support that were both social and material. The November 1939 issue of the *Boeing News* highlights these themes. The template shop reported on a wedding shower of sorts for a newly married Boeing worker: "Monday morning Elton passed the cigars, and the same day at lunch time the boys of the Template Shop presented Braddock with a beautiful set of dishes, two pyrex cooking dishes and a rolling pin, in exchange for the promise that they would all be invited to dinner."[84] *Boeing News* editors included photographs of workers' children, identified as the "Second Generation," and declared, "Of all the 'papas' among Boeing personnel, 100 per cent of them are proud papas and rightly so. If you don't think so, just casually ask any of them how the baby is getting along!"[85] These entries all celebrated Boeing workers' identities as heterosexual married men who supported one another as well as their families and who relished their roles as husbands, fathers, and workers. Such characterizations paint a picture of company stability, cohesion, and camaraderie.

The portrait of domestic harmony presented in the *Boeing News* did not mean that there was no tension in the predominantly white male spaces or in the heterosexual model of workplace organization. Contradiction and tensions within the family metaphors used by corporations in the first decades of the twentieth century were also not uncommon.[86] One 1938 *Boeing News* story, for example, attempted to enlist cutting humor to comment on employee relations and dismiss any notion of homosexuality at Boeing: "Two of our young men have forsaken single blessedness. John Brockway and Bob Hillman have set up housekeeping together on Beach Drive—they really *should* pass out cigars."[87] Boeing's corporate culture did not directly recognize any social relations other than institutionalized heterosexual order. The heterosexual order that was institutionalized in Boeing's corporate culture allowed such stories to be dismissed as humorous. Celebrated relationships that made it into the "Personal Notes" were those within the bounds of heterosexual marriages, such as the report that "a romance in the dope shop culminated September 9 in the marriage of Clara Bercot and Clyde Ault, both members of the shop."[88]

The heterosexual ideal that familialism celebrated was also institutionalized in the family wage ideal that the welfare state upheld. Margot Canaday notes that the Social Security Act of 1935 cemented a "gendered imbalance" into the welfare state by creating a system "designed to shore up men as family breadwinners." In omitting categories of work dominated by migrant workers (farmworkers, casual laborers, and domestics), it also created a system in which benefits went primarily to white men.[89] As she argues, the welfare state "was both gendered and (hetero)sexualized as well. Men were the beneficiaries of marital perks but also the targets of marital imperatives. The latter could be quite punitive, but both types of incentives were necessary to make heterosexuality work as a system that was even more binding for women."[90] Alice Kessler-Harris notes that even into the 1960s "the idea of gender difference remained embedded in marriage patterns and family lives, social tradition and economic possibility." In the family wage ideal, women were supposed to work for their families, not for individual rights: "Women were educated, trained, and taught to earn in order to 'help' their husbands[,] to raise their families' standards of living, and to enable their children to stay in school."[91] Lodge 751, too, reflected the assumptions of the breadwinner family model. In 1939 a women's auxiliary for Lodge 751 was founded. Called the Clipperettes, the women largely organized social events and acted as a support network for Boeing families. The Clipperettes sought "better living conditions for the workers and their dependents," goals that fit within the paradigm and assumptions of the heterosexual breadwinner model.[92] The organization assumed, for example, that members would be a "wife, mother, sister" or "daughter of the Aeronautical Mechanics."[93]

By the 1930s these heterosexual family norms were so institutionalized in Boeing's workplace culture and the company so relied on for a family wage that workers began to talk in terms of "generations" of workers. The engineering department reported in February 1939, "Bert Norberg and George Snyder passed out the cigars, and then took home a couple of employment application blanks for use about twenty one years hence when their young sons finish their engineering courses."[94] Although humorous, the report shows the expectation that shop-floor workers would pass masculine heterosexual shop-floor traditions on to a new generation and keep those traditions in the Boeing "family." One 1933 "Introducing" column told the story of how Albert Walloch came to work at the company: "His parents moved to Seattle—that was in 1920—and he came along. Here his father joined the Boeing organization and a few months later Al Walloch followed in his steps." The publication noted that, while he almost became a bookkeeper, "tradition stepped in" and he became a sheet-metal worker, eventually rising to assistant foreman and then manager of the control surface shop.[95]

Generations of workers were further expanded to include grandchildren as the number of "old-timers" who had been with the company since the 1920s, and sometimes earlier, began to grow. One entry, for example, observed about the birth of a grandchild, "After much questioning it finally came out that Tim Strigen is a proud grandpapa. His reluctance to reveal the secret lies in the fact that a granddaughter arrived instead of a grand-son. Tim claims shyness in any dealings with the ladies. This tiny miss, however, has already caused Tim to trim his 'mustachio' a little closer."[96] While comical, the entry plays on the pervasiveness of masculine norms in the shop-floor departments, making it seem as if women, or anything feminine, were a matter of strangeness.

Masculinity, Boeing "Stags," and Welfare Capitalism

By the end of the 1930s, with the company workforce growing and an institutionalized sense of camaraderie being cemented on the shop floor, company leaders began to institute even greater changes. In addition to cultivating identification of workers with the ideal of the Boeing "family" through venues like the *Boeing News*, the company worked to shape workplace culture by sponsoring company recreation leagues. For large corporations like Boeing, the family metaphor was intrinsically linked to welfare capitalism, in which corporations undertook company-sponsored recreation and social welfare programs. Several scholars have explained the rise of welfare capitalism in American business as a means of combating the rising influence of unions and fostering a sense of loyalty among employees.[97] As Joan Sangster explains, welfare capitalism is an organized system that corporations implemented to maintain a loyal workforce and that was characterized by "the endeavor to create a Company culture of consensus, deference and accommodation" in order to regulate the workforce.[98] A key turning point for welfare capitalism occurred in the 1930s and 1940s, when it began to expand as a result of World War II and because of decreased resistance and influence on the part of unions.[99] In line with these larger changes, as well as the swelling ranks of employees on the company payroll, Boeing added a personnel department in 1939. The personnel department provided assistance with safety and health programs, company insurance, and follow-up for new employees, as well as assistance to current employees in "finding the kind of work for which they are best suited" and resources for further training and education. The new department also helped with the growing number of "employee activities" and was ready to offer "assistance with employees' personal problems, insofar as it is welcome."[100] In 1939 company leaders organized a basketball team to play the Seattle Community League and made plans for an "inter-company basketball circuit" so that various departments, such as the already-organized engineering department, could play one another.[101] The company even had a bowling league that spanned Boeing's plants in Washington and Canada.[102] In 1939 the Boeing Camera Club boasted sixty-seven members and, fittingly, awarded the blue ribbon for the 1939 competition to a picture of a smiling baby.[103] Salmon derbies and ski parties were other popular activities by the late 1930s.[104] The new, expanded corporate culture could serve as a means to attract workers to one another, as well as to the company. Skating parties, for example, which began in the winter of 1939 and were held several times per month, offered a place for social mixing for both Boeing employees and their friends. The *Boeing News* offered pictures of one such party, including one of a young man helping tie the skates of a young woman, and noted that the parties "are thoroughly enjoyed by all."[105]

Masculinity and a sense of shared heterosexual family norms were central to company activities. "Stag parties" held on weekends and after work helped solidify the fraternal networks being built on the shop floor. One purchasing department report provides insight into some of the activities at these parties: "A while back the boys from the department enjoyed an evening in the quiet revelry of a congenial stag party. The evening and morning were spent playing a bit of poker and black jack, and refreshments were served."[106] A report from a year later shows such parties had become an expected part of company culture: "The Purchasing Department's stag party came off as scheduled. The boys attending managed to maintain their equilibrium throughout the evening, even though that was difficult at times probably from lack of sleep. Some left early, intending to ski the next day, but recuperation was more the general idea. All in all, and skipping a few question marks, the party was a huge success, with the promise of more to come."[107] Within the "Shop Notes" feature, celebrations of men's hunting trips and adventures were quite common, though, like the observations about living arrangements, they were always within the context of masculine heterosexual norms. While these were "off-hours" celebrations, the very reporting of them in the *Boeing News* institutionalized them as an important part of shop-floor culture, departmental camaraderie, and loyalty. Other activities, however, were more overtly tied to shop-floor performance and work roles. The inspection department had monthly get-togethers, which were "planned to combine business with pleasure—to promote friendliness within the group and educated old and new members alike in the problems of inspection."[108]

Rising through the Ranks

While humor and recreational activities display the loyalty and genuine affection workers had for one another, many *Boeing News* sections were dedicated to celebrating the accomplishments of workers, especially as workers rose through the company ranks. Thus, the "Personal Notes" were a way to give recognition to other workers, as well as managers. As the company grew and added new workers, the *Boeing News* became a way to mark different generations of workers and celebrate "old-timers." One "Introducing" column noted, "At one time Charles Thompson was just one of three men in the welding shop of the Boeing Airplane Company. Today, he is the foreman of seventy-eight men in this branch of the factory." The column also noted that he "learned the aircraft welding trade by diligently working at it."[109] Another "Introducing" column, published in 1934, compared engineer Lyle Pierce, employed with Boeing since 1922, to a Horatio Alger character; Lyle had "headed west, with no one to see" and "with no promise of a job," though he had heard of the Boeing

Airplane Company and decided to apply.[110] Such celebrations helped cement worker identification with other workers, Boeing career paths, the development of artisanal skills over years with the company, and a sense of workforce stability.

Company leaders, in addition to workers, used the *Boeing News* as a venue in which to promote and celebrate longtime employees and workers who had been promoted. The *Boeing News* functioned as a space in which to celebrate men who were moving up through the ranks of workers. The December 1933 issue of the *Boeing News*, for example, celebrated "Shop Veterans" and listed an "honor roll" of employees who had worked for Boeing for ten to fifteen years. Many of those on the "honor roll" were listed as "foreman," which reflects the growing ranks of the company and the promotion of workers from the shop floor.[111] By the 1930s, many of the company's shop-floor supervisors were men who had joined the company prior to 1920 and worked their way up. For example, W. S. "Dick" Weimar started with the company in 1917, working "on the bench" doing welding and brazing. In 1918 he was promoted to supervisor of the welding and brazing department, and in 1928 he was promoted to supervisor of the machine shop.[112] The "Introducing" section also functioned as a way to highlight workers who had risen through the ranks.[113] The April 1932 issue of the *Boeing News* included a list of shop-floor supervisors throughout the company ranks. Of the thirteen such supervisors listed, twelve had started before 1921 and eight of them were made foremen by 1929.[114] By the early 1930s, then, Boeing had a well-documented cohort of men who had begun as shop-floor employees. Their rise was celebrated in corporate culture in the 1930s as evidence of opportunities for promotion and male advancement.

Aero Mechanic, however, pointed out that managers had the power to parcel out promotions according to their own designs. The wing shop, for example, complained of "favoritism on the part of management" in 1939. The shop noted that managers pulled men from other shops to train them as "lead men for the riveters" despite there being "men in this shop who have considerable seniority and are capable of handling these jobs." *Aero Mechanic* also served as a place where workers could air grievances about the union. "There is a case or two where the lead men receive less pay than the men under him," the contributor noted, asserting that "this department will get things done if the Brothers will use their Union for the purpose it was established to keep and improve conditions and wages."[115] The complaint shows that shop-floor workers increasingly identified the union as a source of power for changing workplace conditions and as a means of fighting for advancement and better working conditions, even while it could also be a source of tension and a site for abuse of power. By 1939 the growing "brotherhood" of the union movement competed with a corporate culture seeking to establish a Boeing "family" based on fraternal associations between employees, managers, and company leaders.

Like other company leaders who used the familial metaphor in the first decades of the twentieth century, Boeing leaders wanted to keep the sense of a small shop even as growth made doing so difficult. As Boeing expanded, it was less and less likely that workers would know one another or mirror a close-knit family. Even by the 1930s Boeing was not really a "family shop" where employees knew one another. News features such as "Introducing" were ironic in that, if the company was indeed a close-knit family, as the *Boeing News* liked to promote, there would be no need for such introductions. *Boeing News* editors sometimes acknowledged this tension, though the publication still assumed a level of familiarity. Even if the realities of the work environment did not allow every employee to know the others, there was an expected cohesion based on ideas of race, gender, and professional identity. Celebrations of Boeing careers, promotions, and retirements certainly gave the impression of stable, long-term employment opportunities.

Boeing's growing links to the University of Washington (UW) helped company leaders build a network of engineers, thus generating an image of the company as a place to cultivate a professional identity and career. By the late 1930s, and even more clearly by the postwar period, UW was seen as a key to advancement through the company ranks, particularly for those who had studied engineering.[116] In the early 1930s the connection between UW and Boeing was still fairly limited compared to later, but awareness of the opportunities available at UW were building in the 1930s.[117] In 1932, for example, the *Boeing News* reported on a former employee in the engineering department who had left to attend engineering school at the

University of Washington.[118] Similarly, some "Personal Notes" entries indicated that some workers viewed education at UW as a way to move off the shop floor and up the ranks at Boeing: "One of our new men, Joe Kearny, is essaying the iron-man role. He is working on the second shift at Plant No. 2, and carrying a full course at the University of Washington so he can get his full and rightful share of sheephide." The entry went on to direct some humor Kearny's way in a tone characteristic of shop-floor submissions: "Unless business is much quieter at night than during the day, he's gonna be a fine example of 'Two Sleepy People.'"[119] The "Introducing" columns often pointed to UW educations. One such case was that of Jack Kylstra, who gave up farming in Yakima to enter the University of Washington's civil engineering program. He started at Boeing in 1924, eventually earning a promotion to project engineer on several different plane models.[120] Alumni of UW often saw their names in the celebratory announcements of shop-floor promotions. One 1939 issue of the *Boeing News* announced the promotion of two UW engineering graduates. R. J. Minshall, who joined Boeing in 1918, was promoted to design engineer in 1928 and chief engineer in 1936, and he then became a vice president of engineering in 1938. In 1939 Minshall was promoted to vice president and assistant general manager. Jack Kylstra took his place as chief engineer.[121]

By the late 1930s Boeing had more than doubled the size of its workforce, and it anticipated continued growth and the need for more engineers. The company had also made the case for its significance to the city of Seattle, and UW, the state's preeminent research university, had paid attention. By the postwar period, Boeing's connections to institutions of higher education, and UW in particular, were crucial to the company's development. Boeing's ties to educational institutions such as UW help to explain the company's ability to support the high level of innovation and flexibility that the airplane and aerospace industries demanded.[122] Boeing's relationship with UW also allowed for the creation and maintenance of the gender hierarchies that upheld Boeing's corporate culture. Boeing relied on UW to provide a stable and skilled workforce. The engineering school in particular provided a steady supply of skilled workers, most of them men, and cutting-edge knowledge and research capabilities. As chapter 2 shows, this partnership took on particular significance during and after World War II, when the company devoted increased attention to engineering.[123]

In the 1930s the view that engineers were the premier workers at Boeing was in the process of being formed. To land a job in Boeing's engineering department was a sign of maturity and increased authority, as the inspection department made clear in one "Personal Notes" column in which it reported that Fred Stover, a former inspector, had "graduated to the Engineering Department."[124] Particularly in the years prior to World War II most Boeing leaders were trained at UW, especially in the university's engineering department.[125] Boeing's links to UW serve as a good example of the company's position in the urban-industrial complex. In 1963 *Boeing Magazine* (a monthly publication produced in addition to the *Boeing News* and geared toward a public audience) featured an article on Boeing's long affiliation with educational institutions.[126] According to this article, "Since 1917, when company founder William E. Boeing hired two promising engineering students from the University of Washington, it has been the company's philosophy to attract and retain the top technical talent from the nation's colleges."[127] Boeing's relationship with UW played an important role in the company's efforts to advance airplane manufacturing and aerospace research. It also helped company leaders navigate capitalist instabilities by providing a reliable and steady network of professionally skilled men.

Boeing News versus *Aero Mechanic*

The *Boeing News* issues of the late 1930s show the central place the publication occupied in corporate attempts to manage growth. Workers were still expected, as part of their work, to report news that fit the family metaphor. The "Personal Notes" section in the April 1939 issue includes all of the traits that characterized the concept of the Boeing "family" by the late 1930s and early 1940s. The bench shop entry reported celebrating the birth of a baby with the established fraternal tradition of handing out cigars: "Carl Lantz came through with cigars last week. It was a husky boy. By the way, Carl, you had better check with Max Estep, who claims he is two cigars behind." In the same issue the assembly shop at plant 2 highlighted the centrality of heterosexual marriage in the lives of shop-floor employees and in maintaining capitalist accumulation: "Our chief shop clerk is looking better now that his wife is home to do the cooking (and keep him in nights)." The wing shop highlighted the established significance of non-shop-floor activities in the lives of employees, and perhaps the skepticism toward corporate management, by using humor to report on men's adventures together: "Extensive plans are being laid these days by Cliff Emery and Roy Burnette who are really planning a big vacation. They are mapping out a fishing trip to Alaska to start in a few weeks, and we hope they bring home the bacon."[128] The reports continued on for several pages, which illustrates the growing numbers of employees.

Celebrations of the breadwinner family model continued into the 1940s. The *Boeing News*, for example, continued to run a series of photographs of the children of current Boeing employees. One "Second Generation" feature, for example, noted that workers in the template shop congratulated a fellow worker on the date of his child's first birthday.[129] Other features highlighted domestic bliss through childrearing and promoted workers as responsible for upholding such traditions. For example, a 1942 issue of the *Boeing News* displayed a picture of a grinning man surrounded by his coworkers. The accompanying text explained how the workers in shop 432 pitched in and presented the man with eighty-nine dollars to mark his new role as a father to triplets. The image and caption depict fatherhood as an experience that bonded men at Boeing and reinforced an atmosphere of fraternalism and camaraderie.[130] As images like this one suggest, in the 1930s workers and management began to identify as members of the Boeing "family." In the pages of newsletters, in hiring and promotions practices, in shop-floor relations, and in both Boeing- and union-sponsored social events, company and union leaders assumed that workers should identify with one another in terms of race, gender, sexuality; the *Boeing News* attempted to create a shared work experience and history. Conceptions of skill, advancement, authority, friendship, and camaraderie all relied on this established social order, which crystallized in the 1930s. The white heterosexual male breadwinner model came to define corporate culture and to provide a sense of order and stability in the workplace, though union efforts showcase the fractures within this sense of order and stability.

Aero Mechanic, too, pushed for fraternal solidarity, but among union members and for the purpose of creating a separate blue-collar shop-floor identity. Like the company and the *Boeing News,* Lodge 751 and *Aero Mechanic* sought to establish fraternal traditions based on heterosexual camaraderie. In 1939, for example, the machine shop reported in *Aero Mechanic* that "the turret lathers were sporting a bunch of cigars on September 12 in honor of the birth of a baby boy, 7½ lbs. to the wife of Herbert Borger."[131] Heterosexual marriages were also celebrated, as when the "great fraternity in the Welding Shop" reported, "Clee Hoffman and Don Simmons, energetic and hopeful men in the Welding Shop, were baptized into the royal and most benevolent order of henpecked husbands."[132] The key difference, of course, between the entries in *Aero Mechanic* versus those in the *Boeing News* is that Lodge 751 encouraged fraternal traditions to bolster the ranks of the union rather than corporate culture. *Aero Mechanic* also talked about "generations" of workers, but, rather than celebrating workers, it called on Boeing workers to sacrifice some of their time to union organizing "for our children" so that the next generation of workers could have higher living standards and better working conditions.[133] The growth of the company, and the spread of corporate management strategies, were making that goal increasingly difficult, though also more urgent in the eyes of union organizers.

By the early 1940s and the U.S. entrance into World War II the growth of the company and changing demographics presented new challenges to both corporate culture and union organization. The May 1942 issue of *Aero Mechanic* reported on the tensions caused by World War II, company growth, and the increased hiring of women:

> It's been a long, long time since 702 crashed the news, but now that we have a new and great active paper we can let the rest of the plant know that we're still alive and kicking. We have a swell bunch of fellows, and oh yes, girl clerks too, with a darned good boss and assistant. But despite this fact, many of the boys have quit and many others are undecided as to whether or not they should. It's quite a temptation when other companies jingle from 15 to 25 cents more per hour in front of their noses, not to mention better traffic conditions and other facilities. Of course, we realize that handling 25,000 people is no picnic and mistakes are

bound to happen, but why is there such a lack of interest in holding good loyal and skilled men? It seems to be a lack of foresight. If these men were the everyday growlers and complainers, we might understand. But, loyalty should be recognized.[134]

As the next chapter shows, World War II exacerbated all of the tensions experienced in the 1930s to an unprecedented degree. Wartime shifts challenged the fraternal order, and both company and union struggled to preserve worker solidarity, particularly as employment levels skyrocketed and the company hired more women than it ever had before. With these changes, white male workers felt a new vulnerability. Company leaders, union leaders, and male employees would look to the social order of fraternalism built in the 1930s to try to weather the challenges brought by World War II.

CHAPTER 2

Manpower versus Womanpower during World War II

In 1939 the *Boeing News* ran an article headlined "Boeing Craftsmen," which pointed out that shop-floor development was a routine part of the Boeing "family." The article noted that men in the cable shop, for example, were "trained in the Shop because skilled men are not available otherwise."[1] Workers were "homegrown" and achieved their skill through time with the company and experience on the shop floor. Aircraft manufacturing, in other words, was specialized work. In fact, 90 percent of those employed in the aircraft industry in 1939 were skilled and semiskilled workers. Thus, men skilled in building aircraft were not easily replaced. Most aircraft workers spent several years as apprentices before achieving the status of fully skilled craft workers.[2] At Boeing, workers could expect to be rewarded for their loyalty to the company with a career and advancement potential, even while the boom-and-bust cycles of the aircraft industry required periodic layoffs. Virtually all of these workers were white men. World War II, however, would fundamentally alter the fraternal standards that had defined the Boeing "family" in the 1930s. This chapter describes how Boeing's white fraternal culture was challenged by the entry of women and people of color into the industrial workforce during World War II, though the idea of "family" helped integrate women and minorities into the company in ways that did not fully challenge white men's authority, or the norms of patriarchal capitalism and the gender division of labor more broadly, because they were positioned as supportive workers rather than primary wage earners and long-term employees establishing career paths. While wartime conditions made it impossible to maintain a stable and homogeneous workforce of skilled white men, company policies and culture approached many changes as temporary and precluded more radical change.

The entry of women into the industrial workforce supported the idea of the workforce as family because women, both at Boeing and in constructions of the nuclear family, were positioned as supportive family members who were not suspending the social care roles that upheld capitalism. This does not mean, however, that women and minorities were easily integrated into Boeing's workforce. This chapter offers an inside view of the internal negotiations that took place as Boeing tried to navigate the challenges of the war years. It also shows the angst and worry that company leaders experienced as they tried to maintain a sense of cohesion and stability despite unprecedented growth, diversity, and disruption.

The war was a turning point for the Boeing "family" in that it required the company to do more with less and to refashion ideas of a workplace built on fraternal networks. As one 1943 Boeing ad explained, "One of the most important jobs at Boeing is . . . simplifying procedures so that, despite shortages of skilled workers, production constantly goes upward."[3] In order to meet ever-increasing production goals, defense plants across the country expanded their efforts to find new industrial workers, including women and African American men.[4] Wartime demands reshaped Boeing's economic and labor policies and offered new opportunities for untrained women and minorities. The labor crisis of World War II forced Boeing's leaders to alter the company image and long-standing employment policies. One promotional pamphlet described the diversity of workers who built Boeing B-17 Flying Fortresses: "Who are these people, the builders of the Fortresses? They are people just like you and your neighbors. They are housewives, students, store clerks, former business men, teachers. They are middle-aged, elderly; they are youngsters in their latter teens. They are a cross section of all America."[5] Although wartime production needs ultimately required Boeing managers to rely on this "cross section" of workers, company officials resisted permanent changes to the tradition of trained white male labor.

The political economy of World War II, and particularly wartime labor shortages, strained the family metaphor that had been the foundation for Boeing's corporate culture in the 1930s. Company leaders tried to adapt to the crisis of wartime changes while still adhering to the capitalist family norm of the male breadwinner model. Family norms outside the plant, built into social policy and gendered capitalist norms in the 1930s, helped sustain and nurture the family culture inside Boeing even during the disruptions of war. The Boeing "family" became a way to maintain gender and race hierarchies and foster a sense of stability and tradition even when the realities of everyday life did not provide the cohesiveness or predictability that company leaders wanted. Understanding how Boeing negotiated the hiring of nontraditional wartime workers lends insight into the absence of women in industrial employment once the war ended, as well as the postwar place of women and minorities at the company. The war years opened jobs for women and African American men but in ways that also facilitated employment discrimination and gendered views of opportunities well after the war was over.

Professionalism and Wartime Growth

During World War II Boeing leaders struggled to balance industry leadership and efficiency with a rapidly growing workforce. The capital and support necessary to maintain such efficiency did not come easily. For the aircraft industry, in particular, it is important to examine the development of professionalism in the industry in the context of government contracts and national security developments. In 1940 Pres. Franklin D. Roosevelt declared the development of American airpower an urgent priority because the United States needed to keep up with German technological innovations. Yet during the late 1930s and early 1940s the aviation industry was still in the process of being created. Despite the horror of the Pearl Harbor attack and the United States' entry into the war in 1941, air force leaders had to work hard to win support for the increased production of aircraft; it was not a smooth transition to wartime production or increased military spending.[6] In addition, American industry was still recovering from the toll taken by the Great Depression. In the 1930s public hostility toward women workers, especially those who were married, grew as work became more difficult to find and women faced accusations of taking jobs away from men. Most employers, including the federal government, barred a household from having more than one job with the same employer. Job opportunities for women in heavy industry, beyond the service, clerical, and trade areas, were especially affected by this hostility toward women workers.[7] Thus, where skilled workers could be justified in a burgeoning industry such as aircraft manufacturing, the jobs were considered work for male breadwinners.

The beginning of hostilities in Europe and the ensuing military buildup led to government contracts that helped pull Boeing and other aircraft manufacturers out of the slump they had experienced during the Great Depression.[8] Boeing began production of the B-17 Flying Fortress in 1935 in response to the army's request for a bomber.[9] In 1939 the U.S. Army Air Corps ordered thirty-nine B-17s, which led to plant expansion and refinancing efforts because of the plane's high production costs.[10] In 1940 Boeing engineers also began designing the B-29 (though the company would not begin production on the aircraft until 1943). To assist in the rapid development of bombers, the federal Defense Plant Corporation funded a new Boeing plant in Renton, Washington, and an expansion of the Seattle plant.[11] During the war Boeing also established eight branch plants in western Washington.[12] Along with expansion of the plants came the need for a larger workforce. The growth at the Seattle plant, the largest of Boeing's facilities, was particularly dramatic. At the end of December 1940 the company employed 8,427 people in Seattle, nearly triple the January 1939 level of 3,000 workers.[13]

During this growth, the company continued to rely on the family metaphor to describe workplace relations and obligations. When Boeing's Seattle plant (plant 2) was expanded in 1940, the company hosted a "housewarming" party for more than seven thousand Boeing workers and their guests. The *Boeing News* reported that workers and their families danced, socialized, and listened to speeches by company leaders, as well as Seattle mayor Arthur Langlie. The publication stressed that the celebratory atmosphere was tempered by the more solemn acknowledgment that the plant expansion signaled the hard work that was needed to complete the new government orders to supply more equipment for the United States and Britain to use in the war: "It was a gay party and a good time was had by everyone, but underneath it all was the knowledge that here was a huge, brand-new building, in which there will be a tremendous amount of activity in months to come." H. Oliver West, who oversaw production and manufacturing in his role as assistant to company president Phil Johnson, gave a speech in which he stated that he "would rather have the party called a housewarming than a dedication" because Boeing was relying on the hard work of employees to complete defense orders and "this job will be the factory's real dedication."[14] West's comments highlight the ways in which references to family functioned as a way to foster employee loyalty during the uncertainty of wartime changes.

Building a Workforce

As the military buildup continued, so did Boeing's need for more workers. Company leaders were faced with a sudden need for a massive workforce to build bombers, which for the first time required the recruitment of workers from outside the Seattle area. People from all over the country, and especially African Americans from the South, came to look for work in the defense industries.[15] Melvin Phillip Winston and his wife, Klara Mae Winston, recalled that, among the new people moving to the area, "most of them came up and wanted to work at Boeing."[16]

By the end of January 1941 the number of Boeing employees in Seattle had risen to 10,510—an increase of 2,000 workers in just one month. In the months leading up to the attack on Pearl Harbor the workforce in the Seattle plant more than doubled, from 10,652 in February to 22,764 at the end of October 1941. At the end of December 1941, its workforce had nearly tripled, to 28,840 workers. Except for a few months during the spring and summer of 1942 and 1943, when the company experienced high turnover and labor shortages, employment continued to climb. Seattle employment peaked at 31,750 in 1945, an almost a 300 percent increase over the 10,652 workers there in February 1941.[17] By the end of the war the total workforce, including employees at the Renton and other branch plants, comprised more than 45,000 people, more than five times the number employed at the original Seattle plant in 1940.[18] By the war's end, 1 out of every 6 people in King County, where the Seattle plant is located, worked at Boeing.[19]

That rapid growth, however, was not enough. In November 1940 Boeing

FIG. 3. Female workers preparing parts for the B-17F bomber in 1942. Courtesy Library of Congress, Prints and Photographs Division, FSA/OWI Collection, LC-USE6-D-008346.

managers reported a dire need for skilled workers, including tool and die makers. In December they called for machinists and welders as well.[20] Competition from the Navy Yard Puget Sound and other defense operations, many of which paid higher wages, hampered Boeing's ability to recruit experienced workers. H. Oliver West, who was promoted to executive vice president in 1941, noted, "Our problem is all in the skilled trades, those that require actual experience over a considerable period of time."[21]

As the labor shortage intensified nationwide after the attack on Pearl Harbor, women began to fill jobs traditionally done by men in a variety of fields. The defense industry and government agencies such as the War Manpower Commission intensified their efforts to recruit women workers in 1942, when it became clear that the number of men leaving jobs for the military was outweighing the number of women entering the workforce.[22] This recruiting effort did not, however, eliminate doubts about women's increased employment in the defense industry or outside the home. As late as 1943, with war production in full swing, *Fortune* magazine reported, "We are a kindly, somewhat sentimental people with strong, ingrained ideas about what women should or should not do. Many thoughtful citizens are seriously disturbed over the wisdom of bringing married women into factories."[23] Similarly, a 1943 *Life* magazine story on victory gardens noted that female students attending a Portland, Oregon, high school were "being instructed in house-wifely virtues," as opposed to receiving training for work outside the home.[24] Despite the need for wartime production and the crises that wartime labor shortages presented, discrimination against women working in blue-collar positions continued across defense industries. African American women in particular bore the brunt of such discrimination, and many employers refused to hire them.[25]

Hiring Women

The war forced Boeing managers to seek unskilled workers, to redefine what encompassed skilled work, and to train new workers to do skilled work, though the necessity of these changes was not immediately evident to Boeing leaders. The company president, Phil Johnson, pointed out in 1941 that significant change would have to take place in order for the company to hire women. Before the war, most wage-earning women in Seattle worked in the service industry. Employers who wished to hire them for factory work would have to obey state laws that controlled matters such as rest periods for women workers. Furthermore, factories would have to expand plants to include more spaces for women's restrooms and personnel services.[26] And, finally, Boeing managers believed they might have to hire a woman to work in the personnel office and oversee women applicants and employees.[27]

At an October 1941 staff committee meeting, company officials discussed several concerns. They determined that the employment office did not have adequate space or personnel to "properly handle women applicants in numbers." Further concerns lay with pay rates and union policies; one manager reported, "There are now a number of women on layoff who are members of the Union and must be re-employed at their rate of 93 cents an hour before we can take on additional women." Overwhelmed by the changes needed before hiring women, and not yet facing a severe, companywide labor shortage, officials decided to focus recruitment efforts on men and "postpone indefinitely the employment of women."[28]

In 1942, however, production increased dramatically, and Boeing needed a substantially larger workforce. The company boosted production from 60 planes per month in 1942 to 362 planes per month by March 1944.[29] From March 1942 to March 1944 Boeing increased the number of Flying Fortresses delivered fourfold.[30] Such rapid growth meant that Boeing's supply of men ran out quickly in the early years of the war. Company managers realized that they needed to hire women to keep up with production. The first female riveters, a group of seven, went to work in March 1942. They were trained in riveting, bucking, subassembly, and general sheet-metal work.[31] The transition to a mixed-sex workplace was not smooth. One Boeing worker, Hellen Nelson, recalled, "Women took an awfully bad beating in Final Assembly. There was harassment and sexism and that kind of thing. It was the first time men and women had worked together. There was a great deal of chauvinism. Women were considered too stupid to know how to do anything."[32] Another worker, who eventually quit, observed, "I had to work with a man who had never had a woman helper before" and he "hated me."[33]

Despite such experiences, many women still enjoyed the work and welcomed the opportunities for economic freedom, mobility, and the sense of independence that wartime work provided. Betty Russell, the first sheet-metal worker hired at Boeing, recalled her time at Boeing fondly. Just out of high school, Russell joined the Boeing staff in April 1942, and she later described her work experience as rewarding: "[I] had a lot of fun. I mean there were no women in the shop when I went to work there, but they allowed two women to work in a tool crib where they kept equipment and tools and so on, but they were boxed in. I worked on the floor, and I was the only woman on the floor for quite some time."[34] Russell's memories highlight both the significance of her work experience in her life, as well as the anxieties of company leaders who were afraid of mixing men and women workers on the shop floor. Russell reported going home to have dinner with the crew boss and his wife because the boss's wife said that if women were going to be employed at Boeing, she wanted to know who

FIG. 4. Women handing out materials for the production of the B-17F in the Boeing warehouse in 1942. Courtesy Library of Congress, Prints and Photographs Division, FSA/OWI Collection, LC-DIG-fsa-8d34408.

they were.[35] Wartime work offered a chance to make more money than was typical for women's work: "There would be days when we would make sixty-two-and-a-half cents an hour. That was good money, five dollars a day was good money, and you worked seven days a week."[36] Unlike during the Great Depression, women's work was encouraged and women valued the opportunity to earn higher incomes.[37]

Despite new attitudes toward women's work, at least for wartime emergency purposes, Boeing leaders continued to resist hiring very many women.

In addition to their worries about tensions on the shop floor, company leaders were uneasy about maintaining production levels with different workers than they normally hired, particularly women. One solution the company tried was to lower the minimum hiring age of men from eighteen to sixteen years old in May 1942 so that the company could employ high school students, as well as teachers on summer hiatus.[38] To many, the male breadwinner model of employment, built on the ideas that males would be long-term employees, carried over from the 1930s and made boys attractive candidates for defense jobs. One 1943 *Life* cover story proclaimed "Boypower" and noted that West Coast manufacturers such as Lockheed were hiring teenage boys to work in riveting, rivet bucking, and drafting apprenticeships, among other jobs.[39] Betty Russell recalled that the different generations of workers stood out on the shop floor but that their presence added a new dynamic to the Boeing "family" and facilitated camaraderie: "We just became a sort of family. One young fellow in our crew that had just been married a short time, when his wife had there [*sic*] first baby. Why we harassed him, gave him a bad time, but it was fun. It was like a big family, you're in the whole of the work at Boeing."[40] At least for some workers, then, the wartime Boeing "family" expanded enough to provide a sense of inclusiveness to the new types of workers joining the workforce. In addition to hiring white women, Boeing also began to employ disabled men, men over forty-five (and thus not eligible for the draft or military duty), and men with various physical traits that would normally place them outside the bounds of preferred hires. One female Boeing worker observed, "I saw several very small persons, some not more than four feet tall. One of these was a mechanic in the final assembly shop, and very well liked. He is able to work in smaller spaces, such as crawling into a wing. Because he is also a skillful worker, he has been advanced in less than five months to an 'A' mechanic's rating." The worker also noted the increased opportunities available due to wartime needs and described such workers as one example of "persons in the plant who in normal times would find employment hard to get."[41]

Despite expanding the hiring pool, by the end of the summer Boeing leaders realized their labor needs would require more aggressive changes to company organization and policies. In September 1942 Phil Johnson, the company president, noted that the "employment of women in the Seattle plant has increased from practically zero to 34% in this period. Studies show that an irreducible minimum of 8,500 male workers will be required in the factory, which places the maximum employment of women at approximately 70%. The shortage of manpower has become increasingly serious."[42] In order to keep up production, Boeing executives decided that they needed to hire more women. By January 1943, just a little more than a year after the October 31, 1941, decision to postpone female recruitment and hiring, 14,876, or 43 percent, of the 34,087 workers employed in the Seattle and Renton plants were women.[43]

Even with increased recruitment, Boeing could not meet the demand for aircraft, so officials tried a new approach: changing processes so less skill was needed to assemble planes. In 1943, while still building the B-17, Boeing began production of the B-29 Superfortress, the plane that eventually delivered the atom bomb.[44] The B-29 was twice the size of the B-17 and more expensive. Company leaders realized they needed to learn how to build it more efficiently. In an effort to increase efficiency, engineers designed the main fuselage of the B-29 in the shape of a straight cylinder. Corresponding parts were then made at various locations and shipped to Boeing's final assembly lines. This simple design change allowed the plane to be built quickly by workers inexperienced in aircraft work.[45] As a result of increased government funding, simplified assembly processes, improved technology, and more efficient worker training, Boeing's production rates soared. In his memoir, public relations manager Harold Mansfield describes the shop floor during World War II and notes the new production strategies, which included new assembly-line formations and changing shop-floor demographics: "There were row upon row of chapped-off sections of bodies and wings, each alive with riveters and installation mechanics, some men, but mostly women in slacks." Company leaders had figured out how to integrate untrained women into the workforce, and, as Mansfield notes, they had "showed convincingly that they were learning how to mass produce."[46] The changes during the war, then, were crucial to company successes in mass manufacturing.

Boeing publicized this new reliance on inexperienced workers. For example, one recruitment pamphlet claimed, "Housewives who have never held a wrench soon make skilled riveters."[47] Similarly, the *Boeing News* characterized a "woman's place" at Boeing as "just like in the home," suggesting that cutting airplane parts corresponded to "cutting cookies," operating blueprint machines mirrored "ironing," and driving a carloader was similar to "bringing home the Saturday groceries in the family car." Boeing's supervisor of employee training and education noted in the same article, "It's surprising how short a time it takes the ladies to learn the fundamentals of mechanical work."[48] Boeing leaders boasted that the company was better prepared to produce planes quickly and efficiently while maximizing staffing power—a significant feat given that increased labor needs were met largely by recruiting vast numbers of new unskilled workers.[49]

Women, too, found the redefinition of skilled work surprising, and somewhat amusing, though it sometimes caused tension between men and women workers. For example, one woman commented on the irony of her holding the same job classification as her husband. He had worked at Boeing for three years as a mechanic and had earned his rank in the company's skilled job classification system through experience; she had been hired right into the same mechanic position with no previous experience. She commented, "Isn't he going to give me a laugh! Here they are putting me to work as a mechanic, and I never had a screwdriver in my hand. Anyhow, I'm not at the same plant."[50] One California woman, who worked as an inspector in two different aircraft plants, in 1943 wrote a letter that reveals the pride many women felt in their newly acquired skills: "I guess I am capable of learning something that I never thought I would be able to do in a thousand years."[51] In a later letter, however, the California woman also reveals the expectations that most women had about the temporary nature of their jobs: "I rather like my job too much but I am not making a decision 'cause I don't think it is going to last too long."[52] Katie Burks, an African American woman who was hired as a mechanic during World War II and ended up staying at Boeing for forty-three years, working her way up to lead mechanic, noted that the job offered new economic opportunities, though men did not welcome or accept women: "My starting wage at Boeing was sixty-two cents. At the time these were decent wages especially considering the men both Black and White did not want us there."[53] As she also noted, layoffs were expected for women who were hired for wartime work.[54] In contrast, some male Boeing employees argued that their wages, with pay scales that began at sixty-two and a half cents per hour (or about one hundred dollars per month for a forty-hour workweek), were too low to meet the cost of living. One male worker recalls, "We were the McDonald's workers, the fast-food chain workers. . . . We were living from payday to payday, trying to make both ends meet."[55] White men, then, were also disempowered by a system in which race and gender hierarchies, as well as company and union politics, set up wage inequities that entrenched inequalities among workers.

Although lack of skill and experience was no longer an obstacle to aircraft manufacturing jobs, ideas about who should have access to aircraft careers, as well as middle-class status, were still rooted in beliefs about race and gender. One Boeing mechanic, a male supervisor who was training a new female employee, commented, "No woman is really worth a mechanic's rating." In his view, "They think they're better than they are. Suppose they can do the work; they don't care about getting the technical training—they just want the money." Men supposedly were looking at the larger picture and investing in long-term careers based on building skills and experience. According to the supervisor, "There are lots of fellows who will drop their good ratings to become an apprentice [in another position]. That means long months of work and going to school twice a week, at low pay, before they get back up to a higher level, but it also means they have a rating for good, in any aircraft factory anywhere in the country. Show me a girl who will do that."[56] Women, in this view, were not dedicated to pursuing work in the way that aircraft manufacturing had typically been organized, especially in the 1930s and early 1940s. This view, however, ignored the structural barriers that kept women out of specific occupations like aircraft manufacturing, as well as the cultural barriers, such as the male breadwinner model, which dissuaded many, both men and women, from pursuing careers. Many shops at Boeing sought to keep women out as long as possible, with varying degrees of success. One worker observed, "Some of the departments, such as timekeeping, held out for all-masculine employees longer than others."[57] One African American woman worker, Ruth Render, recalled that the union did not seem to be a resource to empower women workers because "at that time it was the company's union not the workers' union. That's just how things worked in those days."[58]

Union Politics and Race Discrimination

Union discrimination against women and nonwhite members was common during World War II.[59] Men actively campaigned to restrict white female and minority membership because they feared it would "bring down wages and hinder union effectiveness."[60] Company leaders shared union leaders' desire to continue filling labor needs with skilled white men rather than generally unskilled women and African American men. Archie Smith, an African American worker who moved to Seattle from Mississippi in 1923, pointed out that discrimination against black job applicants was well established: "When I come here, a black person couldn't get a job at Boeing. . . . They'd go there, and go there, and go there, and come back . . . and they couldn't get a job. Boeing wouldn't hire 'em."[61] Another black man described how he had taken engineering classes because he had "an ambition" to be an aeronautical engineer but quit after he decided that "we just didn't have no chance."[62] For black men, as with women training to be mechanics, pursuing a career seemed out of reach while a job, however temporary, seemed more attainable.

Boeing's contract with Aeronautical Mechanics Lodge 751, a branch of the International Association of Machinists, initially delayed the need for company executives to construct new policies based on race and gender. Lodge 751 was organized in 1935, and the company signed a collective bargaining agreement with the union in 1936. The American Federation of Labor (AFL) assigned the union to the IAM, which had a long history of discriminating against women and people of color.[63] Boeing's contract with Lodge 751 prevented the hiring of white women and African Americans until 1941 and 1942, respectively.

Despite increased labor needs and President Roosevelt's 1941 Executive Order 8802, which called for fair employment practices in labor and industry and an end to discrimination by race, creed, color, or national origin, Boeing leaders initially stood behind union rules.[64] They insisted that any discriminatory policies were those of the IAM and Lodge 751, not the company. Under Boeing's contract with the IAM, all employees were required to be members of the union and "questions of eligibility are determined by the association and are outside the company's jurisdiction."[65]

African Americans in Seattle voiced strong opposition to Boeing's adherence to the policies of Lodge 751 throughout the war, even after temporary union membership was granted. The *Northwest Enterprise*, a local African American newspaper, closely monitored and helped coordinate the activities of the Seattle Civic Committee (SCC), which had a membership consisting of "Boeing Boys and Girls"—people who sought employment at Boeing.[66] Several African American organizations and clubs joined forces and created the Committee for the Defense of Negro Labor's Right to Work at Boeing Airplane Company.[67] Many local black labor and social organizations suggested that Boeing was using union policies as a handy excuse for its exclusion of women and minorities. In 1940 the *Northwest Enterprise* charged that Boeing was conspiring with Lodge 751 to exclude blacks from employment with the company. The newspaper reported that the "declaration of Boeing Airplane Company" was "We do not train or hire Negroes." The newspaper also cited the initiation oath repeated at each meeting of Lodge 751: "'I will not recommend for membership in this union any other than members of the white race.'"[68]

Federal and local pressure soon reversed this position, though union infighting and politics continued to hamper efforts to end racial discrimination in Lodge 751. In July 1940, after the secretary of the Seattle Urban League met with union leaders and lobbied for black membership, Lodge 751 voted to admit African Americans to the union. They also voted to propose to IAM leaders that a "whites-only" provision in the initiation oath be removed. Despite Lodge 751's decision to admit African Americans, however, the national union held sway, and the Seattle local's decision was rescinded by the IAM after charges of communist infiltration.[69] Despite these setbacks, the Seattle chapter of the National Association for the Advancement of Colored People (NAACP) reported in September 1940 that the black citizens who "struggle for the right to work at Boeing" had garnered a promise from the union that it would agree to the employment of African Americans at Boeing if company officials allowed it, although no African Americans had yet been hired.[70] As Boeing's workforce grew, African Americans became increasingly frustrated at being shut out of the aircraft company.

African American protest directed at Boeing and Lodge 751 constituted part of larger efforts to end discrimination in wartime industrial plants all over the country. But national leaders targeted Boeing, which reveals the degree to which wartime growth thrust Boeing into national prominence. In October 1940, when the aircraft company announced plans to expand its Seattle plant, NAACP counsel Thurgood Marshall sent a letter to the president of the organization's Seattle branch, noting, "We are striving through our branches to secure our share of employment in those plants receiving Government contracts." In 1941 the NAACP sent a letter to Paul Fredrickson, Boeing's personnel manager, requesting the company's official policy on employing African Americans. Fredrickson replied, "It is our understanding that only those of the Caucasian Race are acceptable to the International Association of Machinists." Characterizing the policy as a "flagrant violation" of Executive Order 8802, the NAACP contacted the Fair Employment Practices Committee and asked it to investigate.[71]

Other civil rights leaders also pressed Boeing for change. In October 1941, at the American Federation of Labor convention, the civil rights and trade union leader A. Philip Randolph stated, "One of the most conspicuous examples in the United States of race discrimination is at Boeing Aircraft Company in Seattle, which from the very beginning of the national-defense emergency has refused to employ Negroes."[72] He argued that Boeing hid behind union rules and used them as the excuse not to hire African Americans.

In response to mounting local and federal pressure the International Association of Machinists, and Lodge 751, finally lifted the ban on African American union membership in April 1942. Union leaders stated, "We have officially gone on record as agreeing to live up to the letter and spirit of the executive order whole-heartedly and without reservation."[73] However, it is clear that union officials begrudged these concessions and continued to oppose African American employment at Boeing. James Duncan, a national union official and international representative of the IAM, stated, "We rather resent that the war situation has been used to alter an old-established custom, and do not feel it will be helpful to war production." Duncan charged African Americans with hindering the war effort with their demands. He insisted, "For minority groups to seek to establish new conditions or change old established customs now will not make for increased production."[74]

As Duncan's comment suggests, the IAM fought against change and worked to maintain a racial and gender hierarchy. The union's system of work permits, in which nonunion members had to apply for special permission in order to obtain work, underscored the temporary nature of employment for white women and African Americans at Boeing and across the defense industry.[75] The practice also protected the union from permanent changes to the membership structure. African Americans were not allowed to purchase work permits until April 1942, and they paid monthly permit fees in lieu of union membership dues. The permit fees were higher than the cost of monthly union dues and were paid directly to the union.[76] African Americans thus had to pay $3.50 per month for a work permit, while white women paid $1.50.[77] Workers holding permits were still barred from union membership, which meant that they were not eligible for the seniority provisions of the master employment contract and could not vote in union elections.[78]

Racial and gender discrimination in unions was prevalent throughout the defense industry. In shipyards along the West Coast, for example, the Boilermakers and other AFL unions set up a Jim Crow system of auxiliaries in which migrants, women, and African Americans were relegated to subordinate status and did not qualify for the benefits and rights of full union membership.[79] A similar system was in place for the aircraft industry, which Marilynn Johnson characterizes as bad, if not worse, than the shipyards in regard to discriminatory policies; in aircraft plants the AFL-IAM banned full membership for African Americans, and temporary work permits were the only way around this restriction.[80]

African Americans in Seattle strongly objected to the work permit system. One advertisement in the *Northwest Enterprise* publicized an antidiscrimination meeting in June 1943 and asked, "Why should Colored workers at Boeings pay $3.50 or any amount of money?"[81] In 1943 Ruby Black, an African American woman employed at Boeing, sued Boeing and Lodge

751, charging that her complaints over the permit system resulted in her termination.[82] In October 1943 Lodge 751 lowered the permit fees for minorities to $1.50.[83] Despite this change, protesters, particularly the Seattle Civic Committee, continued to push local courts to order full union membership for African Americans, though the courts did not do so until after the end of the war.[84]

Boeing officials worried that white employees would object to working with black employees. In April 1942 managers assigned the first African American man they hired to rivet bucking, a job done mostly by white women. Anticipating objections from the man's coworkers, managers laid out a plan to deal with complaints. Any white man who protested working with the African American man would be "discharged for insubordination." Oddly, after three such complaints and terminations, however, the African American man was fired.[85] There was no such plan to address problems between white and African American women employees; perhaps the management believed that no such plan was needed. A 1945 issue of the *Boeing News* portrayed the shop floor as a place of domestic harmony for women by including a photograph of the "Homesteaders in Shop 309," a group of white and African American women riveters and buckers who had worked together as a team for several years.[86] References to the household were part of the larger focus on the familial metaphor and suggested that women had been smoothly transplanted from the home to a new household order on the shop floor at Boeing.

Generally speaking, the defense industry hired more black men than black women. The aircraft industry, however, was more willing to hire African American women than their male counterparts.[87] In 1943, for example, of the 329 African Americans on Boeing's payroll, 285, or 86 percent, were women.[88] The American studies scholar Chitose Sato suggests that both employers and white male employees viewed all women as temporary workers, and so aircraft manufacturers were more willing to hire African American women than African American men. In addition, employers considered African American women less threatening to the established workplace hierarchy. Both African American men and women, however, had an easier time finding employment in the shipyards, which offered more unskilled positions, than in airplane factories. Aircraft company leaders worried that hiring black workers would tarnish the image that employers were trying to promote.[89] Marilynn Johnson notes that several major aircraft companies, including Boeing, instituted discriminatory hiring practices. Some companies, including Consolidated Vultee Aircraft Corporation and North American Aviation, tried to restrict black workers to janitorial positions, which meant the companies had to hire more white than black women.[90]

For many African American women, defense work offered an opportunity for economic mobility. Prior to the war, African American women had been restricted primarily to domestic service.[91] Izetta Spearman Hatcher recalled feeling jealous of her sister, Florice, when she got a job at Boeing in 1942: "My sister was one of the first Black stenographers at Boeing. She was hired and she worked there so that she had an income so that she was able to buy clothing, nice clothing." Hatcher recalled stealing her sister's clothing until her parents caught her and told her that one day she would get a job as well.[92] Another African American woman, Elizabeth Dean Wells, recalled that when Spearman was hired she was "the only one that was able to go into the job" because she was trained as a stenographer. She added that black women had not expected the war to open job opportunities for them: "one reason why girls didn't train for office work, was because there was no future to it . . . office work was just *out* for girls."[93] Despite ongoing discrimination, then, the war did mark a substantial shift in some African American women's expectations about employment opportunities.

Labor Shortages, "Manpower," and "Womanpower"

Even with Boeing's limited acceptance of black and women workers, severe labor shortages continued. In the summer of 1943 the company announced a need for nine thousand additional workers to meet production goals.[94] The Seattle Chamber of Commerce launched a drive to help Boeing meet its labor needs by "put[ting] every idle person in the city to work" and "strip[ping] manpower and womanpower from all non-essential businesses."[95] Although the company held on to federal contracts, production levels and delivery rates declined as a result of the labor shortages.[96] Boeing issued a statement to the Seattle community: "Only the lack of additional labor supply—a factor beyond our control—makes it impossible to meet the increased schedules assigned by the Army."[97] The army canceled nine contracts with Puget Sound–area textile plants and moved the work to other locations in an attempt to move workers from the textile industry to Boeing.[98]

To compensate for labor shortages, company managers began "a race to see if efficiency could be increased rapidly enough to meet increasing schedules despite continually declining manpower."[99] By simplifying manufacturing processes and reducing waste, managers were able to lower the company's operating costs. For example, Boeing reduced the cost of building the B-17 airplane by revising the way workers cut sheet metal. Greater efficiency and lower manufacturing costs did not lead to higher profits, however. Company officials reported a slim net profit of 1.34 percent in 1942 and less than 1.00 percent for 1943.[100] Despite the wartime boom, Boeing in fact struggled to make economic gains during the war years, in large part because of the high labor turnover rate. The Seattle Chamber of Commerce Flying Fortress Committee reported in July 1943 that Pacific Coast aircraft factories lost, on average, eleven thousand workers for every twelve thousand they hired. Boeing leaders believed the problem stemmed from "natural reasons growing out of the war, and to the recruiting of many persons not normally in the labor market, chiefly women with family and domestic obligations."[101] Officials claimed that women were much more likely than men to quit, and such claims were in line with the complaints of other aircraft manufacturers at the time. Many employers argued that women were expensive employees: they had high absenteeism and turnover rates, and they required new services and facilities, such as restrooms.[102]

Turnover and absenteeism among women workers were of special concern to Boeing managers. During the first half of 1943, the turnover rate was between 5 and 6 percent per month, and 65 percent of the workers who left were women. Exit interviews indicate that roughly 60 percent of those women gave personal reasons for leaving, compared with 17 percent of men. Reasons included moving, illness, child-care issues, marriage, maternity leave, transportation difficulties, and domestic duties. Among those who did not quit, absenteeism was a recurring problem. Absenteeism was particularly high on Saturdays, so company leaders considered a shortened work schedule for women on weekends. However, they decided that such a schedule would increase absenteeism because workers would be more likely to skip a short shift than a normal one, so managers abandoned the idea and settled instead on a program of emblems and pins for perfect attendance.[103] They discussed creating part-time options for women based on the fact that, as Boeing president Phil Johnson reported, "Experience in England appears to have been rather excellent in this respect."[104] The union, however, rejected a proposal for a five-hour shift, versus the usual ten-hour shift.[105]

Despite the high overhead caused by fluctuating staffing levels, Boeing officials were reluctant to make the long-term changes needed to accommodate a diversified workforce and to combat absenteeism. Boeing did not, for example, provide services that would appeal to women workers, such as day care. Although Boeing managers considered offering day care, in 1942 they decided that "the Company's policy will be to encourage and afford appropriate publicity for day nursery work but that the Company will not participate in any such activities financially or otherwise and will take no responsibility in the staffing or conduct of day nurseries."[106] There were some options for day care through federal and city agencies, but most of the women who turned down jobs at Boeing cited lack of child care as the major reason.[107]

Rather than making long-lasting structural changes, company leaders focused their efforts on fostering a sense of family among and appreciation for Boeing workers. In 1943, for example, company officials instituted Family Day, for which they shut down the plant (not a small feat during the increased production demands of 1943) and invited employees to bring their families to tour the facilities.[108] At the event company president Phil Johnson addressed Boeing employees and their families, stating, "For many of you who are Boeing workers, this has been your first opportunity to see the plant in its entirety. We hope it has given you a clear picture of the importance of your specific job. There are no unimportant jobs at Boeing—every task has a bearing, either direct or indirect, on production of Flying Fortresses."[109] Events such as Family Day not only tied workers' tasks to larger causes, in this case the production demands of the war effort, but also connected employees' personal and family lives with their jobs.

Workers were also offered parenting, cooking, and nutrition classes and various other services aimed at creating stable and efficient households and healthy workers. For women, the Women's Recreational Activity Council offered classes in "proper dress, makeup, poise, and personality to help women workers maintain their FQ (Femininity Quotient)."[110] Boeing women workers in any position could also purchase "Flying Fortress Fashions," a line of work wear created by the designer Muriel King. The fashions included an insignia indicating Boeing divisions and chevrons to display length of service, thus identifying women not as regular members of the workforce but as a temporary symbol of the patriotic wartime sacrifices that women were making; in this conception women were in "service," rather than building careers or supporting families.[111] Boeing also had a recreational department that offered expanded recreational activities, which included basketball, softball, golf, bowling, badminton, horseshoe tournaments, and archery. Social events included picnics, dances, theater parties, swimming parties, and fishing derbies. Promotional advertisements noted that these services benefited Boeing workers because "this employee participation in outside recreation develops friendly associations at Boeing. When you decide to take a job at Boeing you will find a group of enthusiasts inviting you to join their 'team.' And you'll find these people are just as enthusiastic about building Flying Fortresses as they are keen about their sports."[112] As this advertisement suggests, Boeing's work environment emphasized connections among workers as vital to keeping them happy with their place in the company and motivated in their work. Company leaders may have also presumed that providing opportunities to foster harmony among workers was necessary to maintain a sense of fraternalism and counteract tensions among new types of workers.

Managers viewed a mixed-sex work environment as particularly dangerous and in need of regulation. Company leaders were especially concerned after they discovered that a number of women that had been hired as temporary workers were prostitutes.[113] The family metaphor, however, worked to integrate women into the workforce in ways that bolstered ideas of the heteronormative breadwinner family model. Marriage between men and women workers was celebrated in both the *Boeing News* and *Aero Mechanic*, as had been the case before the war, though now marriages were highlighted within separate "women's spaces" in a way that marked women as temporary workers who were still primarily focused on building heterosexual family units. *Aero Mechanic*, for example, created the "Aero Woman's Page" for the "Sisters in 751," though the publication characterized the endeavor as out of the ordinary and emphasized gender difference as a necessity for a separate female space: "We fully realize that this first attempt at a Woman's Page is rather crude in spots. It lacks the feminine touch that is so necessary and that only you Sisters can give it. So contribute your offerings and suggestions. Let's make it a page worthy of the ability and spirit of the women builders of the Flying Fortresses."[114]

The entry of women into the company and the union threatened to erode the fraternalism of the Boeing "family," though the emphasis on regulating women's sexuality and maintaining white heterosexual norms was an effort to alleviate the fears of wartime changes. Karen Anderson points out that fears over women's sexuality underlay much of the hostility to women's employment in defense factories such as Boeing.[115] Similarly, Eileen Boris points out that "fear of bodily closeness" led employers and unions to resist hiring diverse workers. As Boris argues, "White men sought to reassert control over their women by maintaining the color line."[116] Wartime conditions such as the mobilization of new types of workers and the movement of black men and women out of the South threatened the "racialized gendered regime." From the perspective of employers, maintaining racial, gender, and class categories was also a way to divide the laboring forces and thus retain power over labor.[117]

Company officials knew that hiring more African Americans could result in racial tension on the shop floor. In an effort to mitigate such tensions, as well as fears over the implications of racial mixing, Boeing plants included segregated lunchrooms and restroom facilities.[118] Union officials suggested that Boeing could go further. In April 1942 the Lodge 751 representative, James Duncan, stated that the union would support a separate but equal approach, claiming the union would "have no objection to the government constructing an airplane plant in which Negroes would be employed exclusively." Duncan asserted, "Such a plant would be competitive, but I think the competition would be welcomed and might be a good incentive to both groups."[119]

Duncan's proposal highlights the racial tensions present in the defense industry and in cities across the nation during World War II. These tensions peaked in the summer of 1943, when race riots took place in Detroit, New York City's Harlem area, and Los Angeles. As Quintard Taylor points out, racial tensions in Seattle also grew as African Americans from all over the country migrated to the city in search of work and better living conditions. From 1940 to 1950 Seattle's African American population grew from 3,789 to 15,666, a leap of 413 percent.[120] Clem Gallerson, who worked at Boeing for three years, described the dynamics in his neighborhood as new people moved into the area in search of defense work: "We used to tease a lot of the southerners that were coming up north. . . . Sharecroppers! . . . We called them sharecroppers. Boy, that made them so mad!" Albert J. Smith recalled that the term was widely applied to people moving into the area, and not just to African Americans from the South: "It was a term for everybody then, in a way. A lot of people think it was just for Blacks, but no, it was for everybody." Fred Wingo described an "influx of southerners" who "brought their southern discriminatory ideas with them." Wingo noted that this "influx" produced new anxieties and tensions: "A lot of the natives in Seattle didn't mix well, initially, with the southerners because they had different standards, different ideas about life."[121]

Dana Cloud's analysis of black mill workers in the South explains the conditions facing blacks in industry during this time period. As she notes, they faced "a system of combined race-, gender- and class-based oppression and exploitation, in which an ideology of paternalism, alongside the threat of racist violence, made for a muted, though debilitating, segregation," even as the terms of that segregation were contested and negotiated.[122] As the population in Seattle increased, worried officials braced themselves for disorder and violence. The Seattle police chief, Herbert Kimsey, reported, "We're preparing for anything that might result from a crowded, mixed and excited wartime population."[123] Kimsey's fear reflected larger concerns that social changes brought by war, particularly increased contact between white and African American defense workers, could result in violence.

Although racial tensions at Boeing ran high, the number of African Americans workers there was low. Throughout the 1930s and early 1940s, Boeing did not hire substantial numbers of African Americans. Fred Wingo,

FIG. 5. African American food servers deliver lunch on the shop floor of Boeing's Kansas plant during World War II. Courtesy Library of Congress, Prints and Photographs Division, FSA/OWI Collection, LC-USE6-D-008921.

whose family had resided in Washington State since 1931, described no problems finding jobs in Portland and in various places in the Seattle area in the 1930s and 1940s, except at Boeing: "The only place I couldn't get a job was Boeing. Can you believe that?"[124] In July 1943 Boeing employed 44 African American men and 285 African American women, out of a total workforce of 29,393.[125] Those few workers experienced discrimination. In July 1943 managers reported "continuing racial problems surrounding the use of negroes in present facilities" at Boeing. They expressed concern over the "increasing delicacy" of the employment of African Americans and "suggested that shop supervision intensify their efforts to avert demonstrations."[126]

Echoing union leaders' earlier suggestion, Boeing leaders discussed building a separate plant for African Americans in Seattle's Central District, an area populated predominantly by African Americans. The personnel manager, Paul Fredrickson, thought it "advisable to establish a branch plant conveniently located next to the negro district in Seattle and to staff this plant entirely with negros." Boeing executives decided to check "unofficially" with the local Urban League chapter and with the chair of the Fair Employment Practices Committee to see if a plant staffed exclusively by African American workers would be feasible. Managers expressed vague worries that the plan could not be cleared "from the policy angle." They also raised concerns about the "problem of supervision," and one manager noted that "it would be very difficult to get white supervision to undertake this job." Phil Johnson suggested that "it would be possible to develop negro supervision."[127] Such plans, however, did not develop. It is not clear why Boeing never built a separate plant for African Americans; perhaps the racial tensions of the war years dissuaded them.

Boeing officials, facing so many obstacles to employing African Americans, chose instead to concentrate their efforts on recruiting white women. The focus on turning white housewives into war workers peaked with the onset of severe labor shortages in the summer of 1943; Boeing officials publicly declared that Seattle's "untapped labor reservoir" of women could help.[128] Company advertisements celebrated Boeing's wartime workers as essential, but at the same time Boeing officials and government and union leaders resisted permanent transformations of the company's structure. In 1943 A. F. Hardy, director of the region's War Manpower Commission office, pushed to retain greater numbers of men at Boeing and argued, "It is not that we are trying to evade our responsibilities in supplying men for the armed forces, but we have reached the point where we cannot furnish men and also produce the materials of war for them to use when they go into action."[129]

Boeing executives continued to emphasize the urgent need for men, both skilled and unskilled, throughout the war years. One Boeing advertisement, for example, declared, "Sure! We Need Women—But We Need MEN Just as Much!" The advertisement explained, "There's a lot of work in building the famous Flying Fortress that's ideally suited to women—but there are hundreds of jobs that only *men* can do." Assuring men that past work experience did not matter, the advertisement stressed, "Although we need men who are already skilled—we have here a splendid opportunity for men to learn skills, with good pay while they're learning!"[130]

In this hiring campaign, Boeing competed with the army for men. Company advertising routinely promoted Boeing as vital to victory and Boeing employment as being just as patriotic as army service. Company leaders managed to acquire presidential deferments for some unmarried men working as engineers and supervisors; these deferments were no small matter, because the government typically considered unmarried men first in line for the draft.[131] Regional pressures also played a role in the battle for men. In Seattle the number of new hires could not match the number of men who were leaving for military service. In August 1943 the Selective Service System announced a sixty-day freeze on the induction of men into military service from California and Washington aircraft plants and gave the state board control over the selection of men who would remain on the job. At Boeing, the postponement immediately affected twenty-five hundred men.[132]

Recruiting Women

Despite Boeing leaders' grudging acknowledgment that they would have to hire more women, at the heart of Boeing's recruitment campaign was a steadfast belief that a company dominated by white men was best, and this belief shaped the way managers approached the hiring of women. Boeing executive vice president H. Oliver West emphasized that he "would not like to see the gate open for any unlimited number of women against a small number of new men hires."[133] At several staff meetings in March 1944, company managers discussed the difficulties of maintaining a desirable ratio of women to men. The personnel manager, C. E. French, reported that "all recruitment continues to be heavily overbalanced by women over men."[134] Boeing leaders decided to try to adhere to a 40:60 ratio of women to men. But they were struggling with the increasingly likely possibility that the number of women Boeing employed would surpass the number of men. By the beginning of 1944 nearly half of Boeing's workforce was female. This situation was by no means abnormal for wartime industries; in most California aircraft plants women made up 40 percent of the workforce.[135] Even so, managers were nervous. Although they had surmised in 1942 that

Boeing could operate with a 70 percent female workforce, West was less optimistic: "If it was necessary we could revise our recruitment percentages [from 60:40] to probably 50-50 for men and women."[136]

The company's efforts to maintain a male majority drew negative attention. As Boeing's personnel manager explained, "Due to the attempt of the recruitment teams in the field to adhere to the proposed 60-40 men and women recruitment plan, Boeing is being criticized in the field for refusing to take factory trained women."[137] Despite such criticism, in 1944 executives considered curtailing the recruitment of women. However, they decided that active recruitment of women remained necessary "if we are to avoid criticism in our requests for deferrals."[138] H. Oliver West suggested in a 1944 staff committee meeting that the "large percentage of women employees be more freely used to aid in and justify our request for the recruitment of more male employees."[139] Thus, the employment of women became an important tool beyond filling labor voids and constructing planes on the shop floor; it aided Boeing officials' efforts to negotiate government policy.

Company propaganda reflected these plans. To the public Boeing claimed, "Today Boeing is well in advance of the rest of the aircraft company in percentage of women employed."[140] Behind closed doors, executives strategized their use of employment figures to secure public approval and permission from government agencies to hire and retain men in a time when society perceived women as vital to winning the war on the home front and men as vital to both the military and the home front. Boeing president Phil Johnson requested that reports on women's employment at the company "be gotten in promptly so that we may get the benefit of them in current recruitment." Publicizing women workers would allow Boeing to "advertise more exclusively for men." Furthermore, because of the increase in the number of female workers in relation to male workers, it was "necessary at this time to recruit more men than women."[141]

Boeing adhered to the federal government's suggestions on how to advertise for workers. For example, one 1943 advertisement addressed "Married Men under 38," targeting a category that Selective Service officials had previously identified as eligible for induction. The ad acknowledged earlier statements by the War Manpower Commission, stating that "the services of all men under 38—fathers and childless married men alike—are absolutely essential in making an all-out effort against the Nazis and the Japs." It offered a choice: "What you must decide without delay is this—'I will fight for Victory—in the Army or in the battle of production.' Selective Service has indicated—*You must do one or the other!*" The advertisement assured men that "Building Flying Fortresses at Boeing is 100% War Work" and that the "Flying Fortress is the most vital weapon in the war. It is the spearhead of the entire Allied attack. That is why the Army is calling for more of them." It further emphasized that Boeing workers could influence the direction of the war in the same way as men engaged in active combat: "If you join the workers at Boeing, you will be actually helping our Air Forces *pour it on* the enemy . . . destroy his war industries . . . *win the war.* And the more Flying Fortresses you help build, the quicker Victory will be won."[142] Company advertising promised men that no one would think less of them for building airplanes than they would of men in active combat.

Similarly, an advertisement aimed at women characterized female workers at Boeing as "holding America's Number One job in support of the war effort . . . next only to the work being done by our fighting men."[143] Propaganda also emphasized normalcy in labor divisions based on gender: "Women! Even if you've never done anything except housework there's almost certainly a job for you here at Boeing—a clean and pleasant one. . . . Your husband—your son—your brother or boyfriend will be proud that you are doing your part in building the axis-blasting Flying Fortresses."[144] The supportive role Boeing allocated to women fit easily into the framework of national recruiting campaigns sponsored by the federal government. Maureen Honey argues that women's wartime responsibilities were imbued with characteristics of civic and moral duty and citizenship rather than opportunities for individual financial or personal achievement.[145] Leila Rupp also points out that government recruiting agencies promoted the idea that women could save lives and help end the war, a theme evident in Boeing advertisements.[146] Even after the war was over the supportive role given to women war workers, or "Rosies," continued to hold sway in Boeing histories, as is evident in public relations manager Harold Mansfield's depiction of women's seemingly remarkable ability to pick up aircraft production so quickly: "Most of the women wearing the little Army-Navy

'E' for Excellence pins would tell you there was a reason they were learning so fast, a reason close to the heart. Right now he was somewhere on the sands of North Africa or maybe hitting the beach of Sicily; or in one of Ira Eaker's bombers over Germany."[147] The supportive role fit within the confines of the Boeing "family" theme; wartime changes were not as threatening to the established order when it seemed that women were working to support men, rather than themselves or their families, and would then relinquish the "men's" jobs when the men returned.

Company leaders also enlisted humor in an effort to lessen the impact of social change and to dismiss the threat of women's effectiveness on the shop floor. A striking example is a story from *Boeing Magazine* about women warehouse employees. The article begins by pointing out the uniqueness of these "special" women: "Round one of the battle of women-versus-machines has gone to the ladies, largely (and we do mean 'largely') on account of a team of superwomen who have taken over, of all things, the warehouse jobs." Although intended to be comical in tone, the article perpetuated certain gender stereotypes. Citing the workers' lack of ideal female characteristics, the magazine quipped that such women could be "as feminine as they want to, just as long as they are able to toss a varsity football tackle over their shoulders and run ninety yards with him to a touchdown." The article emphasized that these women were not of "standard size" and represented a curious sideshow in company culture. As aberrations, these women did not pose a threat to men or to accepted ideas about gender identity or men's authority in the firm. This emphasis is further illustrated by the magazine's statement that, although male employees "look up to them," it is only because "they have to. The women are bigger."[148] The article lessened anxiety by making these women into freaks. Such characterizations reveal leaders' efforts to mitigate the disruptive potential of wartime needs and point to the importance of bodies in the war effort.

Pictures and stories of African Americans working at Boeing also played on stereotypes in an effort to minimize the potential of dangerous social change. When mentions of African Americans workers appeared in company wartime publications such as the *Boeing News*, they often were in the context of recreation and leisure as opposed to work. African Americans were often shown entertaining white Boeing employees, as in a picture of two African American women who put on a "spontaneous jitterbug exhibition" during a lunch break at the Renton plant in August 1945.[149] Similarly, a February 1945 issue showed an African American man as he performed a trick during his "one-man show" and noted, "He sings and does parlor tricks." The publication quoted the man as saying, "Watch close now while I turn a dime into a dolla."[150] These lighthearted images masked the fears of disorder that Boeing managers, as well as city officials and union leaders, had earlier discussed behind closed doors. Images of black men as entertainers also diverted attention from them as workers, another element working against their permanence as Boeing employees.

Peace and Postwar Dependencies

The end of the war came abruptly for Boeing workers, and especially for women, who were first to be fired because they had been characterized as temporary, emergency wartime workers. Immediately after the war ended the military canceled its orders for bombers, and Boeing closed many of its branch plants and factories and cut 70,000 jobs.[151] From a wartime peak of 31,750 on February 9, 1945, employment at the Seattle Boeing plant had dropped to 17,722 by February 1948.[152] Most of the jobs cut were women's; one worker, a divorced mother, recalled V-J Day this way: "I kind of panicked, because just like that Boeing closed down. We were laid off that night. We celebrated, great, but meanwhile I didn't have a job."[153] African American women, in particular, were pushed out.[154] These patterns held true at Boeing. One Boeing worker recalled, "I think in general that women understand that in going in there, we were hired for the duration—just for the duration. . . . But most women did not want to leave work at the end of the war. Some might have been relieved if their husbands came home or if they still had a husband who worked. But most of them wanted to stay on. A job was a job, and the whole level of existence had changed."[155] Contrary to the official propaganda that Rosie the Riveter was to be a temporary, wartime factory worker, many women did not voluntarily leave industrial jobs after the war.[156]

Men who returned to the aircraft plants after serving in the military found their jobs completely changed. Because production processes and workplace organization had changed, the men's knowledge and skilled backgrounds were no longer vital.[157] Boeing leaders were keenly aware of this shift. Managers harbored deep anxieties about the future of aircraft production; the future of military contracts was not clear to company leaders. Federal contracts were not guaranteed, and the company's reliance on federal defense contracts now seemed even more problematic than had previously been the case.[158] Edward Wells, Boeing's chief engineer, was so concerned about the postwar future that he selected a group of engineers to work in Boeing's "Hidden Cave," a small downtown Seattle office, to design products that had nothing to do with airplanes or national defense.[159]

Postwar anxieties over the future of work also made their way into relations between labor and management. The first contract that District Lodge 751 had signed with Boeing in 1936 carried over into the war years. In 1947, however, tensions over contract negotiations rose, and the union went on strike for five months beginning in April 1948. Boeing leaders wanted control over layoffs with no regard to seniority. The labor historian Robert Rodden argues that "no self-respecting union could accept such a proposal."[160] According to Rodden, the late 1940s ushered in the "passing of the founding generation of master builders at Boeing" and "a new breed of management." The male camaraderie and fraternalism of the 1930s and first half of the 1940s, when the company was small and company leaders "dealt with employees in the shop in an easy man-to-man way," had disappeared. Rodden's analysis stands out for his assumption that workers would be men who had gained authority and skill on the shop floor and for his view that growth made holding the Boeing "family" together more difficult. After Phil Johnson died, Rodden notes, "a new generation took over, with lawyers replacing engineers and bureaucrats displacing builders. In 1947, for the first time, the company's negotiations were conducted by professionals and technicians."[161] As the company grew, then, some were mourning the loss of the prewar work culture. Some workers felt they were losing power, even while the number of engineers and workers was continuing to climb due to Cold War spending and a new "technocratic political culture" was emerging in the Seattle region.[162]

Despite initial concerns over federal contracts, Boeing emerged from the war a key federal contractor and a top regional manufacturer and employer.

Having built on the reputation it gained during World War II as a leader in national security, the company began to rely on military contracts.[163] More broadly, World War II fostered western cities' dependence on federal spending and federal support for development, thereby exacerbating the boom-and-bust cycles of the aerospace and defense industries.[164] Washington State politicians battled for lucrative defense contracts for Boeing in an effort to facilitate urban growth.[165] Backed primarily by the U.S. Army Air Corps and buoyed by Seattle's interest in urban economic growth, Boeing is a prime early example of the complex relationship Richard Kirkendall describes as the "military-metropolitan-industrial complex."[166] The postwar dependency of Seattle on Boeing and of Boeing on the federal government, and the role of World War II in causing that shift, was not lost on people at the time. As one federal report noted in 1965, "It [World War II] caused drastic changes in the composition of the area's economy and left, as its legacy, a dependence on federal defense spending that still persists."[167] Another study undertaken by the U.S. Arms Control and Disarmament Agency in the 1960s concluded, "Seattle has a disproportionately heavy manufacturing emphasis, but that emphasis is almost entirely the result of Boeing's activities."[168] The study noted that Boeing "dominated the local labor scene."[169]

Cold War military contracts maintained an expanded workforce and also pushed the company into areas beyond aircraft manufacturing, most notably a research and development division that focused on aerospace—Boeing Aerospace Company.[170] Despite Cold War opportunities and growth, particularly after the launch of Sputnik 1 in 1957 ushered in a new emphasis on science and technology research, the company faced several periods of decline in the postwar years, particularly in the early- to mid-1960s, when there were several military contract cancellations.[171] One federal report, however, noted that Boeing was accustomed to layoff cycles: "The history of the relatively young Seattle community is replete with periods of alternately riding the economic crest and wallowing in the trough of economic ill health."[172]

Despite Boeing's ups and downs, the company was celebrated as a symbol of the possibilities of modern science and technology. Even the 1962 World's Fair in Seattle focused on Boeing's dominance and Cold War leadership despite the company's unpredictable employment cycles.[173] By the postwar period, Boeing had developed into a Seattle institution. One city official characterized Seattle in 1970 as "the world's greatest company town."[174] As scholars such as Robert Dean, K. A. Cuordileone, and David Johnson have shown, the Cold War environment fostered a new focus on heterosexual masculinity. Political and economic culture put a new premium on toughness and style, and Boeing's show of industrial might was part of this "cold war cult of masculine toughness."[175]

The Postwar Boeing Family

The Boeing "family" continued to grow throughout the 1950s and 1960s, with some important distinctions from the 1930s "family." Boeing continued to employ women, even promoting women's place in the company in a manner similar to World War II propaganda. In 1951, for example, the *Boeing News* ran an article titled "Women at Boeing on Equal Footing with Men." The article posited that "Rosie the Riveter is back—but now with years of aircraft and other mechanical experience."[176] Similarly, in September 1953 *Boeing Magazine*, a monthly company publication geared toward an "external" audience, declared that "Rosie is back" and that "the era of Rosie, the riveter, and Winnie, the welder, is not over." It went on to explain that out of the 62,200 employees at Boeing, 14,700, or 23.6 percent, were women; that figure was up from 14 percent in 1948. The article declared, "And these are not all taking shorthand and punching typewriters. More than 11,000 of them are hourly employees in manufacturing and production just as women were during the civilian manpower shortage of World War II. That necessary recruitment of the female labor force was the foot in the door in many industries and the door has not closed since."[177] However, this statement masks the tensions surrounding labor changes during World War II and the disappearance of women from the labor force after the war ended; the door did close, or perhaps more precisely, was never fully opened in the first place, even while a greater number of women continued to be employed in the postwar years.

In 1951, the same year that Boeing declared "Rosie is back," one study found that the characteristics of the typical job applicant at Boeing had changed little from the prewar years. The study reported that, between

October and December of 1948, 84 percent of the people who applied for jobs at Boeing were not hired. As was the case in both the prewar and wartime years, skilled workers were deemed the hardest applicants to find.[178] The study indicated that most job applicants were white males, married but without children, between the ages of twenty-one and twenty-five, with a high school education and no military background; women, on the other hand, were described as typically being single and, unlike male applicants, had likely been previously employed at Boeing.[179] Although Boeing was now attracting more and more applicants from outside the Puget Sound region, these characteristics reveal how little had changed during the war years.

Still, there are some important distinctions in the expectations of postwar Boeing applicants. To many black employees, the involvement of the federal government, through the Fair Employment Practices Committee, signaled a new expectation of oversight and regulation to counteract employment discrimination. Reflecting on the changes since World War II, one black man, Albert Smith, credited President Roosevelt with opening job opportunities at Boeing and other defense industries: "See, it takes some pressure, some power to break that thing down."[180] Sampson Valley similarly pointed out how the federal government had forced Boeing's hand: "I remember when Boeing first started. And it was really 'boring,' because they wouldn't give you, give you even a janitor's job. They just were not hiring minorities at Boeing until the Second World War came on. That's the time when the government . . . began to fund these different agencies like Boeing, shipyards and things like that. Well, then the minorities got a chance to get a job."[181] Edward Foulks likewise observed that the postwar employment process was more equitable as a result of wartime federal oversight. He had noticed at least one major change since the 1940s: "I think there've been a lot of . . . changes . . . at least when you fill out an application you know it's going to go in the personnel file, it's not automatically going to hit the waste basket as soon as you turn your back."[182] And yet, Foulks described the continuation of employment discrimination based on race. He recalled how a Boeing supervisor told him about an underground racial "quota system" that was in place when he applied to work at Boeing in 1947.[183] While there is no corroborating evidence from Boeing or other sources about the quota system, the idea of the system is revealing of how Foulks and other minority workers viewed Boeing, namely, as a place where it was tough for them to get a job, even after the war. The rumor of a quota system is also further evidence of the discriminatory practices at play in company hiring decisions at the factory level. Foulks described how managers tried to dissuade black applicants from taking jobs at Boeing, noting that "the fellow that interviewed me did everything in his power to discourage me . . . telling me how bad conditions were, how dirty the work was, how rough it was, and all like this."[184] While World War II did open some opportunities and provide an infrastructure for eradicating discrimination, concerns over race and gender still influenced and drove hiring decisions on the ground and workers' perceptions of hiring conditions.

What had changed after World War II was the organization of work at Boeing. As a result of the shift to Cold War aerospace research and development, the myriad divisions devoted to engineering at Boeing saw a dramatic increase. By the end of 1954 Boeing employed 8,145 engineers, compared to 7,376 at the end of 1953. The 1954 figure represents a 220 percent increase over the 3,700 engineers Boeing employed during the peak of World War II output.[185] Boeing also increased its outreach to students, hosting classes, job fairs, and various other programs that informed UW students about the job opportunities available at Boeing.[186] The company's educational alliances helped it retain access to skilled workers, a significant advantage given the uncertain employment outlook at Boeing and in the aviation industry more broadly.[187]

As the number of engineers Boeing employed grew in the postwar period, so did the number of managers. In 1946 the company organized an association for company managers, the Boeing Management Association (BMA), which was formed to "raise the standards of supervision, improve its quality and encourage a spirit of unity and cooperation." While the association began with only fifty-eight members, by 1965 it had six thousand members. Managers were not required to join, but many did; in October 1965 Boeing reported that nearly 84 percent of Boeing managers belonged to the association. In addition to providing education and training, the BMA sponsored social functions such as dances, "Sports Night," and fishing derbies, among other activities. In 1965 a company-sponsored history and photo album of the BMA declared, "Today, the Boeing Management Association has become a way of life."[188] The BMA also reinforced the notion that the cohesion of the Boeing "family" was defined by white heterosexual men and by social networks of advancement. By the 1970s, however, that was slowly starting to change. One woman manager recalled the reaction of her husband, also a Boeing worker, and the BMA when she was promoted to manager: "When I got reclassified into management, Paul said 'I suppose now I'm going to have to salute you.' We went to a function of the Boeing Management Association—the visit of the B-17. The guard asked Paul for his BMA card. Paul's an engineer. I was the one in management."[189] The reaction to her membership in the BMA reflects the assumptions that only men would occupy the highest ranks of the company, even while the composition of the workforce was beginning to change because of the employment of greater numbers of women.

As the company moved into the "jet age," and particularly as development of the 727 picked up in the 1960s and Boeing began to expand its aerospace operations, Boeing began to recruit workers from outside the United States. Zakir Parpia, who came from India to earn a master's degree in civil engineering at Washington State University in 1975, observed the significance of immigration to Boeing's growing engineering ranks. Parpia recalled that in the 1960s and 1970s "Seattle had its larger share of Indians that were predominantly engineers that worked for Boeing." He also remembered that "they [Indians] came in larger numbers because Boeing needed that category of worker."[190] Part of what drove the increase was the abolishment of national origin quotas, which had restricted immigration by race and ethnicity, under the Immigration and Nationality Act of 1965; this shift led to a wave of immigration from Asia, which in turn diversified Boeing's workforce, particularly the engineering ranks. Cold War military production also meant that defense contractors like Boeing needed skilled engineers.[191] After World War II new opportunities for citizenship among people who had already been in the United States, such as Filipinos, also meant they now had the opportunity to work for defense contractors like Boeing, where employees had to hold U.S. citizenship.[192]

Cold War ideas of citizenship could also cause some tensions on the shop floor. In 1967, for example, Kito Kaneta, a Japanese American engineering aide employed in the missiles and information systems division in Seattle, wrote a letter charging Boeing with racial discrimination and harassment that he claimed was the result of his unwillingness to join a company-sponsored U.S. Savings and Freedom Bond drive, which his supervisor told him was the duty of all employees of a government contractor.[193] Kaneta wrote the letter to the federal Fair Employment Practices Commission and provided copies to U.S. senator Warren Magnuson, U.S. senator Henry Jackson, Rep. Brock Adams, the national headquarters of the Japanese American Citizens League, and the American Civil Liberties Union of Washington State.[194] He described "intimidation of myself and others employed by the Boeing Company who refuse to participate in its Savings and Freedom Bonds campaign."[195] Kaneta's charges provide insight into how the Boeing "family" was redefined in the context of World War II and the Cold War, when wartime threats both propped up the company through defense contracts and also shifted workplace culture to demand a new kind of loyalty. The family metaphor became less about creating an inclusive atmosphere of loyalty and fraternalism than it was about articulating a model of exclusivity upon which power and privilege were asserted. Wartime disruptions made it difficult for company leaders to regulate employees in the same way. As the next chapter shows, even as the rights revolution opened up job opportunities through equal employment opportunity programs, women's place in the Boeing "family" remained elusive.

CHAPTER 3

Women's Place in Equal Opportunity Employment

With Boeing's seventy-fifth anniversary approaching in 1989, company leaders viewed it as the perfect opportunity to take stock. That year, the Boeing Historical Archives began to research what it hoped would be a celebration of "the unique contribution of women at all levels of the company over the course of Boeing's nearly 75-year history."[1] The project went beyond just research. Company historians, public relations managers, and personnel managers, including equal employment opportunity officers, worked together to research and begin to write a monograph tentatively titled *Women at Boeing: Working Partners for Four Generations*.[2] The monograph aimed to celebrate and document women's roles at Boeing, both for the company's historical record and for public distribution. The historical abstract for the proposed monograph noted that although Boeing had employed nearly one hundred thousand women since the company's founding and women had contributed to the success of the company, these experiences had not been recorded. Project participants hoped their endeavor would be a work "unique in the history of Boeing and the aviation industry at large."[3] As part of their research for *Women at Boeing*, company historians and archivists at the Boeing Historical Archives undertook an oral history project, "Talking about Work: Boeing Women Managers on Women in the Workplace ... Then and Now." The Boeing Historical Archives staff surveyed female hourly employees and interviewed fifteen women managers with ten to forty years of work experience at Boeing. All interviews took place in the Seattle area in the spring of 1989.[4]

In the interviews many women identified limited paths to advancement as a source of frustration. One woman with more than thirty years' work experience at Boeing recalled that she and other female colleagues had been channeled into specific areas of the company and that the gender division of labor seemed particularly impenetrable in certain departments: "There weren't many women in Boeing management back in the Sixties. The percentage was something like 'point zero something' ... especially in engineering and manufacturing, which (for women) is probably the most discriminatory section of the company. Where women first got into management were the service organizations ... material, industrial relations, contracts."[5]

Female employees at Boeing, it turned out, were all too eager to express similar concerns. Due to the women's candor, and the unsettling view of workplace dynamics they provided, the monograph project was canceled before the year ended. One manager stated that while the idea of the monograph was good, the evidence was not supportive: "Of some concern is the body of testimony from women who are retired and [from women who are] currently at work within Boeing." He also observed that researchers found "a negative loyalty bias within the hourly population of women" and that project leaders were taken aback by the women's responses and "somewhat overwhelmed by the passion of their concerns and the distance of their patience." The manager concluded that although nothing would be done with the evidence at present, perhaps something could be done in the future: "Please take this as a tentative probe and know that it will remain as a record of history for some future historian to look for reasons ... Why?"[6]

This chapter examines that "why" using the interviews to explore how gendered assumptions ordered workplace relations at Boeing in the context of the push for equal opportunity employment that occurred from the 1960s through the 1980s. Boeing's concept of a company "family," built on fraternal networks defined by the assumptions of heteronormative patriarchal capitalism, challenged the implementation of structural changes in employment opportunities. Company cultures made it difficult to change workers' mindsets about the possibility for equal opportunity employment to function in ways that promoted or allowed for equality, even while feminist politics forced Boeing, and workplaces across the United States, to become less rigid.

The concept of the "glass ceiling," both in terms of historical context and contemporary politics and activism, provides substantial insight into the interviews and workplace politics at Boeing.[7] People in the workplace have been guided by gendered power relations and have identified certain traits as female or male and certain jobs as suited for females or for males not necessarily as an overt exercise of power but often because it seemed like the only appropriate choice.[8] Similarly, Anthony Greenwald and Thomas Pettigrew have found that most discrimination in the United States occurs because of favoritism toward others with similar race or gender identities rather than because of overt acts of hostility or prejudice.[9]

One of the best examples for elucidating the power and complexities of gendered assumptions involves Sears, Roebuck and what Alice Kessler-Harris refers to as the "gendered imagination." The concept of the gendered imagination calls into question women's relationship to capitalism and the way that ideas of gender have upheld a gender division of labor.[10] In 1979 the Equal Employment Opportunity Commission (EEOC) sued Sears, Roebuck and Company for discriminatory hiring practices toward women, particularly in the high-paying commission sales jobs. The EEOC's case was one effort to undo the division of labor and the "sex-segregated labor market that had infected the American experience" and that had remained strong in the 1970s. Sears defended its position by noting that, although it had set up an affirmative action program to recruit more women, the retailer could not find any women who wanted these positions.[11] Sears won its case, with the judge agreeing that women did not seek out commission sales jobs because they preferred jobs that were more social and cooperative and less individualistic and competitive. Kessler-Harris notes that the Sears case "reveals the continuing force and tenacity of the gendered imagination even as it suggests the ways that alternative visions of gendered equity try to write themselves into law and policy."[12]

It is precisely this "gendered imagination" that made change so difficult at Boeing. The interviews and the contextual politics reveal a moment in which it becomes clear that the patriarchal male-dominated model in place at Boeing had been normalized in such a way that to some, it was rendered almost invisible. This invisibility manifests itself when people try to pinpoint exactly what accounts for employment discrimination against women. Boeing leaders, managers, and workers shared a hesitancy to call it premeditated discrimination even as they acknowledged that Boeing had not been a welcoming place for women workers. In one interview, for example, a woman clarifies her position that the discrimination was not necessarily intentional but something to be expected in the short term, based on the company's history. When looking to fill senior management positions, for example, she found that company leaders had simply gotten into the habit of choosing men over women: "It's not because of blatant discrimination. It's that (moving women up) just 'doesn't feel right' yet. It's only a matter of time (until more women move up in the company). But we have to start setting those precedents, and we have to start providing opportunities for more women."[13] The construction of the workforce as a "family" built on fraternal norms made it difficult to reconceptualize the workers' relationship to Boeing's organizational structure and to other employees.

Like the previous case studies, this chapter provides a rare opportunity to look inside the managerial politics of a powerful firm. But unlike the other chapters, this one relies primarily on oral histories, which stand out because of their unfiltered content. Women gave candid critiques of the company and offered straightforward advice to Boeing leaders. It is clear that they did not have the opportunity to do so elsewhere or did not feel that they could outside the format of the interview. Many interviewees described a company that seemed not to know what to do with women employees. They also told stories of a corporate culture that strongly adhered to a gender division of labor and did not provide much room for women's advancement. One woman observed that in her department there were 350 employees, yet only a handful of these were women; she cited Boeing leaders as responsible for such low numbers: "So far, I haven't seen any effort on Boeing's part to help keep (its best) women. I get the feeling the attitude is, 'Oh, well, they're gonna leave to take care of their kids so why take them seriously?'"[14] This forthrightness explains why the women who were interviewed requested anonymity, which allowed respondents to speak without the fear of losing their jobs and to avoid any resentment from their coworkers or supervisors and possible retribution.

The interview transcripts themselves are incomplete, with answers often categorized by theme instead of the order they appeared in conversation, and the questions asked were not always uniform. Thus, the transcripts limit the kinds of information that can be gleaned from the answers, narrow the focus to management/employee relations, and raise questions about the tone and thoroughness of the interviews. In other ways, however, this format enriches the study precisely because women viewed the interview as a rare opportunity to raise their concerns in a confidential setting. Most importantly for the purposes of this book, the interviews captured a moment in Boeing's history when workers and all company leaders were rethinking the place of gender diversity in workplace dynamics. The next section traces the context of changing workforce patterns, including the politics of affirmative action and equal opportunity employment programs, before returning to the particular details of the shifts occurring at Boeing during the "EEO era." The rest of the chapter then focuses on the interviews themselves and the insight into workplace dynamics they provide.

Feminist Politics and the Push for Change in the EEO Era

The 1960s and 1970s brought vast changes to the composition of the American workforce. Women's workforce participation rates went up with the economic crises of the 1970s. Deindustrialization meant that blue-collar jobs once filled by men were being replaced with service sector jobs largely filled by women. Beth Bailey notes that, because of inflation, "women's earnings became critical." By 1976 only 40 percent of the jobs in the United States paid wages that could support a family. The number of women who had children under six years old, and thus not yet in elementary school, began to increase; their workforce participation rate went from 30 percent in 1970 to 43 percent in 1976. In 1985 that figure rose to 50 percent.[15] By the 1970s, Natasha Zaretsky points out, the "two-earner family emerged as a norm for the American middle class," and this changing social order created a wave of anxiety that the nuclear family was in crisis.[16] Bailey notes that, in this changing landscape, "the crux of the problem was that liberation freed women to compete with men and, in so doing, upset what they believed was the proper relationship between the sexes."[17]

Gendered assumptions persisted, closing opportunities for women to enter professions coded male, including management and engineering. As men began to feel increasingly vulnerable due to shrinking job opportunities, unions became more protective of male identities in the labor movement. As Jefferson Cowie points out, new organizations like the Coalition of Labor Union Women (CLUW) and 9to5 attempted to draw feminist politics into labor organizing, though these had an "uneasy relation with unions."[18] Francine Moccio has pointed out that unions resisted opening opportunities to women, and she argues that the legacies of the roadblocks put up by gendered views of women's place in blue-collar jobs from the "EEO era" live on today: "A collusive relationship among male workers, unionists, and employers[,] once used to combat employer exploitation, operate[s] in the twenty-first century to the exclusion of women." Moccio argues that the "Sisyphaean task of changing culture" is not the only barrier to equal opportunity for women but that the government, law, and public all need to have a role in ending women's exclusion from professions that have been coded male.[19]

The period from the 1960s through the 1980s was flooded with legislation aimed at eradicating discrimination in employment. In the abstract for the proposed *Women at Boeing* monograph, researchers characterized 1964–89 as a distinct phase in the growth of women's employment at Boeing; they labeled these years the "EEO era."[20] In 1963 the Equal Pay Act was passed, mandating equal pay for equal work. However, as Alice Kessler-Harris notes, this legislation did not cover comparable work and was not as revolutionary as some feminists had hoped, since women were typically concentrated in specific occupations deemed to be primarily for females. EEO legislation did, however, open the door for further feminist political activism and a push for even greater change.[21] One of the most important pieces of legislation was Title VII of the Civil Rights Act and the creation of the Equal Employment Opportunity Commission (EEOC) to facilitate compliance. Pres. Lyndon Johnson signed the Civil Rights Act in 1964, and its Title VII provisions made it illegal for firms with more than fifteen employees to discriminate on the basis of sex, race, religion, or ethnicity. The inclusion of sex in the list of factors receiving coverage under Title VII was at first introduced into the bill as a joke.[22] Even after Title VII was in effect, the main focus continued to be on race and not sex or gender. As

FIG. 6. District Lodge 751, IAM, union meeting, 1965. Courtesy Seattle Post-Intelligencer Collection, Museum of History and Industry, Seattle.

Kathleen Barry notes, "The press treated the inclusion of sex in Title VII as a laughable diversion from the sober matter of racial discrimination."[23]

Throughout the 1970s and 1980s, however, the EEOC became increasingly involved in wage discrimination suits. Feminist groups such as the National Organization for Women (NOW) publicized the fact that women earned substantially less than men, even when the work was comparable or equivalent.[24] The EEOC found itself so burdened with complaints of sex discrimination that it began to focus exclusively on class-action cases, which gave corporations like Boeing greater ability to resist change and weakened the effectiveness of the antidiscrimination law.[25] As Nancy MacLean notes, "Respect for the law became, in effect, voluntary."[26]

While corporations across the United States circumvented equal employment opportunity laws, further progressive legislation forced company leaders to assess women's positions in company hierarchies. In 1968

FIG. 7. Boeing workers after a labor agreement was reached and a strike called off in 1963. Courtesy *Seattle Post-Intelligencer* Collection, Museum of History and Industry, Seattle.

President Johnson issued Executive Order 11375, which made it illegal for federal contractors to discriminate against women. It also required federal contractors like Boeing to file affirmative action plans with the federal government to address how they would increase employment opportunities for women and minorities. This legislation opened a lot of job opportunities that had previously been closed to women and minorities.[27]

In his study of the working class in the 1970s Jefferson Cowie points out that "diversity and inclusion" were emphasized as new job opportunities opened for women and minorities, though workers as a whole were beginning to lose power. The push for a collective workplace justice movement shifted to "a more individualistic terrain of 'occupational justice,'" including affirmative action and equal opportunity programs. As Cowie argues, "Ironically, as the hope for a genuinely integrated manifestation of working-class identity rapidly faded, the actual sites of work were becoming more integrated than ever before." He further notes the impact of this emphasis during the 1980s, as neoliberalism began to take hold, making workers increasingly vulnerable to capitalist exploitation: "As fundamental as inclusion, identity, and diversity were, an emphasis on gender and racial equity alone tended to allow jobs, pay, and labor rights to fall out of the equation, leaving workers with a set of individual rights to non-discrimination amidst a more brutal economy—a multi-cultural neo-liberalism."[28] In the neoliberal economic context, corporations gained more power at the expense of workers, though in the feminist politics of the era many women aspired to overcome this dynamic. Women, at Boeing and elsewhere, expected change, even as some expressed ambivalence about the possibility of change. Women often demanded access to employment opportunities but did not expect radical structural changes, which reflects both the weaknesses of EEO legislation and the persistence of gender discrimination in capitalist corporate cultures.[29]

Another challenge that limited more radical change was the backlash against feminist politics that emerged alongside EEO legislation. Beginning in the 1970s conservatives, led by the New Right, were particularly threatened by the increased access to jobs that affirmative action provided to women and minorities. The New Right gained ground throughout the 1970s and 1980s with a platform that promoted traditional conservative family values and called for dismantling feminist goals and programs such as affirmative action. Amid the economic decline of the 1970s and 1980s, conservative political rhetoric blamed job loss on affirmative action programs and put proponents of feminist issues on the defensive. The ground that the feminist movement had gained in the 1970s did not end in the conservative backlash of the 1980s, though the political atmosphere became particularly hostile to feminist politics and political influence under Pres. Ronald Reagan.[30] This backlash entered popular culture as a war against "political correctness," in which programs such as women's studies and affirmative action came under attack, particularly in academia.[31] Feminists were put on the defensive.[32]

In addition to a hostile political climate, which Judith Stacey points out was exacerbated by Reagan's promotion of the profamily movement through conservative, antifeminist Supreme Court and federal judiciary appointments that "promise[d] to inhibit the progress of democratic family reform well into the twenty-first century," feminism took a hard hit with the "ravages of postindustrialism."[33] Neither conservative nor feminist politics were able to successfully and fully address issues of structural inequalities between men and women in the workplace. A new emphasis on "traditional" family roles emerged; in this formulation women were valued, both culturally and economically, primarily as caretakers within families. As Stacey points out, neither "family values" and the traditional values of the conservative thrust nor feminism "have been as useful in addressing the structural inequalities of postindustrial occupation structure or the individualist, fast-track culture that makes all too difficult the formation of stable intimate relations on a democratic, or any other basis."[34] Even so, the political backlash against feminism prompted a resurgence of feminist activity in the late 1980s and early 1990s.[35] It was this resurgence, along with predictions that more women would enter the U.S. labor force, that prompted corporations like Boeing to implement changes.

Feminist Politics at Boeing

As a federal contractor, Boeing's ability to conduct business meant it had to comply with and enforce affirmative action programs, report compliance, and undergo periodic reviews, all of which forced Boeing to institutionalize changes that promoted diversity in hiring and promotions.[36] One Boeing advertising brochure suggested that equal opportunity was nothing new at the company: "People of all colors and races have worked at Boeing for as long as anyone can remember. Boeing was among the first eight companies that pledged to take affirmative action to establish equal opportunity under the Plan for Progress program in 1961." The brochure further pointed out that it was not until passage of the Civil Rights Act of 1964 that discrimination in employment became illegal.[37] Yet, previous to 1989, Boeing had no policies in place that specifically addressed development of female and minority career and leadership opportunities. As Janet Anderson, Boeing's EEO manager, noted, "Historically, in an unwritten 'policy,' the Company has supported training (internal and external/paid-time and off-hours) which is mutually available and advantageous in content for males and females."[38] Thus, prior to federal intervention Boeing did not systematically pursue expanding opportunities for women, as affirmative action programs proposed to do. Because of this, and in conjunction with critiques against other corporations and critiques against capitalism, corporations like Boeing were a target for feminist activism.

Feminist critiques were lobbed against Boeing as women employed at the company attempted to push through the glass ceiling. In 1970 one writer sarcastically criticized Boeing for adopting a "fatherly attitude toward its female workers, protecting them from the realities of big business and its attendant worries and responsibilities." She noted, "If you are a woman working at Boeing . . . paternalism manifests itself in basic attitudes toward you and your status within the company." The writer issued a warning to the "Big Daddy on the Duwamish" that women would no longer accept Boeing's paternalistic and discriminatory policies.[39] Her prediction proved insightful, not only for Boeing but also for feminist battles against institutionalized gender discrimination across the country.

This demand for more attention to diversity came not only from the women inside Boeing but from pressures outside the company as well. From June 1983 through October 1984, for example, a group of feminist activists occupied a camp that had been set up near Boeing Aerospace Center, in Kent, Washington, where Boeing produced cruise missiles. They named their encampment the Puget Sound Women's Peace Camp and modeled it after similar sites of antinuclear protest in Canada, England, and the United States, among other places. Participants primarily attempted to raise public awareness of Boeing's link to military weapons and policy and to motivate Boeing workers to join their effort to halt the production of cruise missiles. While their focus was antinuclear protest, they also critiqued Boeing's corporate power and the place of workers in relation to that power.[40] The peace camp participants scrutinized the position of women in society and pointed out gendered inequalities; they characterized the cruise missile as "a terrifying manifestation of the male power structure."[41] Their "unity statement" noted, "We are organizing as women because we feel it is time for women to act together as a powerful force for world peace and justice."[42] One camp member, also a Boeing employee, recalled thinking that the group's feminist politics might attract negative attention in the traditionally male Boeing ranks: "I knew the employees at Boeing would find it easy to dismiss the Camp as a bunch of 'kooks' or 'women's libbers,' people totally unlike themselves." While she expected women's politics to be dismissed, to her "amazement" she found many Boeing employees to be sympathetic, though she noted that many were "kept in line by economic necessity."[43] Others experienced more hostile reactions; one woman recalled that after she passed out flyers at Boeing a male employee spit at her.[44] To some, Boeing could seem an unlikely place for feminist politics.

Defining and implementing equal opportunity employment, however, proved difficult. It was unclear what might be the best way to provide equal opportunity employment opportunities at Boeing, and even the necessity of doing so was a source of debate. Boeing leaders often balked at the implementation of programs for women because they were afraid of creating the perception that they were discriminating against white men, who constituted the majority of the workforce. This stance angered many women employees. One woman interviewed pointed out that Boeing's policies on and attitude toward equal opportunity were often confusing and contradictory. She offered an example in which Boeing cosponsored the annual Women in Business Conference in Seattle yet did not sponsor attendance for any female Boeing employees because doing so would have violated a company policy "to not favor one group over another."[45] Despite the company's objections, some women did attend, though according to one employee, company leaders floundered in trying to determine what constituted gender discrimination:

> For two years now, Boeing has given up to $50,000 for scholarships for high school girls. Well, that buys great PR, but we're not getting any return. Why couldn't the company take that money, and send some of our women to the conference and get something in return. But they won't, because the word "women" is in the title of the conference and Boeing says that sending employees would be discriminatory.... One year, (one of the seminar speakers) pointed out that Boeing was one of the seminar's corporate sponsors. Then, she asked the audience, "Will all the women from Boeing please stand up.["] Nobody did, because no one wanted to admit it. What a commentary that was![46]

Despite its public support for women's opportunities, Boeing leaders had a hard time defining and implementing equal opportunity employment within their own work spaces, even as federally designed and mandated affirmative action programs were instituted to try to combat such inequities in employment.[47] Some began to critique even these legally required programs for going too far. Indeed, for those white males at Boeing who were accustomed to climbing the corporate ladder fairly easily and quickly, with no competition except other white men, sudden competition for jobs and advancement seemed threatening. These fears led to charges of reverse discrimination.

Even while opportunities for women and minorities at Boeing in the 1970s and 1980s were fairly limited, company managers still worried about the effects of a diversified workforce on the reputation for a skilled workforce defined by white men. For example, in 1989 Boeing's EEO manager stated, "We make decisions based on qualifications. And we work to eliminate any misconceptions employees might have regarding affirmative action. . . . You can't just trample on the rights of the white male."[48] Beginning in the 1970s, and particularly when jobs became scarce, affirmative action programs were seen by some as "reverse discrimination."[49] Seattle's reliance on Boeing as the top employer in the region, and the company's turbulent history of massive layoffs, exacerbated such fears. It was clear, however, that women did not challenge men's dominance at Boeing. Boeing's proposed monograph on women in the company noted that in 1989 women made up 26 percent of the total Boeing workforce of 26,300 in the Seattle area; one report on the project noted that this figure was the highest in the company's history except for during World War II.[50] However, in the same year, the *Seattle Post-Intelligencer* looked at the same numbers from a different perspective and reported, "Nearly five decades since Rosie the Riveter worked the production line on the home front during World War II, the aerospace industry is mainly a man's world." The article cited the fact that only 20 percent of production workers were women, with an even smaller number (one in fifteen) working as engineers, while only a handful of executives were women.[51] Both inside and outside of Boeing, some had begun to question how much progress Boeing had made toward equal employment opportunity.

FIG. 8. A Boeing technician works on the 707 in 1984. Courtesy National Archives.

"Gendered Imagination" and Boeing's Place
as an Equal Opportunity Employer

It is clear that at least some Boeing managers harbored concerns about the lack of opportunities for women at Boeing. In 1989 top management had in fact begun a thorough investigation of Boeing's equal employment opportunity programs and then began to formulate policy changes to reinvigorate such programs. Janet Anderson, EEO manager at Boeing, examined career development programs for minorities and females. She also established guidelines for the company's development of affirmative action programs, which she characterized as being aimed at "upward mobility development plans for high-potential minorities and females targeted for executive-level positions."[52] Anderson's affirmative action report recommended more open communication between Boeing managers and women and minority employees; it also suggested the immediate formation of focus groups comprising Boeing leaders, women, and minorities so that all could "openly communicate about business/company issues." The groups would "allow employees to have direct exposure to high level executives and sensitize managers to minority/gender experiences and should result in identifying and resolving conflicts."[53]

As part of Boeing's reevaluation of its diversity programs, company leaders issued an internal report in 1989: "Women in Industry: A National and Company Perspective on Professional Advancement." As the title implies, the report analyzed Boeing's work opportunities for women in comparison with those of other companies. The report noted that 1989 had been a "banner year" for Boeing. Included in the company's successes were an almost 30 percent increase in profits and a ranking by the Society of Manufacturing Engineers as one of the top ten places to work.[54] The report acknowledged, however, that 1989 had not been a "banner year" for women at Boeing and other companies. Nevertheless, it claimed that the problems women faced at Boeing were on the decline: "Despite these pockets of male chauvinism, the overall atmosphere at Boeing is positive and markedly improved." While the report openly acknowledged that women faced a tough atmosphere at Boeing in the 1950s, 1960s, and 1970s, it set the current atmosphere apart from that of the past.[55] The report also positioned Boeing on the cutting edge of career development for women and noted that it was positioned to make even greater strides toward equal opportunity employment, promising a "corporate commitment to bringing increasing numbers of women not only into management, but also into Boeing's innermost decision-making circles."[56] But these claims were not quite as concrete or persuasive as the lived experience of women who worked at Boeing, even for Boeing leaders and managers who were concerned about diversity.

The report acknowledged the oral history interviews and used them as examples of the kinds of difficulties women faced, which included barriers to upward mobility (the "glass ceiling"), lack of social networks, resistance to female power, unequal pay, and unrealistic expectations and double standards for women with children (the "mommy track"). It focused specifically on male attitudes that discouraged acceptance of women in specific positions, particularly in management. The report singled out the engineering department as especially in need of women workers and stated that Boeing, along with other manufacturers, needed to do more to attract women to the "traditionally male-dominated profession." However, the report went on to note that "engineering is just one of the professional and technical fields where an unofficial barrier—now commonly referred to as a 'glass ceiling' seems to cap the careers of women."[57] References to the glass ceiling indicate the feminist politics of equal opportunity that were prevalent in this time period.

The oral history interviews were an opportunity for Boeing leaders to hear about the experiences of women and minorities; yet, because they were archived rather than published, they never really came close to accomplishing the goal set out in the report. In addition, Boeing leaders did not talk directly to the women being interviewed. It was only company researchers and archivists who conducted the interviews, which probably explains the women's honesty. This disconnect helps explain the general lack of communication between Boeing leaders and female employees that many women described in their interviews. Several women noted that they felt alienated from the company. One manager with more than thirty years of work experience at Boeing argued, "(I'd like to see them) mentor a few women in the same way they have done the men. Someone (at the company) has to take it upon themselves to say that it's OK to be a woman and work at Boeing. I don't see anyone doing that."[58] Boeing leaders were certainly aware of such feelings to some degree. In a letter that explained the oral history project cancellation, one male manager wrote, "To paraphrase what I infer from the passion of their comments I hear them say 'Won't someone in the Company join in the dialog?'"[59] This lack of follow-through on important employment issues regarding women helps explain the sense of aggravation with Boeing leaders that many interviewees expressed.

It is important to recognize that the interviews were with women who had decided to stay employed at Boeing. So the perspective of those women who left is not heard, although some interviewees do mention women who had left because of the discriminatory atmosphere. For instance, in one interview a female manager was asked to identify the "most pressing issue" facing Boeing's treatment of women. The manager criticized Boeing for not properly utilizing its female workforce: "I've seen a huge brain drain among young women at Boeing. Women who are just beginning to pay back the company's investment, but they leave because they're so frustrated. Frustrated for lack of support, and because working here is just not worth all the battles."[60] The case of Boeing underscores that such social norms, even while not necessarily overt, were still staunchly and very powerfully defended. Managers and corporate leaders held on to a masculinist corporate culture that rendered these norms invisible even under active pressure to change.

Company leaders addressed the interviews by incorporating them into an internal report on company diversity issues. They used excerpts and themes from the oral history interviews as examples of conditions at Boeing and compared those conditions with regional and national trends on the employment of women.[61] It may not have seemed as if much was changing at Boeing from the oral history interviews and from the composition of the workforce. Indeed, companies since the 1980s have been slow to change and address diversity issues with their unwieldy corporate bureaucracies and corporate cultures. Nevertheless, at that particular moment, Boeing leaders were in fact in the midst of an overhaul of their diversity programs and were becoming much more dedicated to the appearance of diversity, if not the reality.

Of course, this overhaul would not come easy and would most likely take a great deal of time. Toward that end, several women argued that achieving equal opportunity was going to be a battle in Boeing's masculine work environment despite the changing political climate that had opened some doors for female advancement. One noted that equality did not require special treatment, just treatment that was similar to what males at Boeing received:

> We don't want anything special, just to be one of the guys. We just want the company to treat us like everyone else. That's really what we want. That would be a big change . . . just treat us like one of the guys. Sometimes I think there are men here who don't [know] what to think of women . . . whether we can really talk, and that we're just normal people. . . . Y'know, it would be nice to have a nice, nurturing environment here so that I can go out and see my customers. Do you know, it's easier (for me, as a woman) to deal with executives on the outside than inside my own company. And I keep asking myself, "Why is that?"[62]

Such comments reveal a belief that ideas about women's capabilities hindered job opportunities and advancement potential for women at Boeing. The latter comment also hints at tensions between a belief that women need to be given a fair chance, which would mean access to the same networks of advancement and mobility that men had, and a feeling that equal employment opportunity programs could require special accommodation or preferential treatment that would be unproductive.

Although many women saw the atmosphere as discriminatory toward women, they offered few solutions to a problem they saw as larger than Boeing. In other words, the "gendered imagination" was a problem that pervaded society, not just Boeing. In many ways this attitude normalized such discrimination. For example, in one interview a woman was asked what the company could do to "improve its relations with women employees," and her response reveals a sense that the answers were fairly simplistic, though not often heeded: "Fairness, that's all that's required. Just plain fairness. I've seen so much unfairness. It's not just a Boeing problem, it's probably like that all over."[63] Some women did compare Boeing to other companies. One interviewee argued that Boeing's pace of change seemed glacial compared to that of other companies: "I have a friend at Hewlett Packard (and from what I understand), things that seem like breakthroughs here have gone on there for years."[64] In another interview a woman reported that from her discussions with other women who belonged to the Society for Engineers, she believed that Westinghouse and Lockheed were "more supportive of women" than Boeing was.[65] She shared her opinion that Boeing was missing out on an opportunity to be a leader in providing opportunities for women: "Essentially, Boeing is a very conservative company, and because the rest of (corporate America) hasn't made moves, they don't think they should. That if they do, they could be held up for ridicule."[66] Another manager, who had an MBA and twelve years at Boeing, offered some advice to women who wanted to improve their work situation: "Bottom line, you've just got to be more focused. Boeing offers tremendous educational opportunities. But no one at Boeing is going to take you by the hand like they do at IBM and say, 'Ok, here's your career path.'"[67] This manager's perspective highlights the complexity with which women addressed the problems facing women at Boeing; women cited individual consciousness and motivation as well as systemic and ingrained social inequalities and attitudes about women workers.

Advancement at Boeing and the Politics of Affirmative Action

Part of the difficulty in generating change in corporations like Boeing was the dominance of male networks that propelled men to the upper ranks of corporations. Advancement at Boeing was both a result of time with the company and a worker's place within the established company hierarchy. From the company's earliest days the careers of Boeing leaders were cultivated within the ranks of the company workforce. In 1988 the *Boeing News* acknowledged that affirmative action programs still had work to do in this climate: "Training and recruitment toward increasing the number of women and minorities in management and upper-level positions is the direction of the 1980s."[68] Boeing's vice president of human resources, Joe Peritore, noted the power of corporate culture in stalling women at the lowest ranks of management and in hampering affirmative action programs: "Part of that is our culture. We promote from within, and it takes many years in The Boeing Company to reach those levels. So just the progression of time will take care of some of that problem. But we think we can do more."[69] As a result, in the late 1980s the company implemented a program to identify "high potential" women and minorities and to try to provide opportunities and mentoring for them to reach the management level. The company also instituted an apprenticeship program to provide more training for women in the machine shops. One employee noted that this awakened a nostalgia for the "Rosies" of World War II: "Guys are pretty tickled that qualified women are coming into the machine shops again."[70]

Machinists, however, because of the burdens they were carrying in the Boeing "family," felt a sharp divide from upper levels of management. In October 1989 fifty-seven thousand machinists launched the "biggest strike in IAM history" and walked off the job in what one union publication described as a "family crusade."[71] Citing "family" and "family issues" as primary reasons for the strike, workers pointed out they were working long hours of overtime, sometimes lasting years, in order to meet new plane orders. In the newspaper of Lodge 751, *Aero Mechanic*, lodge president Tom Baker noted that, before the strike, "the Company was telling everyone within earshot that management and workers were one big family, and that the workers were the Company's most important asset."[72] Strikers also used references to familialism to critique the company's stance on refusing to increase wages. Baker argued, "The Company seems to think that the people who build the finest flying machines in the world are a foolish bunch of children who cannot count!"[73] Strikers walked the picket lines with their families and told of the sacrifices their jobs were requiring. For men, as well as women, management seemed to be taking advantage of workers and not upholding the obligations that a familial model would suggest. One worker, a new father, observed, "My baby is one month old and this strike is the most time I've gotten to spend with her."[74] In addition to being emotionally draining, the strike was also financially draining for many machinists. One worker noted that by the time the strike was over, his family was left with just eighty dollars. Some workers found part-time jobs to help tide them over.[75]

In 1989 business was booming at Boeing. The company had record profits and was trying to produce one new commercial jet per day, a 400 percent increase in production rates from just two years earlier. The *New*

York Times reported on the pressures that the neoliberal economic environment put on workers as the company tried to navigate the boom in Boeing's orders during the 1980s: "The machinists make up less than half of Boeing's nationwide work force of 145,000, but they are the ones who actually assemble the airplanes, including the jumbo-sized 747 and the smaller 737."[76] Workers argued that company leaders were unfairly profiting from their hard work and sacrifices. One female worker noted that her loyalty was shifting to the union: "The company can afford to pay us better in the good times. We stuck with them in the bad times. . . . They should be willing to share. This is the first union I've ever belonged to and it's great."[77] In a time of booming profits and expanded administrative and managerial ranks, both men and women machinists were acutely aware that they were losing power. In his 1989 book on union politics John McCann argues, "The important questions which faced workers in the 1930's are still the questions facing workers in the late 1980's."[78] For the increasing number of women entering the workforce, however, the issues were new. For many men, the demise of the family-sustaining wage and the tensions between union and management signaled that the Boeing "family" needed to be strengthened. To many women, however, "family" at Boeing meant exclusion, especially from those jobs coded male. By the 1980s women were still rare in the engineering ranks of the company.

The engineering program at the University of Washington provided the social network that helped uphold a familial sense of cohesion and male camaraderie in the ranks of management. Women were noticeably absent in this network. Between 1980 and 1988 an average of 845 women per year enrolled in UW's engineering program, while only 138 per year graduated. Suzanne Brainard, a member of the UW engineering faculty and director of the Women in Science and Engineering Program, argued in 1989, "We're looking at incredible retention problems, massive dropouts—30 percent more women dropping out than men."[79] Throughout the postwar period white men remained "the traditional people in the field."[80]

At Boeing, the shortage of women in engineering reinforced a corporate culture in which white men's shared social status ordered the workplace. The fact that many managers and company leaders had started as employees of the engineering department limited women's advancement potential.

In addition, many of the managers had graduated from the same engineering programs at UW, and some hunted or socialized together on weekends. It was this fraternal support network, called the "old-boy network," that facilitated a built-in sense of common identity at businesses across the United States. It is also what made the Boeing "family" retain some characteristics of the 1930s even though the company had changed dramatically since earlier times. In 1971 there were only 50 women managers at Boeing, and by 1980 there were 659. Still, this brought the ratio of female to male managers to 1:16. The *Seattle Post-Intelligencer* noted, "These 659 women have either been singled out or have carved their own niches in the mystical and often annoyingly traditional Boeing corporate hierarchy."[81] Women were employed in all sectors of the company in the postwar period, but not in ways that challenged traditional constructions of the Boeing "family."

Many women engineers at Boeing were discouraged by the male atmosphere and left Boeing after only a few years of employment. One woman manager who was interviewed in 1989 recalled that women still seemed a novelty within company ranks and were easily overlooked: "They're not necessarily harassed; it's worse. They're ignored. And I know what it feels like; I've been in meetings where the men behaved like I wasn't even there."[82] Another woman described how entrenched the gender division in labor seemed to be and how there seemed to be no way for women to move up to the higher ranks: "When I was in the clerical work force, the lack of opportunity for women was absolutely the biggest issue. There just didn't seem to be any way for a woman to move up, to get into management...to move up. (Back in the Fifties), the feeling of being a second-class citizen was normal among the women I worked with."[83] A manager with forty years' work experience at Boeing blamed the company's desire to maintain a masculine image for the lack of opportunities for women in the 1950s: "Back then, everybody knew no woman could be a manager where it was visible to the outside. Y'know, to vendors. I'm telling you, that was the policy! In fact, two supervisors *told* me they would have made me a manager if I'd been a man. But that [was] because I was a woman, I was going to hit the ceiling (in Material)."[84]

Similarly, a woman with more than twenty-five years' work experience observed that Boeing had little experience dealing with women because of the company's long history of having a majority male workforce. She recalled a case in which the company refused to let her go on a business trip because the client was known to use "bad language." She had worked at the company for two years before Boeing finally allowed her to travel to a sales presentation, and even then the company worried about how clients would perceive female representatives: "Y'know what Boeing did? My boss called the [client] to ask if it was all right if they sent a woman along! You see, Boeing thought the client might be insulted if a woman was sent on a presentation." Although the woman was eventually allowed to go on out-of-town business trips, her coworkers insisted on calling her "Charlie" on the trips rather than by her real name. She explained the tensions they were hoping to avoid with this tactic: "You see, they figured it wouldn't look good if they went home and told their wives they went out of town with a woman. So, from that very first trip, I was 'Charlie.' And that nickname stayed for years."[85]

In another interview a manager described Boeing's stance on women traveling out of the country and stressed that company leaders' concerns about women traveling were often old-fashioned. This manager recalled making a sales call on a female executive from a "Third World Country" who was surprised to learn how behind the times Boeing was: "Over lunch, we talked about women's issues, and it turns out (her company) had us beat on every single issue. . . . I think Boeing thinks it's much more progressive on women's issues than the rest of the world. But that just isn't the case."[86] Company leaders' concerns were also evident to a female engineering manager in Boeing's commercial division. Over the course of more than thirty years at Boeing, she faced difficulties in traveling as a representative for Boeing. Prior to her departure for meetings in the Middle East, North Africa, and Latin America, Boeing leaders sent telegrams to "gauge the climate toward a woman's participation," even though, as she observed, it often seemed that Boeing managers were out of touch with other cultures and public perceptions of women: "What they [the clients] wanted was the information we were bringing. And as long as they got what they wanted, they didn't care who did it. Boeing had the problem with women. They were so afraid that they might get into trouble (with the client), that they wouldn't make a move. And all it took was someone with a few guts to say, 'This is the way it's going to be.'"[87]

With the development of affirmative action programs, women at Boeing gained a sense that they had permission to speak out against the inequalities ingrained in their work environment, yet they still had mixed expectations on their ability to alter the established order of the Boeing "family." Even though Boeing had some equal opportunity programs in place, women expressed a belief that they were too weak to make meaningful, widespread, or lasting changes. Interestingly, despite Boeing's denials that the federal mandate accounted for policy changes, some interviewees cited gender visibility as the reason for a promotion. As one woman explained, the very need for Boeing to have increased visibility of women in leadership positions because of civil rights and women's rights legislation resulted in her advancement. She explained the circumstances that led her to achieve promotion on paper but not in reality: "I was a token. I got into management because of the (Civil Rights Act). So Boeing could raise its quotient of women managers. Later, after I was appointed supervisor my manager wouldn't let me to [sic] sit in for him while he was on vacation, or wouldn't allow me to do special projects. His prejudice just couldn't allow a woman to represent his organization to another. . . . And that's terrible. You have to develop your knowledge and skills, but first you have to be given the chance."[88] When asked about tokenism, another manager with more than twenty-five years at Boeing answered similarly: "When I was first made a manager, my husband said, 'Well, they've met their quota.' It hurt, but, yes, I think I probably was (a token) in the beginning. That's not true anymore. I get things done, and everybody knows it."[89]

When asked about the company's stance on women in management prior to government intervention, another woman replied that little had changed. She noted that the men at Boeing proved resistant to change because, back in the 1950s, they believed women shouldn't be placed in management positions that would be visible to the outside. They could hold traditional managerial roles, such as in nursing, personnel, and the library, but not where clients or the public could see them. She believed the problem had persisted despite the changing times: "That was back in the 50s. But I still have a big problem with the company today for that same reason. There is not a single woman on Boeing's executive board. Boeing has been very backward in promoting women, and they are today."[90] To many, inequalities had to be addressed in order to meet the challenges of the future.

Affirmative Action and the "Skills Gap"

By the late 1980s there was a growing recognition among Boeing leaders, managers, and workers that things had to change, even though change was slow to modify corporate culture and women's experiences at Boeing. While implementing affirmative action programs in 1989, Boeing leaders made upward mobility for women and minorities a goal and targeted management positions in particular. Managers sought to implement changes that promoted diversity, though such efforts were often framed as future endeavors rather than present battles. These discussions often lacked a sense of urgency and any recognition that there were any wrongs in the past that had to be rectified with modifications, such as those the affirmative action programs entailed. Changes were often predicated on the future need for labor. For example, EEO manager Janet Anderson's 1989 report notes that the company had recently created seminars for Boeing managers to attend. The first course was titled "Affirmative Action: Managing a Diverse Workforce." These seminars were designed to "assist in further understanding the challenges which lie ahead in managing the diverse workforce of the future."[91] Anderson predicted that demographic changes in the workforce would require a different corporate tradition regarding employment opportunities. Boeing's report on affirmative action programs noted that minorities would make up 29 percent of the new entrants into the labor force between 1990 and the year 2000—twice their current share of the workforce—and that immigrants would represent the largest share of the increase in the population and the workforce: "Sixty-one percent of all females of working age are expected to have jobs by the year 2000." Her report also warned of an impending "skills gap," in which "unskilled, entry-level jobs, where many minorities and women have historically been assigned, will decline dramatically."[92] The "skills gap" would require corporations to provide more training to workers.

The report implied that managers should not risk alienating potential workers. In addition, Boeing leaders had to act or risk a labor crisis: "The underutilization of minorities and females in all levels of management is a fact and one that Boeing cannot afford to ignore."[93] Similarly, in 1988 the national director of the Office of Federal Contract Compliance Programs observed, "The old assumptions—2.2 children and the wife stays home—are antiquated. Companies that are going to attract the best and the brightest might recognize this."[94] Such sentiments echo the labor crisis of World War II, when labor shortages and increased production forced Boeing managers to reconfigure definitions of skill, training methods, and recruitment of the "ideal" worker. Just as in World War II, then, employers would have to provide more training and education opportunities to allow more than just white males to obtain jobs classified as skilled. Employers would also have to rethink the male breadwinner model.

Women at Boeing predicted a labor problem would develop if company leaders kept turning a blind eye to diversity problems. One interviewee, for example, commented that the company's fortunes depended on its ability to incorporate a more diverse workforce: "Boeing better start training its managers to be more sensitive to the needs of women. Make the environment better for women and minorities. Otherwise, it's going to be hard-pressed to have the work force turn out the airplanes it needs."[95]

Changing the Old-Boy Corporate Culture

Changes proposed in 1989 posed new challenges to the Boeing "family." In its original conception, the Boeing "family" was held together by a social network of men who identified with one another as fathers, skilled workers, and masculine white men. For those Boeing employees in management or leadership positions, this fraternal network, which many labeled the "old-boy network," was even more exclusive. It was also cited as one of the biggest obstacles to more open access to Boeing employment opportunities. Challenges to masculine organizations in the 1970s and 1980s were widespread, particularly because of the precedents, tools, and language provided by the civil rights movement. As Barbara Arneil argues, the 1970s constituted a "critical juncture" in American organizational history, a time when a "fundamental value change" occurred as more, but not all, organizations began to embrace diversity.[96] Boeing's inability to more fully open its corporate culture meant that, in the remaining decades of the twentieth century, women continued to face challenges breaking through the barrier of company culture. In his study of masculinity and inequality within organizations Mark Maier argues that the "old-boy network" has worked alongside other mechanisms of masculinist organizational cultures to restrict women to the lowest levels of power within organizations:

> In their roles as organizational colleagues, men at the top have often felt uncomfortable relating with women as equals. The glass ceiling within organizations—the negative stereotypes and basic skepticism that men have of women as managers, their reluctance to accept women into the informal networks upon which advancement to the highest levels so vitally depends, the subtle and overt manifestations of sexual harassment, the segregation of jobs, less access to off-the-job training opportunities that groom managers for powerful positions, and the persistence of the "old boy network" and women's restriction (either by design or by consequence) of access to the inner sanctum of senior management—pose formidable barriers to managerial women.[97]

As Maier further argues, organizations that embrace "masculinist values" do not function as effectively as they could. He argues that "the corporate masculinity inherent to organizations is an example of structural dysfunctionalism."[98]

The old-boy network was widely known throughout Boeing, and many women pointed to an expected "structural dysfunctionalism" based both on the old-boy network and on the neoliberal capitalist policies that empowered company leaders at the expense of workers. In one interview a woman was asked where she saw the company in ten years with regard to women's advancement. Her answer reveals just how deeply rooted in the old-boy network Boeing's corporate culture really was: "It's a tough fight to get into management, and once you get there you find it's not a warm and fuzzy place to be. You can't get around the ol boy's network, because it's there . . . and worse in some places than others."[99] As they had been in the 1930s, informal networks were vital to getting a job at Boeing and navigating company policies and culture once inside the company. In the context of the company's growth over the postwar period, these networks became even more important.

In the "old-boy network" men rose through the ranks together and lent support to each other, both in their work and in their personal lives. Those who worked in Boeing's highest ranks fondly remembered the camaraderie and support lent to them by their peers. For example, Carl Cleveland, a Boeing manager who eventually became an assistant to the president, wrote a collection of short stories based on the many humorous adventures and memories of former and current Boeing workers. Cleveland fondly recalls that Boeing president Bill Allen used to give a lawn party each year for the company's top management. He also describes episodes in which support went beyond work; he relates a story of a Renton plant supervisor being arrested for driving under the influence and promptly calling one of the top Boeing leaders to bail him out of jail at two-thirty in the morning.[100] He also explains groups such as the "Staggering Stags," a group made up primarily of Boeing engineers whose purpose was "to provide relief from work tensions with an occasional two-day bash at some remote site."[101] Except for the World War II period, it is difficult to find stories about Boeing women engaging in these types of activities. While it may be easy to dismiss these stories as inconsequential, they in fact get at the heart of the supportive network that existed for and among men at Boeing, one that many argued did not exist for women.

What these stories illustrate is the significance of corporate culture for the everyday operations of Boeing as a firm, something both its leaders and workers realized was important as they tried to institute diversity beginning in the 1970s. Both the EEO report and the women interviewed identified the ability to change or even shape corporate culture as a crucial avenue toward equal opportunity employment. Anderson's 1989 report argued that corporate culture—its values and goals—must facilitate upward mobility for minorities: "Without the appropriate climate, little, if any, progress can be made to equalize the representation of minorities/females in management." Although she placed this onus on corporate leadership, she also called for holding the individual accountable for "evaluating his or her role within that environment."[102] Her report also acknowledged that it was no small feat to alter corporate culture and the long-standing climate of white male privilege at Boeing. She observed, "Boeing's longstanding position of not providing special training for minorities and females is deeply ingrained.

A policy change may be controversial."[103] The fact that Boeing's corporate culture was so deeply immersed in patriarchal traditions explains why, even with the pressures exerted by the women's movement, Boeing remained slow to change. Affirmative action programs faced a major hurdle in the long-established social networks at Boeing. These networks were built on long-term relationships among white men and were the foundation of Boeing's corporate culture. Even Boeing leaders were aware of how significant these informal networks were for employment and advancement. The 1989 Boeing report on affirmative action, for example, cited "lack of informal 'networks'" as an "organizational barrier" that discouraged advancement of minorities and females.[104]

Similarly, many of the women interviewed for the oral history project commented on the existence of an old-boy network that prevented the hiring and advancement of female employees. One interviewee noted that, in addition to doing "double duty" with jobs and kids, women do not become managers because "they don't go hunting, fishing or golfing with their bosses like a lot of guys do, so it's understandable why they (senior managers) would look to their friends first."[105] When asked about obstacles for women at Boeing, a female manager in the company's commercial division commented, "The ole boy's network; now, there's an obstacle. Sometimes I think it's my age, or the fact that I don't have as many years with the company. But when a young guy hires in AFTER me, and is invited to join the others for lunch, it concerns me."[106] Those women privileged enough to be in direct proximity to the old-boy network by virtue of their job soon discovered that their presence was barely acknowledged: "There was a general lack of support after my promotion was announced. I mean, I think it's strange when you get a (promotion) and no one acknowledges it. Nobody offers congratulations or 'good luck.' It even affected some of my friendships. Some men felt they couldn't continue to be friends without being considered a traitor to the other men in the office. Because chumming with me was a lack of loyalty to the 'Boy's Network.'" This manager went on to note that even other male coworkers expressed surprise at the harsh response: "A few weeks after the promotion, I told my boss, 'I wasn't expecting this much turmoil.' He said, 'I wasn't either. But give it six months.' Six months later things died down."[107]

Many interviewees emphasized that in order to counteract and circumvent the power of the old-boy networks women workers at Boeing needed to create their own social networks and support groups. The topic was of such relevance that one woman noted it invariably came up whenever she got together with other Boeing women.[108] Indeed, some interviewees argued that women needed to act more forcefully to create such networks; others argued that women needed to toughen up and beat the men at their own game. As one woman put it, "Women have a lot to learn as far as being team players . . . not being complainers. Not expecting special privileges. But to really make a difference, they've got to learn how to maneuver; how to play the political game. Y'know, women can be quarterbacks just as easily as anyone else."[109] Another woman, a manager for ten years, noted that the struggle for a sense of camaraderie and acceptance, particularly as buoyed by support networks, was an uphill battle and that although there had been a few gradual changes it was still a struggle for recognition and comfort:

> It was real lonely those first few years. I couldn't play cards at lunch with my old friends because now I was their boss. And I wasn't accepted by the male managers, who had their hunting and fishing groups. It's only been in the last two or three years that I've felt really accepted by male peers. . . . It's lonely, although it's getting a little better now because there's a few more ladies in management. It's tough on some of the women when their bosses [don't] take the time to listen to them. We're closer to our emotions, and we're not always able to hide them.[110]

Another interviewee with more than thirty years at Boeing similarly described the loneliness that came with being a female manager. When asked, "What was the most difficult aspect of moving up in the company?" she pointed to the isolation and lack of networking opportunities: "Back then (the 60s), there were so few other women managers in the company that I was usually the only woman at departmental meetings . . . or at retreats. The situation is much easier now, but back then a woman manager had a lonesome job."[111] Similarly, others saw substantial room for improvement and noted that social networks were an important means for such improvement. Women were encouraged to volunteer for causes such as the Special Olympics, the Boeing Employees Good Neighbor Fund, and the Boeing Management Association. As one woman saw it, "It gives them the same kind of community network that men have."[112]

Although there were no visible, formal networks for women, there were some very loosely defined informal networks that operated outside Boeing's organizational structures and corporate culture. Such networks were the direct result of a discriminatory work environment. Women often bonded with each other by feeling isolated from the dominant male corporate culture at Boeing. One woman recalled being actively discouraged from starting a networking club at the plant. As she recalled, "We were denied the use of a room because the company said it couldn't support that kind of activity because it was exclusive."[113] Still, women found ways to meet and network. Another woman recounted the camaraderie she formed among her coworkers, who met for dinner every three or four months: "It was a sounding board for some of the problems we had at work . . . and we'd share thoughts about how we would handle the situation."[114] One woman described the revolutionary impact just the secretarial pool could have if only their consciousness could be raised: "If the secretaries ever banded together and went on strike, the Boeing Company would be on its knees in three days. Fortunately for Boeing, the secretaries are just as unaware. Or they would (have gone [on] strike) a long time ago."[115]

Gender and Generational Assumptions

Several women pointed out that while policies were in place that encouraged equal opportunity, it was not easy to change the attitudes of coworkers. One woman described this atmosphere as in some ways more stifling and having a much more subtle form of discrimination behind it: "It wasn't like the Fifties where they could just say, 'Hey, we don't want you.' There was nothing hidden about that; that was just policy. Not written, but spoken. Today, (the policy) is not spoken, but their actions (of the old guard male managers) show their real feelings."[116] Several women mentioned a similar generational gap between older managers and those who were younger. One woman predicted that the real change would come not with institutional policies but through attrition, as a younger generation of managers whose wives were also in the workforce took the shop floor: "The younger (managers) don't have that problem. They usually treat women like the rest of the guys."[117] The "gendered imagination" of men seemed to some women interviewed to be changing, if slowly. In one interview a woman linked this gradual shift directly to altered gender roles within the home, claiming that the younger men "have different ideas about women; they help at home, they share responsibilities at home. So, things are evolving."[118] Likewise, another interviewee remained hopeful that there would be even more such changes in the future; when asked what advice she would offer to other women, she urged patience, since the company was slowly realizing that it needed to do whatever it could to attract a quality workforce. "You're [not] going to get the best people you can unless you have an environment that is good for minorities, good for women, as well as for men," she said, adding that one bright spot was that "the company's managers are getting younger all the time. And let's hope that those younger men have different attitudes than the generation I was working with."[119]

The interviews also make clear that it was not just men who had ideas about how women would fit into the company. Women also promoted ideas about skills that came "naturally" to women. Much like the issue of gendered imagination that underlay the Sears case, these depictions render women as better than men at being soft and conciliatory rather than aggressive and forceful. One woman noted that female workers tended to be more compassionate and therefore better with personality issues. She recalled being in meetings in which she was the only female in attendance: "(My presence) probably kept them from being more at each other's throats than if I hadn't been there. I think nurturing is needed in a corporation; you need a 'softening' touch. And many a secretary has lent an ear to a frustrated boss, and helped them through that trauma."[120] When asked how women have "affected the development of the company," one woman said she thought she brought sensitivity to her dealings with customers: "(As a woman), I helped raise the customer's comfort level. You see, if I sat between two airline people at lunch, a friendship would develop. They could tell me about their wives, their kids. There was a softness."[121] The Boeing interviewers asked specifically about gender differences between men and women managers. Another woman talked specifically about the "special qualities" that women brought to management because they were better team players than men. She also indicated that women often had nontraditional approaches to difficult challenges. As she put it, "There are few women (managers) and minorities in this particular division and it's too bad. They need more of a balance here; just like in real life."[122]

Things got even more complicated when trying to figure out how to incorporate women fully into a male-dominated company while adhering to seemingly natural gender roles—a challenge for capitalism more broadly. Even Boeing's report acknowledged that women were expected to adhere to sometimes confusing standards of behavior based on ideas about gender and sex norms: "Women are expected to be tough, decisive, independent, risk-taking and goal driven. They must display the commonly accepted attributes of the highly successful corporate male, and at the same time be demure, unassuming and attractive."[123] In the oral history interviews one support division manager who had been at Boeing for more than twenty-five years related a story about the strange position women occupied because of this double standard: "The other day, my boss said, 'Y'know, you're just like my wife . . . aggressive, right on top of things. But (here at work) that means you're pushy and a bitch.' And he was right. We can't be aggressive without being called bitches. We want to get things done same as men. And the only difference in our management style is that we're women."[124] In the ranks of management, then, despite the mandate of affirmative action programs that posited that women could be managers on an equal level with men, ideas about gender still shaped views of women's efficacy in managerial positions.

The Legacy of the EEO Era and Feminist Politics

The resurgence of feminist activism in the late 1980s and early 1990s corresponded with a flurry of discrimination charges against Boeing that began in the 1980s. For example, in 1984 the number of discrimination charges received by agencies outside the company and through lawsuits totaled 75; by 1988 that number had shot up to 170, a 126 percent increase.[125] In addition to filing suits in federal courts, thus generating broader publicity, workers also filed complaints with the Seattle Human Rights Commission (SHRC). Many of the cases charged Boeing with discrimination in hiring and in the way workers were treated on the job. Most of the complaints were filed by minorities or white women.

There were several cases in which employees charged Boeing with race discrimination and filed complaints with both the EEOC and the SHRC.[126] Some of these suits described a work atmosphere that appeared to be getting worse for women and minorities. In one complaint filed with the EEOC and SHRC in 1981, a black male charged his white supervisor with terminating his employment based on race. The worker observed that his department had witnessed a sharp decline—more than 50 percent—in its number of African American workers over the years: "I believe my Race was a factor because I believe the supervisors are trying to get rid of Blacks."[127] In another case that exposed white patriarchal corporate culture, in 1981 a black male complained that, after his white girlfriend visited him at work, his supervisor, a white male, "stated to me why don't I get a Black girlfriend."[128] A black female reported that she had been interviewed several times by white men but had never been hired, which she attributed to her race. She reported that one of the men who interviewed her "told me it was difficult to get into Boeing and people try to get their family [and] friends and neighbors into Boeing."[129] Lawsuits and the EEO influence there had tangible effects on the way the workplace was organized. One woman recalled that at Boeing Commercial Airlines the executive dining room included only a men's restroom; after some EEO lawsuits were filed, however, Boeing installed a women's restroom.[130]

These cases reveal the very real impact that the "EEO era" had on workplace relations at Boeing; they illustrate the pressures from the women's movement and civil rights movements to more effectively incorporate diversity into Boeing's corporate culture. Finally, such cases also reflect the growth of institutionalized spaces for employment discrimination grievances. Yet, as one study of corporate responses to employment discrimination cases found, firms often respond to charges of gender and sex discrimination with anger and respond to charges of race discrimination with fear.[131] The next chapter highlights the anger that arose when a woman attempted to challenge Boeing's prescribed corporate culture in ways that EEO policies did not address. The case exposed the degree to which ideas about sex and gender segregation were by the 1980s entrenched both in Boeing's work spaces and in the concept of the Boeing "family."

CHAPTER 4

Jane Doe v. Boeing Company

Beginning in the early 1980s there were new challenges to Boeing's corporate culture that made clear the company's role in the policing and
surveillance of both gender and sexual norms. Jane Doe, a self-identified
male-to-female transsexual who desired anonymity, was a Boeing engineer
from 1978 to 1985.[1] During those years Doe worked in several different
departments and divisions at Boeing, including Boeing Aerospace Company
(BAC), Boeing Commercial Aircraft Company (BCAC), and Boeing Computer Services (BCS). She spent the majority of her time at BCS in Renton,
Washington, including the period up until Boeing fired her in 1985. BCS
provided support for—and shared office space with—just one customer,
BCAC. Thus, Doe worked not only among her fellow engineers but also in
the same physical space as her customer, which was significant given the
normative masculinist culture of the engineering profession. Even in such
a large corporate setting (there were more than eight hundred employees
in her office complex alone), Doe worked closely with the smaller work
group that came to be known as "Bob Masters's area," named for Doe's
floor supervisor, Robert Masters.[2] Of the fourteen people working in "Bob
Masters's area" only a few were women, including two who sat near Doe.[3]
The rest, including Doe's immediate supervisors, were men.

Doe excelled at BCS, and her work performance was never called into
question. She consistently achieved good work performance reviews and
recognition for her engineering abilities. In addition, her supervisors testified that, even at the time of her termination, Doe's work performance

was not at issue.[4] What Doe's managers and Boeing leaders did question, however, was the gender and sex image Doe began to present in the mostly male engineering department beginning in 1984. Doe was fired for violating company standards of dress, which were understood through the framework of masculinist norms and traditions. This chapter examines Doe's experiences and the subsequent lawsuit, *Jane Doe v. Boeing Company*, in which the issue of employment discrimination was scrutinized in the contexts of both the emergent transgender rights and disability rights movements and the neoliberal politics of corporate power expansion and surveillance of employees. Doe, as a transgender woman, essentially disrupted Boeing's organization of work along sex and gender lines. Doe was not only disrupting this male-dominated environment but also doing so from a position that rejected normative sex and gender identity. Boeing's firing of Doe typifies what Robert McRuer refers to as "compulsory able-bodiedness," in which "people with disabilities embody for others an affirmative answer to the unspoken question, 'Yes, but in the end, wouldn't you rather be more like me?'"[5] As Lennard Davis's analysis of normalcy shows, the construction of the norm assumes that most people are or should be included in the norm.[6] In the minds of some coworkers, Doe was not able-bodied nor was she within the homogeneous gender and sex norms of Boeing engineers. Doe confounded Boeing's corporate culture and the disciplinary mechanisms of capitalist work that were based on patriarchal gender and sex norms.

LGBTQ Politics at Boeing

There were other challenges to the normative sex and gender traditions of Boeing's corporate culture in the 1980s. For example, several gay and lesbian employment discrimination cases were brought against Boeing. One of the most publicized cases was that of Bruce Kleiman, a Boeing aerospace engineer who tested positive for AIDS in 1985 and was subsequently laid off. Kleiman, with help from the state's Human Rights Commission, filed a lawsuit against Boeing on the grounds of disability discrimination and was eventually rehired at Boeing.[7] One local gay publication noted that, while Boeing hardly had a reputation as a gay-friendly employer, the company's large workforce made it "hardly a surprise . . . that Boeing does employ a large number of lesbians and gay men."[8] Increased attention to workplace rights stimulated efforts to fight against patriarchal heterosexual sex and gender norms in the workplace, such as refusal to hire lesbians and gay men.[9] In the Seattle area several activist groups began to target top employers, including Boeing. For example, in 1985 the Greater Seattle Business Association (GSBA), a gay and lesbian advocacy group, undertook a regional effort as part of a national corporate outreach project run by the National Association of Business Councils. The GSBA's initiative, which it characterized as "knocking on the corporate closet door," identified three goals: to assess existing corporate policies in regard to gay and lesbian employees, to inform corporations about gay and lesbian issues, and to provide information and resources for corporations on areas of concern to gay and lesbian employees.[10] Fourteen Seattle corporations were asked to take part in the initiative, and only Boeing and Microsoft "declined to participate."[11]

The transsexual movement, which overlapped with the gay rights movement in important ways, also attempted to transform sexual politics in the workplace and challenge discrimination based on sexual and gender identification, even as corporations resisted these attempts. As Susan Stryker points out, "Like other queer militants, transgender activists sought to make common cause with any groups—including nontransgender gays, lesbians, and bisexuals—who contested heterosexist privilege." Importantly, however, she also points out that homosexuality could sometimes share more commonalities with heterosexuality in terms of gender constructions.[12] People who identified as transgender faced particular difficulties in fighting against ideas of gender that were deeply entrenched in corporate organization and bureaucracies.

Descriptions of transgender experiences at Boeing varied. They were localized and highly dependent on one's immediate work surroundings because there were no corporate policies that recognized transgender rights. One male-to-female transsexual worker who had been laid off in the 1970s transitioned after being laid off and was then rehired as a female employee.[13] In 1982 another male-to-female transsexual approached Boeing management to inquire about company policies on transsexuality and transitioning on the job.[14] She was instructed to use the men's restroom and prohibited from wearing feminine attire.[15] These cases, because they were negotiated largely on the shop floor between the managers and the workers, did not produce the kind of historical and legal records that the case of *Jane Doe v. Boeing Company* did.

While at Boeing, Doe met several other Boeing employees who were positioned outside the male heterosexual norms that dominated her engineering unit at various LGBTQ support groups she attended throughout the late 1970s and 1980s. At the Seattle Counseling Service for Sexual Minorities, Doe befriended "transvestites, transsexuals, and people that were professionals, doctors, lawyers, Boeing employees, as well as carpenters and blue collar and unemployed, and just the whole spectrum of careers and skills and education level."[16] In 1982 Doe met, at a support group, the previously mentioned male-to-female transsexual, who told her about her experiences transitioning at Boeing; while managers had instructed this employee to use the men's restroom and not to wear feminine attire, according to Doe, she looked like a female both at work and at the support group they both attended and thus appeared to not be following Boeing's directive to avoid feminine dress.[17] Significantly, at least in Doe's view, there was a known example of a Boeing employee who had transitioned on the job. To Boeing managers, however, this was not an accepted precedent, nor was it compliant with Boeing's workplace regulations and the gender and sexual norms on which these regulations were based. The underlying fear was that sexual and gender identities that fell outside normative definitions would disrupt employee camaraderie, thus hampering workplace productivity. One senior personnel manager, for example, later reported that Boeing workers who had transitioned while on the job had proven "disruptive to the work force" because the sex change process "causes complaints from other employees."[18] Thus, when Doe began her transition in 1984, she was facing some hostility because of the challenge to gender and sex norms she presented.

Jane Doe and Transgender Politics

Although Doe's decision to change her appearance was the culmination of decades of conflicted feelings about her gender, she cited 1984 as a pivotal year in her transformation, recalling it as the point when she "reached that dramatic conclusion" that she was a woman.[19] In late 1984 she decided to pursue sex reassignment surgery. Her decision in 1984, however, had widespread and immediate ramifications for both her personal and professional life. She began seeing a doctor for hormone therapy and a psychologist for counseling in preparation for her surgery.[20] On the basis of several recommendations from friends, Doe went to Colorado in 1985 to consult with Dr. Stanley Biber, one of the leading physicians in gender dysphoria and sex reassignment. Dr. Biber advised Doe on the specific guidelines that the medical profession had established for transgendered persons who wanted sex reassignment surgery. More specifically, he cited the Harry Benjamin International Gender Dysphoria Association's *Standards of Care: The Hormonal and Surgical Sex Reassignment of Gender Dysphoric Persons*, which advised patients to live full-time in the social role of the sex they identified with for at least one year prior to surgery.[21] Doe described her reaction to Biber's instructions to live as a woman as one of relief. She also emphasized the deep reflection that went into this decision: "Gender dysphoria is not just something I read about and thought would be fun to try."[22] At the same time, however, the Benjamin Standards conflicted with Boeing's requirements, and Doe could not simultaneously fulfill both.

The choices Doe faced cannot be fully understood without taking into consideration the trajectory of disability discourses and litigation and their intersections with transgender and medical discourses. The creation of the Benjamin Standards and the emergence of "gender dysphoria" and "gender identity disorder" as terms of "diagnosis" reflect the growth of the medical profession and its views of transsexualism in the 1970s and 1980s. Doe relied on the recommendations of psychologists and counselors to deem her ready for surgery. But medical diagnosis of gender dysphoria and gender identity disorder remains complicated, controversial, and inextricably connected to developments in the history of disability more broadly. As Susan Burch and Ian Sutherland explain, until the 1980s disability studies and conceptions of what constituted a "handicap" followed a medical model positing that disabilities were equated with pathologized dependency or a deficiency that could be rehabilitated through medical intervention.[23] In the case of Doe, the diagnosis of gender dysphoria allowed her to gain access to sex reassignment surgery and also served as the platform upon which her legal claims of employment discrimination against Boeing were built. But while the diagnosis of gender dysphoria can sometimes allow people to receive medical care and legal protections, it can also undermine individual autonomy, reify dominant gender norms, and reinforce the idea that transgender people are sick or pathological.[24] The search for an "authentic" self can also reinforce the idea that gender is stable, fixed, and coherent. As Judith Halberstam points out, transsexuals are often represented both "as 'empire' and the subaltern, as gender dupes and gender deviants, and as consolidated identities and fragmented bodies."[25] Joanne Meyerowitz argues that these classifications are problematic because, for transgender people, "varied presentations of gender were no less 'authentic,' and no more 'free,' than other sincere attempts to express a sense of self."[26]

Doe's desire to follow her gender identity was at odds with Boeing's investment in rigid gender divisions in the workplace and masculine norms in the engineering department. She was therefore placed in the impossible situation of needing to express her gender but being banned from expressing it, of being categorized as either normal or pathologized, and of conforming to a homogeneous corporate culture or being an outlier relative to it. For the most part, Doe relied on a language that explained her postoperative gender as fixed and in line with an "authentic" gender. She later argued in court, for example, that "only those that are still in the early stages of dealing with their issues" would present themselves as transsexuals.[27] At the same time, however, Doe also relied on the legal definitions of gender dysphoria as a handicap or disability when she had to make adjustments for having a gender that did not match her body: "My understanding is that the legal definition of a handicap . . . is a condition that prevents one from performing one of life's major functions," and, as she noted, "I still can't have babies. I can't menstruate. . . . I have some maintenance that I have to do that biological women don't do in terms of I have to dilate on a weekly basis, and I have to take hormones." Doe further described herself as "emotionally handicapped" because of her "history as being raised as a male, and not many women have that history, so my history is part of my mental handicap."[28] Doe's language illustrates the complexity of her relationship to the diagnosis of gender dysphoria; she both rejected the idea that transsexuality was fixed or a permanent state at the same time that she affirmed transsexuality could never be fully erased.

In the summer of 1985 Doe made the decision to officially inform her managers and coworkers of her intention to transition and told them that her physical appearance would change. She later testified that she was nervous about telling her coworkers but felt she had to because she was afraid of the attention she could attract, particularly after she informed her supervisors.[29] She noted that while she "had hoped to transfer to a new job as a female because there would be less chance of disruption and less fingerpointing," she was not offered a new position. Nevertheless, she stated, "It has been a smooth transition however in my work group. Everyone was made aware that I would be dressing as a woman on 1 June 1985 and going by the name [Jane]."[30] Doe noted with surprise that, in most cases, relationships remained "very professional" and many of her coworkers proved supportive.[31] Others, however, had difficulty accepting what they perceived as Doe's disavowal of male privilege, which included a place of belonging and authority within the masculinist engineering department. Some reactions were exceptionally harsh. A lead engineer in Doe's department, for example, later testified that he reacted with "disgust," that Doe was "rejecting his male birthright" and was "so fouled-up mentally that he would even contemplate such a thing."[32]

Boeing, like other organizational cultures, put a premium on predictability and certitude, particularly with regard to gender.[33] And, like other women at Boeing, Doe had to negotiate the gendered hierarchy in a male-dominated workplace. Corporate cultures thrive on values of stability, predictability, and conformity.[34] Boeing was no exception. In addition to challenging the normative organization of labor power as a woman engineer, Doe also confounded organizational and state norms in transitioning to a woman. Most state, legal, and corporate definitions of gender and sex are conflated with anatomical or chromosomal tests.[35]

Doe tried to negotiate the boundaries of Boeing's request for "gender neutrality" while simultaneously attending to her doctor's preoperative instructions to dress as a woman for up to a year prior to surgery. The coercive gender norming Doe faced was reinforced through corporate disciplinary measures that amounted to compulsory gendering. Boeing leaders forced Doe to choose a "normal" gender that was part of larger patriarchal heterosexual prescriptions. As C. L. Cole and Shannon L. C. Cate note, this "compulsory gender binarism" is inherently limited and discriminatory under patriarchal systems.[36] Women are disadvantaged under patriarchal processes that posit women as less worthy of rights and privileges than men and in which males determine what constitutes normal in the culture.[37]

The events leading to Doe's discrimination suit began in March 1985, when she informed her managers that she would begin to dress as a woman, which she began doing in June of that year. While there were no complaints about her clothing, except from management, in September 1985 a coworker complained that Doe had used the women's restroom. The complaint prompted managers to reexamine their response toward Doe's transition, though it was her clothing and appearance that became the central issues in the case. Doe, her managers, and corporate leaders held a series of meetings in September and October to negotiate attire.

Doe's supervisors and managers investigated company policy but did not uncover a specific written corporate policy applicable to her case.[38] The absence of a written policy was critical; it meant a lack of recorded institutional precedent, which in turn privileged and empowered the norms of Boeing's corporate culture. Company leaders struggled with how to respond to what seemed to them to be new, potentially dangerous, issues. Boeing's personnel department asked Doe's supervisor, Barry Noel, to "formulate a company position on it." Lacking both precedent and policy, Noel described his responsibility as "plowing new ground," a comment that exposes the entrenched position of gender discrimination in corporate culture and policies, which the women managers of the 1980s had also pointed out.[39] After several months Boeing leaders eventually concluded that while there was no policy, there was an "unwritten *position* that people were to present themselves according to their biological gender at most recent date of hire."[40] This extralegal response by Boeing leaders reflects what Stephen Whittle calls the "default assumption," that is, the belief that gender is fixed and corresponds to anatomical sex.[41] For transgender people, this assumption can mean discrimination both before and after transitioning. In leaning on an unwritten position that conflated gender with anatomical sex, Boeing managers adamantly refused to recognize gender presentation as fluid and understood sex reassignment in normative binary terms. They rested their power to discriminate against Doe on the false understanding of gender as a static state of embodiment. Boeing managers asked Doe to dress in a "gender neutral fashion" and wear either male or "unisex" clothing, because, per the requirements of company policy, she had checked the box marked "male" on the job application she had filled out in 1978. She would not be considered a woman to them until after surgery was completed.[42]

Interestingly, there were no Boeing company rules about employee name changes, and Doe had no trouble taking that first symbolic step. Similarly, she found latitude in changing her name within the governmental arena. In 1984, even before she began wearing feminine attire at work, she changed her legal name, got a new driver's license, and had the Department of Defense reissue her security clearance at Boeing to reflect her new name.[43] Doe was even able to change the sex designation on her driver's license with a letter from her doctor.[44] Boeing changed the name on Doe's employment records, and one of her supervisors changed the male pronouns in her work performance review.[45] Doe's name change went through without controversy.[46] In the security clearance interview, which was a requirement for changing the name on her security badge, Doe presented her transsexuality as established both at home and at work: "Everyone I associate with on a regular basis as well as some that I don't are aware that I am a transsexual. My co-workers and supervisors at the Boeing Company, Seattle WA, as well as my immediate family are aware of my transsexuality."[47] Nonetheless, although the company allowed the name change without controversy, Boeing leaders refused Doe's requests for accommodation, such as a medical leave of absence, though corporate leaders did tell Doe that if she quit they would consider rehiring her after surgical reassignment.[48]

For Doe, matters of image and presentation proved more difficult to navigate than matters of record. After she announced her transition in March 1985, managers informed Doe her attire required regulation in order to "prevent disruption in the workplace." They defended this regulation as nondiscriminatory by claiming that all employees, not only Doe, were required to wear clothing that was "appropriate" to their gender at the time of hire.[49] Boeing managers specifically prohibited Doe from wearing dresses, skirts, and "frilly blouses."[50] Although managers sometimes touted neutrality and ambiguity in dress as a solution, they clearly also sought to strictly enforce binary gender. For example, managers further instructed Doe to maintain a "male image" through her attire, which suggests that "unisex" or "neutral" functioned more within the terrain of "male."[51]

Understandably, there was some confusion on what precisely characterized "feminine attire" and a "male image." The corresponding lack of a definition of sex that upheld Boeing's instructions on attire has been crucial for how discrimination operates, particularly under nondiscrimination laws.[52] According to the logic of one Boeing manager, the criteria for judging Doe's attire was "if someone would be uncomfortable with that individual going into the female bathroom, that would be the criteria. That would be the measure."[53] Doe was told that, under this definition, feminine attire referred to dresses and skirts.[54] Doe expressed frustration at such criteria because she had no clear guidelines when getting dressed in the morning and thus remained unsure whether her attire on any given day was acceptable.[55] Doe sought further clarification from her supervisor, who told her "that my overall appearance, if viewed by someone that didn't know me, should not be female. It could be male or neutral."[56] As feminist scholars have revealed, the assumption that "neutral," natural, or normal is a default position for "male" has ordered much of the way the world has been constructed.[57]

The ambiguous and decidedly subjective nature of the criteria for judging Doe's attire was compounded by the fact that Boeing did not have a formal, documented dress code. In the engineering department, typical dress for men included ties, jackets, and sometimes jeans, while the smaller number of female engineers typically wore dresses, skirts, or jeans. Yet these normative modes of employee attire were enforced by company culture and traditions, not by managed regulation.[58] This situation reflects the role of convention in Boeing's workplace organization; the fact that the conventions were both unspoken and assumed thus privileged and empowered them as "neutral," normal, natural, and invisible.

Many of the unwritten rules at Boeing were enforced at the discretion of individual supervisors and managers. Thus, regulation of inappropriate dress remained in "local" control. As Geoffrey Stamper, an EEO administrator who was promoted in 1985 to corporate manager of employee relations and services, characterized the situation: "It's usually the line management that exercises the prerogatives."[59] Even so, corporate rules exercised ultimate authority, and the rules on dress were inarguably vague. According to Boeing leaders, by dressing in a feminine manner, Doe did not violate a dress code but instead violated the "preamble of the company rules which stated that ordinary reasonable common sense rules of conduct applied in the workplace."[60] Unsurprisingly, Boeing's vagueness on the topic of dress led to variation. Doe recounted seven other cases of transsexuals working at Boeing in the mid-1980s and argued that management treated them differently depending on the department and the supervisors. She noted that in two cases in particular the treatment differed on the regulation of dress and access to use of the women's restroom.[61]

It is clear, however, that in 1985 corporate policy in regard to dress and gender performance was still being negotiated among Boeing leaders. The company had a bureaucracy in place for dealing with discrimination and equity issues, which included personnel representatives, a discipline coordinator, human resource managers, EEO officers and administrators, and a corporate manager of employee relations and services. Even with this bureaucracy, however, Boeing managers still had difficulty in handling the issue.

Ultimately, by September 1985, Doe's supervisors had decided that disciplinary action was needed. The impetus for this decision was a complaint filed by a female employee regarding Doe having used the women's restroom after business hours. The complainant had not actually seen Doe use the women's restroom but had instead heard about the occurrence secondhand while gossiping with a male employee. At least two other female employees were aware Doe had used the restroom but did not complain.[62] Management had wide latitude to interpret the corporate position on transsexuality, but this complaint illustrates that employee surveillance of other employees also determined the ways in which the corporate position was reinforced and the limitations of (as well as reach of) bureaucracy and formal policies. Although Boeing's work spaces were organized in a top-down centralized bureaucracy, local work dynamics prevailed.

The complaint prompted Doe's supervisors to push for stronger regulation of Doe's gender performance. In an attempt to resolve the problems, Boeing management determined, once again, to specify prescriptions for Doe's gender performance, but this time they specified their prescriptions in writing, and they included severe consequences for any transgressions. Doe's warning came in October 1985 in the form of a "Corrective Action Memo," which was a typical step in Boeing's disciplinary process. The memo instructed Doe not to use the women's restroom (even though she typically used an off-site restroom) and, despite the fact that Doe had worn none of the prohibited items such as skirts and dresses, ordered her to avoid dressing like a woman. Finally, it gave Doe two weeks to comply or face termination.[63] In response to Doe's disciplinary warning, more than a dozen of Doe's coworkers signed a petition and presented it to her supervisor stating support for Doe's transition. The petition did not go beyond her supervisors, although corporate leaders became increasingly involved with regulating Doe's transition. They were not happy with the amount of time that they had allowed to pass without addressing Doe's attire. One corporate director told Doe's human resources manager that he was "very upset that nothing had been done about [her] attire before this time."[64] Corporate leaders wanted the situation tightly managed so as not to set a precedent of accommodating what they considered to be gender transgressions.

Corporate Efficiency and Workers' Rights

The corporate instability that plagued American business in the 1980s helps explain the bureaucratic infighting and struggles for control. The case of Jane Doe occurred during a time of economic reforms and corporate organizational woes, both at Boeing and in business generally. In the 1980s corporations struggled to achieve "efficiency" and managerial streamlining in the midst of a wave of mergers and rapid expansion.[65] The proliferating bureaucracy of Boeing's divisions was typical of the development of firms in the United States in the post–World War II period, particularly in the 1970s. Boeing had developed increasingly dispersed chains of command in order to deal with the growth of new facets of the company and a marked expansion of middle management.[66] In an organizational culture in flux, there was less resiliency in confronting a fundamental challenge to routine administration.

The neoliberal turn in the 1980s and 1990s also left workers with little room to bargain for workplace rights. As modern welfare capitalism declined, corporations offered fewer services and benefits for workers. Workers could no longer expect to have the same kind of relationship or identification with their corporate employers.[67] President Reagan's focus on tax and budget cuts, deregulation, and the disempowerment of trade unions and professional organizations in the 1980s set the stage for a full-scale commitment to neoliberalism in the 1990s, an era characterized by privatization and a decrease in social services provided by the state.[68] While the power of workers declined, the power of the CEO, at Boeing and at other corporations, grew.[69] In this new business environment, corporations as a whole gained more power.[70] Reflecting these broader changes, Boeing's bureaucracy reordered workplace structure and altered the company's traditional culture. For example, by the 1980s the "All in the Family" section of the Boeing News, which had been introduced in the 1930s, was long gone. The Boeing News of the 1980s routinely reported on airplane orders and government contracts rather than highlighting the news of employees. One 1986 issue, for example, promoted a new "corporate creed" in which job security would be based on performance and Boeing, in turn, would work to foster a "team spirit."[71] The sense of the Boeing "family," then, was on the decline by the mid-1980s, though one 1985 issue of the company publication noted that an employee referral program helped keep jobs "all in the family," which suggested the maintenance of employee connections for company opportunities even as the company diversified.[72]

As Boeing's bureaucracy expanded and the company announced that its Puget Sound–area workforce was expected to hit seventy-nine thousand by the end of 1986, workers began to feel their loss of power and felt increasingly alienated and distant from upper management.[73] Throughout her transition, Doe attempted to talk with the corporate leader responsible for establishing company policy, but she was not entirely clear on who that person was.[74] Not surprisingly, Doe felt particularly alienated from Boeing's hierarchical leadership structure. She asked to meet with Boeing leaders and two doctors on the Boeing medical staff, but these requests were never filled and Doe never met with anyone at a level above her supervisors and human resources representatives.[75] Doe also wrote to Stamper, the corporate manager of employee relations and services, and to Stanley Little, the vice president of industrial relations, but she testified that she was unsure if they were the appropriate people to contact.[76] As she explained, "I wasn't real clear on who reported to who at upper management. It seems like a lot of vice presidents that were under other vice presidents and stuff. So I wanted to send it to at least two people and I just thought that—I wasn't sure who was the right person, but I felt if I sent them to a couple people that were fairly high up that it would filter over to the appropriate people."[77] Doe attributed part of the confusion to a sense of organizational instability and the fact that her work environment seemed in flux. She noted that the organizational structure of her work group was in transition and she rarely saw her supervisor because he was located in a different building.[78] In the new neoliberal order, company leaders were less responsible for the day-to-day operations of firms like Boeing.

Increased pressure from corporate leaders to monitor Doe's attire heightened the managerial resistance she faced. Doe's managers asserted that, by the time they issued the Corrective Action Memo in the fall of 1985 (roughly six months after she changed her appearance), she had pushed them too far. One supervisor testified, "[Jane] had really changed from a point of reasonableness to one of a crusader for the transsexual cause."[79] Doe, however, testified that she had not attempted to make a political statement, claiming that if she had wanted to get fired she would have worn a dress or skirt. To Boeing leaders it did not matter if Doe was making a political statement or not; in their view, Doe had crossed an established line of workers' rights and sociability at Boeing by making demands with significant consequences for legal and medical policy at the company. In the context of a decline in modern welfare capitalism, such demands seemed particularly threatening. Firms were trying to rein in costs by providing fewer services to employees. While the new era of political economy seemed to offer "globalized, turbo-charged capitalism" in which firms were all-powerful, firms were, in fact, as Suzanne Bergeron points out, "limited and potentially vulnerable" because of the economic changes caused by late capitalism.[80]

Under the terms of the Corrective Action Memo that regulated Doe's
appearance in her final weeks at Boeing, her transition was marked as a
site of heightened power for her supervisors. Doe's supervisor had the
power to decide if she was in compliance, that is, if she was, in his view,
dressed like a woman.[81] These reviews provided justification to fire Doe if
her supervisor decided she was not in compliance. At a follow-up meeting
regarding the Corrective Action Memo in October 1985, Doe requested
that her supervisor assess the outfit she wore to see if it met company
guidelines and was surprised when he found her appearance, which he
described as follows, to be in compliance: "shoulder-length, curly blond
hair; earrings—salmon colored, behind hair; no finger nail polish noticeable;
may have had some makeup base—not noticeable; pale blush—had to look
for it; no lipstick; blue plaid shirt—open at neck; salmon colored sleeve-
less sweater; gray slacks/pleats; gray women's flats."[82] Doe was surprised
that her supervisor found her in compliance, so she was still confused by
the characteristics that defined feminine dress. She was anxious to both
keep her job and make a successful transition and argued that clothing
and appearance were a vital, and competing, part of both desires: "I was
terribly frustrated, confused, stressed, distraught. I wanted to dress in
feminine attire. Boeing was accepting my dress that I thought was feminine attire . . . but since they were accepting it and they weren't accepting
feminine attire then, I felt that they were saying it wasn't feminine attire.
So I was very confused and I wanted them to accept what I was wearing
as a feminine attire or let me wear more feminine attire or actually both.
I wanted to look professional."[83]

At the same time that Doe worked to stay within the bounds of acceptable
attire at Boeing, then, she also attempted to adhere to normative gender
order to meet the requirements of her transition. Doe's compliance reviews
occurred on a daily basis. Doe recalled that her supervisor would "stand in
front of me first thing in the morning, and look me up and down, head to
toe, and take notes."[84] This ritual reflects gendered bureaucratic organizational norms more broadly. As Karen Ramsay and Martin Parker note,
in corporate organizations, "The privacy is often male and the surveilled
are often female—but not vice versa."[85]

It is clear that, as Doe and her supervisors negotiated the company position, the possibility of a court battle was not far from their minds. Both Boeing and Doe indicated an awareness that the conflicts they experienced might end up in court or at the very least require legal counsel. In notes prepared by Bob Masters to document a meeting with corporate officials and human resources personnel on October 22, he noted that "Boeing will defend me if I am named a co-respondent and will pay the damages if Boeing loses the case." His notes also contain the line, "Handicap is best defense," likely in reference to Doe's anticipated tactic should she choose to file a discrimination suit.[86] For her part, Doe had been in contact with lawyers throughout the meetings and in fact consulted with her lawyer before signing the Corrective Action Memo Boeing issued to her in October 1985.[87]

On November 5, 1985, Doe's supervisor decided she was not dressed "androgynously, male, or neutral," particularly because she was wearing a pink pearl necklace, and she was immediately fired.[88] The lack of a written, published dress code makes the pink pearl necklace an inauspicious catalyst for termination, while at the same time it reinforces the power of clothing in organizational culture and administrative routine.[89] A Boeing spokesperson told the press that Doe had been fired "for violating company rules" and also stated that she "would be rehired after the sex-change operation."[90] It was not until 1989, well after she was fired from Boeing, that Doe could afford to undergo sex reassignment surgery.[91]

After she was fired, Doe sued Boeing for employment discrimination based on gender dysphoria under state disability discrimination provisions.[92] The suit, *Jane Doe v. Boeing Company*, was filed in 1986. Company leaders were reluctant to talk publicly about the case, and certainly the surveillance of employees' gender and sexuality that occurred on the shop floor was not publicly acknowledged. One Boeing spokesperson stated in 1986 that lawyers were working on the case and that the company didn't "normally make pronouncements on hirings or firings."[93] The case did not reach court until 1990, and the final ruling was not handed down until 1993.

Jane Doe v. Boeing Company, 1986–1993

By the time Doe filed her lawsuit in 1986 there was legal precedent for her claims. The case emerged during a period of growth in transgender activism.

In the 1970s and 1980s activist groups such as the American Civil Liberties Union were pressing for legal recognition of transsexual rights.[94] In 1974 the city of Minneapolis passed an antidiscrimination civil rights ordinance that included transsexuals; shortly thereafter Margaret Deirdre O'Hartigan used the ordinance to successfully sue the state of Minnesota and have them pay for her sex-reassignment surgery. In California the outcome of a suit granted transsexuals the right to change their names and sex on their birth certificates.[95] More broadly, increased attention to workplace rights stimulated efforts to fight against patriarchal heterosexual sex and gender norms in the workplace.[96] Joanne Meyerowitz notes that by the 1990s the transgender movement had "emerged in force."[97]

Beginning in the 1980s, there were a handful of legal filings that charged corporations with discrimination against transsexual persons based on state disability discrimination provisions. For example, in *Jane Doe v. Electro-Craft Corporation* (1988) the New Hampshire State Supreme Court ruled that, under the state employment discrimination statute, transsexualism qualified for disability claims. While similar cases were tried in the 1990s and early 2000s, *Jane Doe v. Boeing Company* was one of the earliest.[98]

The case went three rounds in the courts. In 1990 the trial court ruled in favor of Boeing, finding that Doe had been accommodated. On appeal, the court ruled in Doe's favor under state disability discrimination provisions. In the final review, in 1993, the Washington State Supreme Court reversed the Court of Appeals and ruled that Boeing did not discriminate against Doe.[99]

During the three rounds, particularly when Doe won the second round in the appeals court, local newspapers, including the *Seattle Times* and the *Seattle Post-Intelligencer*, reported the rulings. Although neither newspaper devoted substantial attention to the case, both printed several articles on the case and both narrated it as a battle over a "pink pearl necklace."[100] In the final Washington State Supreme Court ruling, the judge, Frederick T. Rasmussen, pointed to the complexity of the case and noted it was not "a case about pink beads." Rather, he ruled that the case was about "the need to strike a balance between the company's duty to respect human dignity and the human condition and the need for the company to be respectful of others and the obligation of the company under the law to draw a balance."[101]

There were two very closely related issues that shaped how Judge Rasmussen arrived at his decision. The first was whether or not gender dysphoria fit the definition of a handicap. Significantly, the case played out just as the Americans with Disabilities Act (ADA) was being debated in Congress and in the media. The ADA was passed in 1990 to protect the rights of people with disabilities, but it explicitly excluded transsexuality as a category of protection. Nevertheless, Doe and her lawyers won the argument that gender dysphoria was a "handicap."[102] The judge relied on the medical diagnosis of two medical experts to "prove" she was gender dysphoric and thus handicapped. He ruled fairly easily and quickly that Doe's gender dysphoria was a handicap under Washington State law and noted, "It seems to me that the facts are really pretty clear as to handicap. There is a condition, gender dysphoria, which is medically and psychologically recognized. It is referred to in DSM III."[103] He further characterized gender dysphoria as a "lifelong condition" and an "abnormality" that is "not a static thing but a continuum."[104]

Under Judge Rasmussen's ruling, however, Doe's handicap was conditional; he ruled that gender dysphoria was not always a handicap but that it became a handicap in Doe's case because of her psychologist's advice that she live as a woman for a year, which "caused conflict with the work environment," as evidenced by complaints from other workers regarding feminine dress and use of the women's restroom. This situation corresponds with many disabilities scholars' arguments that "disability is often less about physical or mental impairments than it is about how society responds to impairments."[105] According to Judge Rasmussen, however, it was a temporary handicap that would be alleviated upon Doe's surgery since Boeing's policy dictated that after surgery the company would treat Doe as a woman and allow her to dress in a feminine manner and use the women's restroom.[106] Overall, this aspect of the case remains an important legal precedent for the resulting court recognition of gender dysphoria and for using state disability statutes to argue for employment discrimination based on transsexuality. Nevertheless, this tactic remains controversial as it rests on an assumption that the disability can be "fixed" through sexual reassignment surgery, while also reifying categories of disabled/"handicapped" and "normal."

The second, and more decisive, issue that the case hinged on was whether or not Boeing reasonably accommodated Doe if indeed her gender dysphoria could be considered a handicap. Doe and her lawyers argued that she suffered discrimination because her supervisors did not use female pronouns, did not allow her to use the women's restroom, and did not permit her to wear feminine attire. The judge's ruling was complicated by the fact that under Washington State law there was little established legal precedent for ruling on reasonable accommodation for claims of employment discrimination; it was not clear what degree of accommodation was legally reasonable or, as the judge put it, "whether or not the employer is obligated to provide any reasonable accommodation sought by the employee, or whether the employer is only obliged to offer a reasonable accommodation."[107] Judge Rasmussen ruled that the test of reasonable accommodation was "if the employer bends far enough to permit that individual to work."[108] Rasmussen's ruling illustrates the ways in which ideas of normalcy have been constructed in the workplace; ideal workers have historically been those who are free from disability. Thus, to "reasonably accommodate" Doe meant doing so within the confines of a narrow and homogeneous view of "normal" working bodies.[109] Conversely, Doe and her lawyers also appealed to normative gendered order to make the case that Boeing discriminated against her while at the same time trying to negate the notion that gender should matter to workplace order; Doe argued, for example, that she needed to dress as a woman in order to successfully transition: "I had to know that I could be comfortable in public as a female. I was certain that I was not comfortable in public as a male."[110] At the same time, one of Doe's lawyers argued that Boeing's restrictions regarding her attire constituted discrimination because "in a work place situation it makes no difference how a person presents pre- or postoperatively."[111]

In the end, it was the second issue of reasonable accommodation that swung the ruling in favor of the defense. During the case Boeing spokesperson Russ Young stated, "We continue to maintain our accommodations were reasonable. I think this underscores the difficulty of trying to balance the needs of an individual with those of the rest of the work force."[112] Young's statement reveals the fundamental assumptions about gender and normalcy that formed the basis for Boeing's unwritten policy position. To Boeing leaders, Doe stood outside organizational norms.

Judge Rasmussen agreed with Young's assessment and ruled that Doe had "failed to cooperate" with the directives of her supervisors and the accommodations they had provided to her.[113] Clearly the judge recognized Boeing's right to regulate appearance to preserve the company's ability to regulate the workplace environment. His ruling is an implicit acknowledgment that gender and sex, and their regulation, were at the center of the way corporate life at Boeing functioned and could be profoundly disruptive, not only of Boeing's corporate culture but of patriarchal corporate capitalism. The evaluation and uneven regulation of Doe's behavior and appearance reinforced the more general idea that all Boeing employees regulate their own self-presentation at the same time that it reinforced the idea of male privilege. The compulsory gender binarism that Boeing leaders required, and which patriarchy is built on, stands at the heart of corporate culture and power.

Tellingly, in the midst of Doe's case, another male-to-female transsexual employed at Boeing questioned the meaning of gender difference at Boeing and the ability for workplace organization to change in a meaningful way. She pondered, "One can only wonder what Corporate will do when the inevitable female-to-male transsexual announces his intention to use the men's restroom."[114] To her, unsurprisingly, a woman claiming rights and access to male spaces seemed even more problematic to Boeing's workplace organization than a man (at least as so defined by Boeing leaders) choosing to enter female spaces. Those who disrupted this structure (Doe in this case) paid in material ways to an extreme degree. Doe faced multiple sources of discrimination; she was positioned both outside the realm of normalcy and able-bodiedness as well as outside Boeing's male corporate culture. As Susan Wendell points out, "Disabled women struggle with both the oppressions of being women in male-dominated societies and the oppressions of being disabled in societies dominated by the able-bodied."[115]

Despite the challenges posed by *Jane Doe v. Boeing Company*, it was not until 2006 that Boeing instituted an antidiscrimination policy covering gender identity; sexual orientation had been covered in the antidiscrimination policy set in 1997.[116] In adding a clause specifying gender identity, Boeing was following the lead of other U.S. corporations. Between 2000 and 2007, for example, the number of companies instituting employment discrimination protection for transgender employees jumped from 3 to 125. A few of these companies, including Kodak and IBM, provide insurance coverage for transgender employees' medical expenses.[117] The fact that Boeing and these other companies made these changes does not necessarily mean that they committed themselves more broadly to issues of gender and sexual equality. Even as transgender and transsexual employees (mostly in the Global North) have faced fewer restrictions, major corporations, including Boeing, now rely on flexible labor arrangements, with increased part-time and temporary labor, and greater financial speculation. For workers, this change has meant that men and women workers began to face similar circumstances, as white men lost high-paying career jobs. Nevertheless, white men continue to be concentrated in the highest-paying and highest-ranking jobs.[118] In this new order, many workers have been left vulnerable because they are easily replaced as jobs are increasingly outsourced and layoffs become more commonplace.[119] In addition, the new "preferred workforce" is young women of color; these women, especially those living in the Global South, work outsourced jobs that pay low wages and offer little security.[120]

Thus, even as transgender people have been increasingly recognized within corporate bureaucracies, new regimes of control and exploitation have emerged to undermine their power and the power of all workers more broadly. Overall, *Jane Doe v. Boeing Company* exposed the everyday assumptions, based in gender and sex, that have ordered capitalism and workplace organization, while at the same highlighting the changing work dynamics under neoliberalism that have reinforced the power of corporate bureaucracies to regulate workers even as workforces become more diverse.

As the case of Jane Doe suggests, support groups have offered employees a way to try to navigate the gender and sexual norms of Boeing's corporate culture. Advocacy groups, for example, have worked to create support networks for gay Boeing employees. In 1989 a group of fifteen Boeing employees founded BEAGLES, "an association for Gay and Lesbian Employees of the Boeing Company" designed to "serve both as a social group and as an advocate of gay and lesbian concerns at Boeing."[121] By June 1989 BEAGLES had more than fifty members. Yet there were still concerns about how such a group would be accepted at Boeing, and the *Voice Northwest* cautioned readers to "please respect their privacy" as they prepared to meet with Boeing management and EEO officers.[122] BEAGLES later revised and broadened its targeted membership as the Boeing Employee Association for Gays, Lesbians, and Friends. One BEAGLES representative, a Boeing process engineer, observed in 2008 that such groups had improved Boeing's work environment: "When you come to work every day and know that there are people like you there—well, it makes the environment a lot more pleasant."[123] Workers' unions have been another source of support for charges of discrimination, and in the case of Doe the engineering union SPEEA provided Doe with union representation at meetings between Doe and her supervisors. The union, however, was not involved in the ensuing court battle. To some workers, Boeing's unions have reinforced the heterosexual masculine norms of Boeing's corporate culture; as one gay union member observed in 1999, both the union and the company could serve as spaces that reinforce heterosexual norms. The worker described "routine harassment of gay men especially" at Boeing and noted that the union did not seem to prioritize fighting for gay rights. It did not, for example, include domestic partner benefits in contract negotiations: "A lot of people don't talk about the issues; we avoid arguments about this issue."[124]

There has been greater visibility of and communication regarding transgender identities at Boeing in recent years. Boeing received the Human Rights Campaign's Innovation Award in 2009 for its guidelines on transgender employees.[125] While these guidelines show improvement in Boeing's handling of issues regarding visibility and awareness of the difficulties transgender employees face, they also indicate that transgender people are not fully integrated into the company in ways that promote ideas or practices of equality.[126] The guidelines, instituted in 2004, mirror the shift away from the familial metaphor to the neoliberal focus on teamwork; transgender employees seeking to change their gender identification are labeled "Transitioning Teammates," a name that reflects the neoliberal context in which all workers are outsiders relative to the increased corporate power of CEOs and managers.[127] The label "Transitioning Teammate" also points to the continuance of the idea, evident in *Jane Doe v. Boeing Company*, that transgender employees stand outside of corporate culture and are thus not full or true members of the workforce.

Marilynn Laird, a transgender woman who worked for Boeing for more than fourteen years, offered important insight on Boeing's corporate culture in recent years. Laird began working at Boeing as a machinist in 1988, moved to the salaried ranks as an engineer in 1998, and was laid off in 2002. She began to transition in 2003 and then returned to Boeing as a contractor on projects from 2009 to 2011, working in Charleston, South Carolina, and San Antonio, Texas.[128] In Laird's view, conditions for transgender employees had improved, though conditions remained difficult for all women. While she had some difficulty with one manager using the wrong pronouns when she returned to Boeing as a woman in 2009, she observed, "Boeing did have clear policies for GLBTQ employees and contractors." Laird noted that at Boeing there were "transgender females there who are still under the radar." In her experience, identifying as transgender had proven problematic in the hiring process at companies besides Boeing: "Getting hired is where the issues are. I know that of the 400 plus jobs that I applied for after transition the majority of jobs I did get interviewed for I was fully or over qualified for I did not get because of my diversity." In Laird's view, the power of male managers at Boeing has been propped up by the fraternal and patriarchal network of white, heterosexual men: "Diversity has improved but it will still be a struggle until a large number of male managers who are products of the BFI system Brothers, Friends, and Influences are gone."[129] Tellingly, Laird maintained that she would "not ever work for the Boeing Company again," even as she pointed out that the problems go beyond just Boeing: "To this day women are treated as second-class citizens by the majority of the male population."[130] Her comments underscored the work still to be done in dismantling the links between patriarchy and capitalism.

Jane Doe v. Boeing Company remains a landmark case in the historical record on transgender and worker rights, illuminating how transgender identities, and gender and sex norms more broadly, were constructed and maintained through legal, medical, and corporate discourses. Moreover, it provides a valuable opportunity to go beyond a focus on gender and to analyze transsexualism within historical capitalist relations.[131] The case is also crucial for understanding the contemporary legal relationship between transgender and disability and the normative organization of labor power under neoliberalism.

The company's everyday operations and traditions, upheld by the enforcement of heterosexual gender norms, placed Jane Doe outside the Boeing "family." While equal opportunity legislation did change expectations, it was not in ways that could fully eradicate the gendered expectations built into Boeing's workplace culture. As Katharine Bartlett points out, "Despite the progress made under Title VII [of the Civil Rights Act of 1964] in eliminating barriers to women's access to equal employment opportunities, the Act has never kept up with the expectations many have had for it."[132] The case of Jane Doe revealed the norms upon which Boeing's corporate culture were based and the authority of the company's managerial and engineering ranks in overseeing and helping to shape, in conjunction with company leaders, the sexual division of labor. Company leaders, and some coworkers, were unable to recognize a way for Doe to be productive and function outside of company norms and the gender binaries that had guided the company since the 1930s. The more recent evidence, as well as the silences of those still "under the radar," to use Laird's description, suggests that surveillance of gender continues to be a guiding directive for managers and company leaders looking to discipline workers under the new norms of neoliberal capitalism.[133]

CHAPTER 5

Employing Teamwork

By the end of the twentieth century the familial contract that Boeing leaders and workers had tried to uphold, often unsuccessfully, since the 1930s had been irrevocably altered. As Dana Cloud notes, by the mid-1990s the company had "completed its turn toward lean restructuring," which disempowered workers and union organizing in new ways: "The realities of neoliberalism—manifest as rampant off-loading, offshoring, speedup, and layoffs—made these tasks profoundly difficult, as union leaders in this time period assumed the necessity of concessions."[1] Workers observed that the "rhetoric of teamwork did nothing to assuage the stress of perpetual job insecurity."[2] Cloud points out that in the past unions provided a "class-specific alternative to managerial 'teamwork,'" though in this particular context the International Association of Machinists and Aerospace Workers (IAMAW) collaborated with Boeing on the teamwork concept, which in turn inspired the "rank and file" to view their work, and unionization, differently, as the 1995 strike revealed; in that strike, workers realized "their own power" and voted against the IAMAW bargaining committee's recommendations to accept Boeing's contract offer.[3] As Cloud argues, "The 1995 strike demonstrated that when workers push from below, they can win gains from the company and hold the union, their fighting organization, accountable to the interests of the workers they represent."[4] Cloud's study reveals that the neoliberal capitalist shifts of the 1990s reframed workers' relationship with company and union leaders. Relations between Boeing workers and company leaders grew especially tense after Boeing acquired

McDonnell Douglas in 1997 and became the biggest aerospace company in history. This chapter examines the tensions over the neoliberal shift from family to teamwork. Both male and female employees have reported feeling increasingly alienated and disrespected by company leaders since the mid-1990s. For some workers, especially male engineers, the neoliberal shifts of late capitalism brought a newfound sense of vulnerability, and for women of all ranks these shifts offered an opportunity to articulate older frustrations of inequalities within Boeing and the company unions. By 2000 these feelings had boiled over.

This chapter focuses on two unprecedented acts of employee resistance to companywide changes. These acts occurred in February 2000, and, like the 1995 strike, they offer evidence of employees' resistance to neoliberal imperatives.[5] On February 9, 2000, more than seventeen thousand members or about three-fourths of the Society of Professional Engineering Employees in Aerospace (SPEEA) decided to go on strike. The SPEEA strike lasted forty days, which may seem short until one considers that in fifty-six years SPEEA had gone on strike only once, for a single day in 1993. A historically tame union, SPEEA joined with the International Federation of Professional and Technical Employees, of the AFL-CIO, in 1999 and was newly radicalized and energized by its affiliation with a traditionally blue-collar union. The second unparalleled event, which emerged in part out of the increased strength of SPEEA, was a class-action lawsuit filed February 25, 2000, a little more than two weeks after the start of the strike. In the suit, *Beck v. The Boeing Company*, twenty-eight women, both current and former employees, filed charges of wage discrimination against Boeing.[6] The case was named for Mary Beck, who had done tooling and wiring work at Boeing for eighteen years. Beck was laid off in 2003 and argued that the case was "not about the money" but instead was "about the injustice that all the women have gone through."[7] The employees who filed *Beck v. The Boeing Company* alleged pay discrimination on the basis of sex and argued it violated Title VII of the Civil Rights Act of 1964. They pointed out that they received lower salaries, less overtime, and fewer promotion opportunities.[8] They also argued that male managers had free rein to offer promotions, workplace opportunities, and pay information, which exacerbated and upheld gender discrimination against women. Ellen Schaff,

employed in the electrical department for twenty-two years, observed in
court documents, "There is a cone of silence over (job) information; men
are allowed within the cone, women are not."[9]

As the suit gained momentum, the claims grew beyond SPEEA to encom-
pass a class-action suit made up of all women employed by Boeing in the
Puget Sound area.[10] Boeing reported that the class potentially totaled
twenty-nine thousand women. The case was settled out of court in 2004,
with negotiations proceeding that spring and summer. In May the two
sides issued a joint statement indicating that they had "made considerable progress toward resolution of the case." Boeing announced that a
monetary settlement was reached in May, and terms of the settlement,
including revised promotion and employment policies, had been agreed
upon by July. One Boeing leader, the executive vice president of internal
services, stated that the settlement contained "enhancements" with regard
to performance evaluations, salary reviews, and promotions, as well as other
"employee relations" policies that would "strengthen our already robust
suite of employee-focused processes." Noting that "Boeing has been and
will continue to be firmly committed" to equal employment opportunities,
company leaders were unwilling to acknowledge the inequalities that the
case exposed.[11] The *Seattle Times* pointed out that, if the case had gone to
court, it would have been "the largest gender-discrimination class-action
lawsuit to go before a jury."[12] Thus, even while all workers were renegotiat-
ing relations with company leaders via the union, gender still determined
how workers experienced their position at the company.

The issue of respect was the driving force behind both the SPEEA strike
and the class-action lawsuit, though what precisely that meant depended
on one's perspective and position within the company hierarchy. Other
issues lay behind the strike as well, including pay, work hours, and working conditions. To the striking SPEEA members, respect meant preserving
their place within the Boeing "family"; engineers in particular often viewed
themselves not as industrial workers but as an elite group of white-collar
workers. This view had been reinforced, and cultivated, by Boeing's corporate culture, which gave them a unique and celebrated place in the
company hierarchy. While engineers and technical workers wanted a better
contract, pay increases, and better benefits (especially since members of

District Lodge 751 had received these concessions in their recent contract negotiations), they also wanted the emotional connection to the company that seemed to have disappeared since the mid-1990s, especially after the merger with McDonnell Douglas. Many described feeling that Boeing leaders no longer recognized the centrality of engineers to the company. One engineer, Bruce Anderson, noted, "I think upper management needs to take a change of direction in the way they treat their employees. For several years now, I personally have felt like I haven't been valued with this company. I'll be 21 years with this company next month, and here I am holding a picket sign."[13] Another striking engineer, Cynthia Cole, described a sense of abandonment and alienation from Boeing leaders: "Things that pushed us over the edge were some of the comments" from corporate leaders that "made us realize that they didn't value us as assets and we could be easily replaced."[14] While the "we" in Cole's comment refers to SPEEA, it could just as easily have referred to women at Boeing.

While women experienced union solidarity, especially in identifying as workers who felt dislocated from company leadership, their work experiences were unfairly shaped by gender. To women at Boeing, respect meant receiving equal opportunity and equal pay. Neoliberalism deploys gender difference by relying on the social reproduction norms of capitalism; as state social services have decreased, women's burdens have increased and pay and benefits for all workers have gone down. Mimi Abramovitz argues, "Neo-liberalism reversed the trend toward greater equality, exposed the nation to the perils of slavish reliance on market forces, and increased the cost and burdens of women's care work in the home."[15] Women at Boeing had never had the sense of stability and respect that male union members had achieved, though the inroads made through equal employment opportunity programs had moved women closer to equality. One worker involved in the suit noted, "Boeing has a good-old-boy system that is pervasive and longstanding."[16] *Beck v. The Boeing Company* publicly revealed the persistence of gender discrimination at the company despite the requirements of Title VII of the Civil Rights Act of 1964. Title VII, however, was often thought of as a means to combat racial rather than sex or gender discrimination. Furthermore, for women, individual cases were hard to pursue, and organizing as a class provided a means to address the inadequacies of the Equal Employment Opportunity Commission in dealing with gender and sex discrimination charges.[17]

Women at the center of the class-action suit felt disrespected not only by company leaders reacting to the economic shifts of the late twentieth century but also by Boeing's corporate culture and shop-floor traditions, which hampered their ability to achieve a status equal to that of their male coworkers. While the SPEEA strike called for solidarity among all Boeing workers and showed a widening gap between labor and management as a whole, the class-action suit revealed the other divisions among workers that had been growing over the course of the postwar period. These divides were also evident in union membership. In 2000 the *751 Aero Mechanic* observed, "Women make up only 24% of the hourly bargaining unit—making it clear that it is very much a man's world at Boeing."[18] Union efforts have faced tense reactions when incorporating women and addressing women's issues, even while, as Cloud points out, workers of diverse identities recognize "the incredible importance of the union to their power and voice at work."[19] Women and minorities found themselves up against corporations with multiple avenues for disempowerment and discrimination. For women, then, the neoliberal shifts of the 1990s constituted a point at which gendered and racialized identities as workers, women, and union members could collide, forcing women to prioritize their identities in new ways by 2000.[20] Neoliberalism also required a new way of thinking about workers' relationship to the company, a way that did not imply the kindness or sense of responsibility that the family metaphor evoked.

The "New Economy" and Boeing Employees

The economic context of the 1990s partly explains the depth of workers' concerns after the Boeing merger with McDonnell Douglas and during the SPEEA strike. In the 1990s people began to question Boeing's economic and cultural viability. The company began to lose ground to Airbus, Boeing's biggest competitor for the production of commercial aircraft. There was also a sense that the company was losing ground in the Seattle area to the growing high-tech industry. The *Economist* opined in 2000 that "Boeing's somewhat military factories feel as if they are part of a different century from the sprawling 'campus' at Microsoft."[21] *PacificNW* magazine noted that "with the decline of unions, tech revolution, the rise of global commerce and the advent of smartphones and laptops that can connect workers to the office at any moment, even miles away from it, the very idea of a structured job week that ends at quittin' time on Friday afternoon seems quaint."[22] Boeing, and its workers, seemed out of date. The Boeing "family," which had once seemed to offer a refuge against economic shifts, now appeared to be a liability that limited global competitiveness by holding corporations responsible for workers in a way that could hinder profits and flexibility to reduce or expand the workforce at will.

As corporations grew ever larger, workers lost power. Numbers, not workers, seemed to take top priority. Familialism no longer resonated with corporate leaders or managers, who were increasingly focused on the mandates of investors and financiers. The neoliberal turn of the 1990s was characterized by deregulation, privatization, and state withdrawal from social services. In the context of these changes, a new premium was placed on the financial sector. The imperatives of Wall Street were now placed above corporate family values and practices.[23] As the striking engineers noted, workers had been thrust into an outsider position. The demise of a sense of family also occurred at other companies.[24] The history of corporations like Boeing reflects a shift in corporate capitalism whereby both the scale and the scope of businesses have changed. For certain aerospace workers—that is, white men—the postwar period had seemed to promise stability, but that sense of security had eroded by the end of the twentieth century.

In the 1990s business leaders also began to institute new corporate practices that threatened the power and autonomy of both workers and unions. Business leaders, particularly in high-tech companies in the Pacific Northwest and California's Silicon Valley, moved away from management strategies focused on bureaucracy, hierarchy, loyalty, and lifelong careers.[25] In this new business environment, work was redefined. More corporations focused on flexible labor arrangements, with increased part-time and temporary labor, and greater financial speculation. For workers, this shift has meant greater similarities between men and women workers as they lost high-paying career jobs, though white men continue to be concentrated in the highest-paying and highest-ranking jobs.[26] In this context, both women and men have been left vulnerable because they are easily laid off and replaced. Ironically, corporate cultures that seemed to promote employees' best interests and tout freedom and flexibility could in fact be even more controlling and regulatory.[27] As *PacificNW* reported in 2012, "The 40-hour workweek feels like a vestige from a time when the labor movement proudly distributed bumper stickers proclaiming, 'Unions: The folks who brought you the weekend.'"[28] One Amazon employee observed that the workday is no longer "nine to five" and "there's no such thing as a 'workweek' anymore."[29] As Dana Cloud notes, Boeing enacted "team programs" in order to combat growing union militancy; these programs "train workers to work more efficiently and to combine jobs—thus spelling future layoffs." The "lean production" measures enacted in the aerospace industry reveal the neoliberal "pressure for concessions in bargaining, speedup of production, and increasing job insecurity."[30]

At corporations across the country, engineers experienced disrupted work patterns and felt increasingly vulnerable as their job security and status as professionals were threatened.[31] Sanford Jacoby notes that "the layoffs of the 1990s received enormous publicity because they represented a qualitative transformation: a shift away from high levels of security for previously protected white-collar groups."[32] Regarding the Seattle region, the *Economist* labeled this shift "the slow death of the Boeing man," referencing engineers who had lost power not only with the company but also within the larger regional competition for professional and technical workers: "Seattle man has given way to Redmond man in the local hierarchy."[33] Companies like Microsoft and Amazon began to dominate the Seattle area and to change the dynamics of both the local economy and the local labor market. In the process, engineers lost power and prestige. While Boeing engineers could expect to make an average of $63,000 a year, high-tech workers living in King County were taking home $236,000 a year in salary and stock options. The *Economist* further observed that "house prices have soared out of the reach of young aircraft engineers."[34] The breadwinner model of the 1930s Boeing "family," in which white men at Boeing could expect to enter into a lifelong career that would provide access to a middle-class lifestyle, was gone. Unions, as well as shop-floor labor, also seemed antiquated in this new high-tech Seattle environment.

In an effort to stay competitive in both the aerospace industry and the labor market Boeing leaders focused their energy and business strategy on globalization, rather than preserving a regional identity associated with family norms. Globalization held appeal for Boeing leaders because it seemed to promise an even more powerful version of capitalism that placed far less emphasis on the corporation having responsibility for employees and their needs. But while the policies of late capitalism seemed to offer a "globalized, turbo-charged capitalism" in which firms were all-powerful, as Suzanne Bergeron points out, firms were in fact "limited and potentially vulnerable" because of the economic changes caused by late capitalism.[35] By embracing globalization in both rhetoric and structure, Boeing leaders often felt they were adopting a defensive posture and were fearful of being left vulnerable by increasing labor costs, an uncertain market, and tighter regional competition for engineering talent. Company leaders posited global growth as a move that benefited workers and not just the company's bottom line. In 1997, at the Paris Air Show, Boeing commercial airplane group president Ron Woodward asserted that global collaborations in the aerospace industry benefited everyone. He noted, "Aerospace is truly a global business in which we all have a stake."[36] Yet, as the 2000 SPEEA strike illustrates, it is clear that workers did not feel included in this process. Exacerbating the anxiety over Boeing's future was the fact that in 2004 and 2005 Airbus sold more commercial planes than Boeing did. Aviation writer John Newhouse surmises, "Boeing's troubles were traceable partly to arrogance—a tendency to take the market for granted, to coast on its laurels—and partly to changes that developed in the corporate culture." According to Newhouse, Boeing began to fear risks and investment in new technologies. He cites a "legacy of obsolescence."[37] In 2004 *BusinessWeek* claimed that the tighter competition for federal contracts in the 1990s and Boeing's merger with the more aggressive McDonnell Douglas in 1997 had changed Boeing's corporate culture and "shifted Boeing's emphasis to the bottom line."[38]

The economic shifts of the 1990s explain the attention given to the SPEEA strike and the concern of engineers that Boeing was in a state of declension. The striking workers were not necessarily concerned with the state of the company but about the place of engineers within the company; engineers were losing ground, and power, to CEOs and financiers.

Engineers, Growth, and Union Organization

The 2000 SPEEA strike would have been unthinkable just two decades earlier. While discontents were certainly present throughout the postwar years, the power and prestige of being a Boeing engineer, which placed one firmly near the top of the Boeing "family" hierarchy, mitigated most complaints. Boeing engineers believed themselves to be an integral and respected part of the company for nearly all of the postwar period. David Noble points out that in the early twentieth century American engineers adhered to the dictates of corporate management systems and became not only technical experts but also professional corporate leaders and managers, an identity that resonated with many engineers into the twenty-first century.[39] As journalist Michelle Dunlop of the *Everett Herald* noted, they traditionally held a position of authority within company culture: "They're the nerds behind the birds. They're the innovators, the visionaries behind Boeing Co. aircraft."[40] The *Economist* described Boeing engineers of 1990 as "the princes of the Seattle economy," with "secure, well-paid jobs and the respect not just of the company but of the town."[41] In the 2000 strike, engineers themselves embraced their identity as the brains of the company. One of the cries on the picket lines was "No nerds, no birds!" To many, the picket lines looked and felt decidedly different from the picket lines of shop-floor workers. One of the striking engineers noted that the strike might warrant the title "March of the Dilberts" or "Revenge of the Nerds."[42] As Michelle Rodino-Colocino points out, "geek" culture was celebrated in the 1980s as white-collar high-tech work boomed for white male information technology (IT) workers and computer professionals: "'Geeks' have been a cultural and political-economic preoccupation since the diffusion of personal computers in the 1980s."[43] By the 1990s, however, as these "geeks" began to experience job insecurity and layoffs, they viewed the economic restructuring of neoliberalism through "the wages of white masculinity," which precluded a more inclusive class consciousness.[44]

The esteem and respect engineers received tempered any union activity among them for most of the postwar period and nurtured a widely held belief that SPEEA members would not strike. A 1972 study of SPEEA, for example, concluded that engineers' status as professionals made them

FIG. 9. SPEEA poster from the 2000 strike at Boeing. Courtesy Washington State Historical Society.

unlikely to go on strike or identify with shop-floor workers' sense of class consciousness; the report characterized them as a group with "no viable strike potential."[45] It also noted that Boeing engineers were "not very aggressive in their relations with management."[46] One engineer stated that relations were so good between engineers and the company that SPEEA had a reputation for being a "wuss" when compared to the IAM. SPEEA was "Boeing's 'tame' union" and was "tolerated, even nurtured to some extent by the company."[47] They were also known as "a particularly coddled bunch" because they had a history of cordial relations with company leaders.[48]

In fact, many company leaders, including CEO Phil Condit, had been SPEEA members. Because Boeing leaders had historically been cultivated from within, many had been engineers who had risen through the ranks of the company. Aviation writer John Newhouse describes CEO and company president Thornton "T" Wilson as successful because of his blue-collar roots and history of working on Boeing's shop floor as an engineer. A successful Boeing leader by this definition was one who could identify with, and thus better manage, Boeing workers.[49] Boeing presidents, CEOs, and those in the upper ranks of management were held responsible for Boeing's ability to remain on the cutting edge of the airplane and aerospace industries, but they were also charged with upholding harmony among Boeing employees.

Over the latter half of the postwar period, however, relations between company leaders, managers, and workers had become more fragmented as the company grew larger and more bureaucratic. The ranks of middle management had grown to an unprecedented degree. By the early 1990s Boeing had fifteen thousand managers.[50] In 1987 Boeing had hired an outside consultant, Gary Jusela, who held a PhD in organizational psychology from Yale, to assess Boeing's structure and corporate culture, particularly with regard to management. Jusela noted the presence of a "formal boundary drawn between Seattle and the off-site divisions."[51] CEO Frank Shrontz was so concerned about the splinters within the company ranks and divisions that he began to conduct meetings with various Boeing employees to hear more about their complaints. He heard several comments that management was "too preoccupied with other things" and that some supervisors simply "weren't people-oriented." These accusations were especially troubling to him because "when management leaves a leadership vacuum, the union obviously is going to step in and fill it."[52] Boeing employees had been feeling increasingly alienated from management even before the company acquired McDonnell Douglas. By the year 2000 even the unlikeliest of Boeing's unions, SPEEA, had become more vocal as the distance between company leaders and workers grew.

For the striking SPEEA workers, as well as the IAM, the merger with McDonnell Douglas was particularly egregious; many employees noted that it changed corporate culture and workplace relations, and not for the better.[53] As Cloud notes, CEOs Phil Condit and Harry Stonecipher "agreed in 1999 to shift Boeing's organizational culture away from a warm and quasi-familial atmosphere (which put a kinder face on the exploitation of workers) to a more open 'tough, lean, and team oriented' environment."[54] Public Broadcasting Service reporter Mike James noted that the primary concern engineers raised in the strike was the demise of the Boeing "family" after the merger. The striking workers complained that, especially since the merger, the family culture had become "more impersonal, more focused on profits than quality." Many also expressed concern that the special status of engineers "began to erode" after the merger.[55]

In becoming the largest aerospace company in the world, Boeing also started to feel less like family. In response to the engineers' concerns, company chair and CEO Phil Condit noted that global growth and economic changes necessitated a very different version of corporate culture than the family model on which the company had been built: "We are not a family; we are a team." He went on to state it was "not an easy transition, but it is a very important one."[56]

To the striking SPEEA members, the rhetorical shift from family to teamwork was deeply troubling and signaled a larger problem with their place in the company and the relationship between company leaders, managers, and workers. Many of the striking engineers were also not happy with the leadership changes and in particular Harry Stonecipher's employment as president and CEO after Condit's retirement in 2003. Stonecipher, like Condit, emphasized teamwork over family. As the *Economist* noted, he had a "blunt, it's a business-not-a family approach to Boeing as president of the larger company."[57] The expected consistency that had held the

Boeing "family" together was no longer applicable, and the new emphasis on teamwork stressed working together despite differences, rather than fraternal bonding based on shared similarities. Teamwork suggested that workers were easily replaced and that their gender, sex, race, and networks of affiliation did not matter to the company in the ways they had previously. A shared social status would no longer order work or place people in particular positions in the company. Indeed, a shared familial status was impossible to guarantee in the context of bureaucratically streamlined, but geographically scattered, sites of production.

Engineers equated the rhetorical shift to teamwork with a loss of respect. One SPEEA staff member argued, "When you spend years working for an organization, dedicating yourself to doing your very best, part of your reward is (or should be) the respect of your employer."[58] Engineers were historically the heart of the company. Older engineers had weathered the boom-and-bust cycles of the postwar period, and younger ones wanted to be able to weather the storms of the twenty-first century. When they could no longer count on the Boeing "family" concept to uphold a sense of job security and respect for their work and place with the company, they responded with anger and hurt. The emphasis on teamwork implied that Boeing's focus would now be on "winning" the global competition and suggested that workers, especially engineers, no longer played a central role in the company hierarchy. In talking about the transition to teamwork, Condit emphasized that skill and winning, rather than loyalty and defined roles, were now at the center of corporate culture: "We're looking for the best performers on that team. We're looking for the best performance from that team."[59] In this new formula, SPEEA members felt a sense of loss and abandonment, which confirms the emotional depth that Boeing's familial corporate culture held for workers.

As the labor activist and historian Ross Reider notes, while the company's merger had left many mourning the loss of a sense of familialism it also mobilized workers to respond to company leaders in new ways: "The merger also introduced new volatility into management-labor relations by diluting Boeing workers' sense of 'family loyalty' and by creating new union organizing opportunities, especially among white collar employees."[60] The merger of Boeing with McDonnell Douglas helped usher in new expectations not only for Boeing leaders but also for employees. For unions, it meant radicalizing their organizing activities, no small feat for SPEEA and the "strike-skittish engineers."[61] As one engineer, Ron Want-taja, observed, "No one really thought a strike would happen . . . people were used to seeing SPEEA cave in."[62]

The radicalization of SPEEA was not readily apparent at the time of the merger, perhaps because most news of the merger focused less on how workplace hierarchies were upended and more on Boeing's consolidation of market power. The *Seattle Times* reported that the merger seemed to be a perfect match. Referring to the company as the "new Boeing," the newspaper acknowledged what a tremendous business move the company had made, at least in terms of sheer growth, size, and market share. The merger made Boeing "the most powerful company in the history of aerospace," with $50 billion in annual sales and 220,000 employees at locations all over the world. The *Times* posited, "It will command the attention of airlines, governments and military establishments around the globe." The newspaper did acknowledge, however, that the merger might put a strain on workplace culture: "The toughest challenges for Boeing now could prove to be inside, rather than outside, the vastly expanded company. Staying nimble, meshing the corporate cultures of the two behemoths, finding common ground and positioning the new company for the future will be no easy tasks."[63] Given the vast power Boeing had acquired, it is noteworthy how vulnerable workers felt after the merger. Yet, it is also understandable; many workers did lose power in this shift and their spot in the company hierarchy; the "new Boeing" troubled them. For many, the rhetorical shift to teamwork exacerbated their concerns, which opened the way for stronger union organizations.

To Boeing leaders, grievances over respect and a decline in the sense of family seemed antiquated and associated with an old-fashioned way of doing business. Boeing leaders stated that "competition in the global economy requires a different culture inside the factory."[64] After Boeing and SPEEA reached an agreement, Condit expressed hope for improved relations between Boeing engineers and company leaders based on the new teamwork model. He stated, "One day I hope we can look back on this time as a turning point—a time when we more clearly recognized the importance of listening to and seeking to understand each other." So that the company wouldn't lose sight of these lessons, Condit promised to set up a "new 'working together' joint-task force" that would "focus on the issues impacting the engineering and technical communities."[65] A task force, while perhaps helpful in facilitating communication between labor and management, could not make headway toward better working conditions and the resolution of equity issues that workers wanted. After the strike Boeing leaders increased their efforts to restructure and reimagine the company as a global "team" company, as opposed to a regionally based family company with strong local roots.

The Radicalization of Union Organizing

In a relatively short period of time, SPEEA had morphed from a relatively weak and ineffectual organization to a union that had demonstrated resolve, bargaining power, and an affiliation with the labor politics traditionally affiliated with blue-collar shop-floor workers. The economic context of the 1990s, reflected in the rhetorical shift to teamwork, provided the momentum for greater attention to union organizing among all Boeing workers and all of Boeing's unions.

By the late 1980s District Lodge 751 had strengthened the union presence at Boeing.[66] The economic instability of the company made union representation an important source of stability for many Boeing workers, though it challenged the tradition of familial loyalty that company leaders had historically tried to foster.

Shortly after Boeing's merger with McDonnell Douglas, SPEEA took steps to strengthen its organizing position. As one engineer surmised, "This, in itself, may have triggered Boeing's hardnose position" in contract negotiations.[67] The union's affiliation with the AFL-CIO challenged the view that SPEEA would be less aggressive in union organization. Margaret Levi, of the Center for Labor Studies at the University of Washington, has noted, "The affiliation with big labor and the strike 'transformed SPEEA'" by making it "a militant union capable of affecting Boeing's profits and hurting Boeing in the pocketbook."[68] Not only did the affiliation signal SPEEA's new identity as a tougher, more determined union, it also put a lot more people in SPEEA's corner.

SPEEA received support in the strike from Boeing's other union, Lodge 751. Representatives from Lodge 751 marched with SPEEA members. The *IAM Journal* noted, "For 40 days, IAM members contributed financial, political and moral support to some 26,000 Boeing engineers and technical workers waging the largest white-collar strike in U.S. labor history."[69] One striking engineer described the support from IAM as "touching," noting that "their contract requires them to cross our picket line. But they seldom do so without a wave and a honk. They often stop and leave doughnuts, pizzas or cups of coffee. They doubted our resolve in the beginning, but now seem to be proud of us."[70] While on the picket line, one SPEEA member and technical worker, Jon Sergeant, observed, "In the past, we haven't looked like much of a union. But today, we're starting to look like a union."[71] The strike signaled a new relationship between Boeing's unions and between labor and management.

SPEEA's affiliations with other unions widened the effects of the strike on Boeing's bottom line and ability to do business. While the IAM possessed a contract stating it could not cross the picket line of any other Boeing union, other unions were not under the same obligation. Members of the Teamsters, including United Parcel Service and FedEx employees, and various others refused to cross picket lines, which had a significant negative impact on Boeing's business. As Wanttaja explained, "737 fuselages from Wichita sit on a siding in Renton, because the trainmen won't enter the plant. The fuselages sit there until the railroad sends a manager to drive them onto the plant. . . . A mainframe IBM computer crashed recently[;] the IBM repairman refused to cross the line."[72]

In early March, Boeing public relations personnel announced that negotiations had stalled and were at an "impasse." Yet, as Alan Mulally, a Boeing senior vice president and the president of Boeing's commercial airplanes group, announced, work opportunities at Boeing were expanding because of new plans to produce a long-range version of the Boeing 777. Mulally observed, "We have a wonderful future ahead of us," and he emphasized that teamwork would provide ample work opportunities because "we are moving forward to capture many new market opportunities. We're asking our talented technical team to join us for the journey."[73] It was not to the company team, however, that workers began to flock but to the company union.

Coming off the heels of the SPEEA strike, all of Boeing's unions were motivated to push for greater change. Boeing employees began to view SPEEA as an outlet for their frustrations. Membership in SPEEA increased more than 50 percent during the strike; before the 2000 strike 42 percent of the engineers and technical workers had been members.[74] After the strike, membership in SPEEA jumped to 65 percent of those employees. As Professor Levi notes, the effects of the SPEEA strike extended beyond the forty days on the picket line, because SPEEA members demonstrated that they were "extraordinarily successful in mobilizing their members and nonmembers in a sustained and difficult strike."[75] The self-described nerds had created a new space for themselves in the Boeing hierarchy, one alongside Boeing's shop-floor workers rather than beside the managers and company leaders with whom engineers had traditionally been affiliated.

In addition to spurring union activity in SPEEA, the strike and the changes at Boeing after the merger with McDonnell Douglas led to greater efforts in 2001 to solidify union power in Lodge 751 through better integration of workers and unions.[76] Lodge 751 led a membership drive to organize clerical workers alongside shop-floor workers. In the "largest organizing drive in Pacific Northwest History," the IAM attempted to organize 16,500 "white-collar professional, technical and clerical employees at Boeing into the IAM." The clerical workers voted not to join, but IAM president Tom Buffenbarger stated that this failed vote did not diminish the vision or fortitude of union organizing: "Boeing's top brass may be leaving Seattle, but the IAM is here to stay."[77] At the same time that Boeing leaders were making plans to move company headquarters to Chicago, then, Boeing employees were consolidating their position within a company that was increasingly dispersed.

Women, Union Politics, and Pay Discrimination

For women at Boeing, sharing in company prosperity seemed even farther out of reach than it did to many male employees, especially those white male "geeks" who were drawing on the "wages of white masculinity" at the expense of a larger class consciousness that would have offered room for diversity in race and gender.[78] While both men and women workers felt increasingly vulnerable in the face of greater job displacement and insecurity, women continued to be paid less than men. In addition, while union organizing efforts at Boeing were enjoying some success, women felt vulnerable within the union ranks as well. Amid the economic dislocations of the 1990s, women sought to strengthen their place not only within Boeing's ranks but also within union hierarchies. Women in District Lodge 751 organized the Women's Committee in 1996 to support women, encourage their union membership, and implement programs to help them achieve equality both within the union and at Boeing. In 2000 the Women's Committee organized a conference that it called the "I.A.M. Women Hear Us Roar Conference," during which women would share their work and union experiences. Concerns over economic vulnerability and inequality permeated the conference. One Boeing employee reported feeling that her education, which included two master's degrees, "intimidates her supervisors, which has caused problems in her job."[79] An AFL-CIO survey conducted at the conference noted that of particular concern to women were paid family leave, equal pay, affordable health care, pensions, and Social Security.[80]

Women at Boeing had reason to worry about economic vulnerability. In the Boeing "family," women had never been at the top of the company hierarchy. But pressure from unions like SPEEA and class-action lawsuits pushed Boeing to redefine its corporate culture, even amid the push toward globalization and the immense growth of the company following the merger with McDonnell Douglas. While the growth of the company seemed to take away some workers' power and security, it also emboldened many to push the company for greater equality on the basis of race and sex. Teamwork, after all, meant embracing diversity and working cooperatively to create a globally competitive Boeing. Teamwork, then, could work both as a metaphor that displaced some workers, notably the striking engineers, and as one that also allowed for a greater awareness of Boeing's need to diversify its workforce. While this situation did not necessarily offer increased power to workers or unions, it did allow for greater attention to diversity and equal employment opportunities. Consequently, Boeing settled several large employment discrimination cases in the 1990s, most notably one in 1999, when the company settled for $15 million with a group of African American employees who had charged Boeing with discrimination in promotion and hiring practices.

Moreover, in a survey conducted a year before that case, Boeing recruiters had reported feeling uncomfortable traveling to black colleges and universities to recruit workers and that they were not encouraged to do so by their supervisors.[81] Most of the $15 million settlement went to employees who had filed racial discrimination charges. A portion of the settlement was designated for improving the company's equal employment opportunity bureaucracy and processes. In the press release that announced the court's approval of the settlement, CEO Phil Condit expressed Boeing's apparent relief at having the matter settled: "We are very pleased with today's court ruling. The court's approval today allows Boeing to continue its movement forward not only on the commitments outlined in the settlement but toward the company's vision of a culture of inclusion, where diverse groups and ideas flourish."[82] It is striking, and perhaps telling, that Condit said the company was envisioning a "culture of inclusion" as opposed to claiming that it already existed.

In February 2000 twenty-eight women filed a class-action suit alleging pay discrimination on the basis of sex. They cited lower salaries and fewer overtime and promotion opportunities going back to at least 1997.[83] Women also described an uncomfortable work environment that included harassment based on sex, gender, and race.[84] The total number of plaintiffs that the class-action suit involved was twenty-nine thousand, nearly matching the ranks of SPEEA membership; thus, at least some of the women interviewed for the 1989 oral history project were likely involved in the suit. Even if they were not directly involved in bringing the suit, women in the company could not have been surprised by it. One of the main issues of the class-action suit was discrimination in pay; the suit charged Boeing with paying women less for doing the same job as men. Many of the women interviewed for the oral history project had mentioned this very problem. As one woman put it, "There's a line about money that it's not a motivator, but that if you don't think you make enough it's a demotivator. Well, I know I'm payed [sic] less than all my colleagues. And every time I get a pay raise, it just raises this issue: that women at Boeing are payed less than men."[85] Another woman described how she had been in a position for four years, yet her successor, a man who worked under her, immediately made five hundred dollars more than she did when she had the job. The news, of course, infuriated her: "I told my boss, and I got a pittance of a merit raise . . . and had to wait a year to get it. I'm a first-line supervisor in our group. And I feel I should earn more than the newer, younger male supervisors. And why won't I? Because I'm a woman."[86]

A third woman discovered she was making six thousand dollars less per year than any of her male counterparts even though she was doing the same work.[87] Because of their tone of resentment, these interview excerpts stand out with respect to the many issues that the women identified as problems at Boeing. Despite affirmative action, one woman noted, pay inequities were at the root of Boeing's discriminatory practice: "The company probably would like to think it treats men and women equally, but they don't really get down to where the discrimination is being done. Like in advancement, and in salary."[88] This assessment of Boeing's affirmative action programs depicts a company with only superficial commitment to equal employment opportunities. The court documents from the subsequent class-action lawsuit make such comments seem generous.

As the case developed, details emerged that proved Boeing leaders had in-depth knowledge of pay inequalities and had worked to hide them from public view. In response to the lawsuit, Boeing denied the charges. A Boeing spokesperson reassured the public, "When the jury has the full story, they will find that the company did not practice discrimination of any kind." He also stated that statistical data on pay disparities between men and women "can't capture all of the critical factors that go into pay or promotion decisions."[89] To women workers, the most significant "critical factor" was gender. One Boeing manufacturing engineer, Patti Anderson, testified that she made two thousand dollars less per year than men performing the same job. More poignantly, she made less than her male family members, who also worked at Boeing: "My husband, brother and dad also performed the same job as me and consistently received higher raises than I. I know this to be true because I saw their pay stubs."[90] Boeing leaders, in response, argued that gender was never a consideration in pay disparities between men and women: "These disparities are the result of quantity or quality of work, seniority and/or merit-based pay systems, or other factors other than gender."[91] Boeing's public denials, however, masked what company leaders and managers already knew. Although Boeing tried to seal the court documents, the presiding judge ordered them to be opened, and more than twelve thousand pages of internal documents revealed that Boeing paid men more than women for the same job. Internal correspondence also revealed that racial minorities, both men and women, were paid less than white men were.[92]

More alarming is the fact that Boeing leaders and managers had been aware of these disparities since at least 1994, when they had actually been forced to perform several internal studies on the issue. In the 1990s a government agency responsible for making sure federal contractors followed affirmative action mandates began to audit Boeing sites.[93] In 1998 the Labor Department's Office of Federal Contract Compliance Programs (OFCCP) initiated an investigation of Boeing based on the agency's findings, which suggested "systemic discrimination concerning compensation of females and minorities."[94] In response to the audits Boeing also organized an internal investigation into pay discrimination. The company organized the Diversity Salary Assessment Team in 1997 to study inequities in promotions and pay. The study concluded that "females . . . are paid less" and that "gender differences in starting salaries generally continue and often increase as a result of salary planning decisions."[95] These "planning decisions" included determining who would be promoted into the ranks of management. A May 1998 report from Boeing's internal investigation noted that gender was a primary determinant in who got promoted: "few persons, especially women and minorities, are hired into management."[96] From 1997 to 2000 women at Boeing were paid an average of $1,000 less per year than their male coworkers.[97] In some departments the dollar figure was higher. Women employed in the commercial airplanes group, for example, made an average of $1,742 less per year than men.[98]

During the audits, Boeing refused to hand over its internal studies on pay inequities, and the Labor Department case was eventually settled for $4.5 million. Company managers who had brokered the settlement were reportedly relieved, as they had anticipated worse liabilities. Boeing's director of employee relations, who had been a key player in settlement negotiations, tellingly observed, "The fact that our compensation comes up . . . negative, negative, negative would suggest that there's something generally not right about the way we're doing it."[99] Boeing leaders, then, as well as Labor Department investigators, were aware that Boeing's corporate culture created and maintained gender pay disparities.

In response to this trouble, Boeing began to try to temper the pay inequities without drawing too much attention to the issue or to Boeing's role in it. Because Boeing leaders were "worried about a major lawsuit," they attempted to hide the pay discrepancies beginning in the mid-1990s by increasing women's salaries.[100] They also attempted to hide the efforts to compensate for pay discrepancies. A senior compensation manager testified that he organized a secret compensation plan designed to mitigate legal risks; the plan was so secret that even senior-level managers were not privy to the information. Laura Yamashita, a labor law attorney who had once worked for Boeing on the pay studies, testified that Boeing hid the studies in a "secured office location" that included precautions such as a locked cabinet with a "special electronic cipher lock" that had its combination changed regularly; not even janitors or security personnel were allowed access to the room. Yamashita also testified that all meetings regarding the studies were held in a "secure, limited-access conference room" and that corporate leaders had to hand over all meeting notes when they left the room. Boeing spokespersons dismissed the secrecy by stating, "It is company practice to keep confidential information secure, particularly when it comes to salary information."[101] The court disagreed, however, and ordered Boeing to produce documents it had been keeping secret, which pushed the company toward settlement of the class-action lawsuit in 2004.

Despite the secrecy around specific documents and numbers, the salary adjustment plan was well known to Boeing employees. Some employees nicknamed the program "Bucks for Babes," underscoring both the systemic awareness of claims of disparity and the more cynical view that women's pay increases amounted to tokenism.[102] The court documents revealed that Boeing's own reports admitted that the wage gap would be difficult to close. In 1999 Boeing leaders found they would have to pay out an additional $30 million in salary adjustments to equalize just *some*, not all, of the wage gap. In the end Boeing funded only a dismal one-third of this amount, at $10 million.[103] This payout was enough, however, to stop the Labor Department audits in 1999. However, even the semisecret program to adjust women's pay could not undo the institutionalized discrimination embedded in Boeing's corporate culture. The plaintiffs' lawyers in the 2000 class-action suit argued that, even after the salary adjustments, pay disparities still existed.[104] Plaintiffs' experts argued that Boeing's business practices and corporate culture "permitted gender stereotypes or gender-biased opinions to infect Boeing's employment decisions, and disadvantaged women throughout their Boeing careers through arbitrary restraints on pay adjustments." They also argued that "Boeing permitted a corporate culture or environment hostile to women" because those who did act inappropriately received no punishment or consequences and that gender or sexual harassment was underreported because women who did report problems suffered retaliation.[105]

Ironically, despite proclaiming innocence, Boeing had, in its effort to avoid litigation, produced an enormous paper trail documenting widely known, pervasive, and systemic gender discrimination.[106] After the paperwork was brought to light, a settlement agreement was reached. Boeing paid $72.5 million to the twenty-nine thousand female plaintiffs to settle the case in 2004. The settlement report noted, "By the time of the settlement, this was among the most hotly-contested matters of its kind."[107] The matter may have been hotly contested, but it was certainly not an isolated case. Boeing joined the ranks of several other large corporations, such as Home Depot, Coca-Cola, and Morgan Stanley, that had settled discrimination suits in the years leading up to Boeing's case. As part of the settlement terms Boeing admitted no fault but agreed to change some of its policies and practices, including monitoring overtime and salaries and conducting annual performance evaluations.[108] Boeing was also ordered to report salaries more frequently, collect information on compensation and report it to the plaintiffs' counsel for three years, reevaluate and restructure decisions on overtime and promotions, and strengthen the power of investigators of EEO and sexual harassment complaints to enforce decisions. Prior to the settlement, managers were able to "veto any sanctions proposed by the EEO investigator."[109] The EEO Commission, then, had little to no authority when compared with Boeing management. Boeing's corporate culture had outweighed federal mandates, which reveals the power of corporate culture to both block equal opportunity employment and perpetuate employment discrimination despite institutional changes designed to prevent employment discrimination.

Global Teamwork and the Pacific Northwest

The scandals of the late 1990s focused public attention on employment discrimination and corporate culture just as Boeing was planning for the release of the new 7E7 passenger jet, later known as the 787 Dreamliner. A *BusinessWeek* writer declared, "Troubling headlines are a comparatively new problem for Boeing. A company dominated by engineers, it tradition-ally focused on innovation and design." The magazine reporter further opined, "The company's tactics in the pay-discrimination lawsuit, Beck v. Boeing, also raise broader questions about the health of Boeing's corporate culture."[110] The scope of the lawsuit and the settlement that resulted also drew attention. The plaintiffs' attorney noted, "It's revealing that over 60 percent of female employees filed claims—in most class-action suits a 30 percent response rate is typical."[111] The strength of women's response to the class-action suit reveals the depth and breadth of gender discrimina-tion at Boeing.

The class-action lawsuit forced a very public reworking of Boeing's cor-porate culture just as company leaders were strategizing the restructuring needed after the merger with McDonnell Douglas. It did not, however, immediately place men and women workers on equal footing or eliminate charges of discrimination based on race and ethnicity. In 2001, for example, a group of 1,850 Asian American engineers sued Boeing on the basis of racial and ethnic bias. The engineers, who had come from Afghanistan, Pakistan, India, Cambodia, Vietnam, and the Philippines, charged Boeing with paying them less and giving managers unfair discretion in assigning pay scales, a charge also made in the class-action lawsuit filed by women. In a 2004 ruling that came only days after the Beck settlement was announced, however, a federal judge dismissed the claims and stated that Boeing did not discriminate against Asian Americans. A Boeing spokesperson stated that the ruling was not a surprise to company leaders because, in their view, "We've demonstrated that the company has gone to great lengths to be a good place for all employees to work."[112] The number of employees involved in lawsuits charging racial and ethnic discrimination, however, shows that many nonwhite employees had problems with managerial practices on the shop floor and with the power given to managers.

Gender, too, remained a point of contention. Gendered cultural expectations mattered a great deal in how women's employment was perceived. Those women who were promoted to managerial and executive positions were often stigmatized as representing tokenism. In 2003, for example, one male manager who had been with Boeing since 1987 described a "widely held belief that women were sometimes promoted to meet diversity requirements." In 2006 another male engineer, who had started working at Boeing in 1991, characterized the hiring of women and minorities as insincere and based only on a need to appear to be an equal opportunity employer. He noted, "There has been company-wide promotion of women and minorities over equally or even better qualified personnel."[113] To engineers who had weathered the shifting landscape at Boeing due to globalization and the SPEEA strike, enforcement of equal opportunity programs were part of the larger demise of power and rights for white-collar workers. White male engineers were losing power and rights within the ranks of the company; highly paid, highly skilled workers were being replaced in the company ranks, and white male engineers vocalized their sense of loss amid these shifts.

In the midst of increased scrutiny of Boeing's corporate culture, however, the company was also widening the gap between company leaders and workers, which included making plans to move the company headquarters from Seattle. The relocation plans did not sit well within the traditional family framework, which had fostered a sense of belonging and place.[114] Boeing leaders' new emphasis on teamwork was a calculated rhetorical move that individualized business and work and held the company less responsible for the fate of workers, a fate that seemed increasingly precarious because of a new focus on global business and financial speculation. The family metaphor suggested a fixed home headquarters, patriarchal responsibility, and stability—notions that were not easily portable to the competitive global or transnational corporate world. Although Boeing had long endured boom-and-bust cycles, the familialism of Boeing's corporate culture and the social hierarchies upon which it was based offered a compelling sense of stability, authority, and control to help workers weather the changes. The striking SPEEA engineers wanted to hold on to the familial model because it offered a promise of inclusion, at least for some, and a predictability that the new model of teamwork did not.

Boeing was beginning to alienate not just individual workers but the entire city of Seattle. As the aviation journalist Sam Howe Verhovek has noted, this "new Boeing" was a sharp departure from the business practices that had built the company over the course of the twentieth century. He references those glory days when the occasional labor dispute or strike could be worked out with management. As he observes, "The dominant feeling in Seattle was one of immense, almost viscerally parental, pride in the company's airplanes, especially the Boeing 707." Verhovek also claims that this familylike atmosphere facilitated innovation, creating a stable workplace where employees felt free to share their ideas. As he recalls, "In interviews more than fifty years after the fact, one hears over and over that Boeing's workers believed—knew—they were involved in a great enterprise."[115] However, the SPEEA strike in 2000 and the class-action lawsuit illustrate that workers did not think they had a stake in the "new Boeing" and in the focus on globalization.

Workers began to feel even more isolated from company leaders in the years that followed. Company leaders lost credibility amid a series of scandals, which reinforced the message that Boeing's unions, rather than company leaders, were the family members to be most trusted. In March 2005 Boeing Company executive board members forced CEO Harry Stonecipher to resign after a coworker reported an illicit affair between Stonecipher and a female executive. Boeing board chair Lew Platt commented, "It's not the fact that [Stonecipher] was having an affair. That is not a violation of our code of conduct." He further explained that Stonecipher had been asked to resign based on "issues of poor judgment surrounding the affair" that "impaired his ability to lead."[116] In a move that seemed well timed, especially after more scandal involving business deals made by Phil Condit, Boeing began to recruit leadership from outside the company.[117] In June 2005, for the first time, Boeing chose a leader who did not come from the company's own workforce and Seattle networks. W. James McNerney, former head of 3M, earned the dubious distinction of becoming the "first outsider to run the Boeing Company."[118] The fact that the first "outsider" was not hired at Boeing until 2005 attests to the strength of the fraternal corporate culture at the company and the strength of the institutional bonds it had forged with the military, the city of Seattle, and the University of Washington.

The processes of globalization, most notably the growth that went along with it, changed the dynamics of the Boeing "family" and made it difficult, and eventually impossible, to maintain the company's links to Seattle in the same way that it once had. As Dana Cloud notes, "A number of workers saw the move [of the company headquarters to Chicago] as a desertion of a community Boeing was preparing to 'trash,' without having to look workers and their families in the face."[119] Most of the company's newspapers and magazines, relics of the 1930s family-based approach, were shifted to online formats. A monthly magazine, *Frontiers*, became an in-house publication in 2002. The audience for such publications had also shifted in the twenty-first century. In 2012 Boeing announced that it would partner with the Seattle Times Company to offer the magazine as an advertising insert in the newspaper. James Albaugh, CEO of Boeing Commercial Airplanes, stated that the magazine, and the company's distribution of it as a monthly "advertising insert" in the *Seattle Times*, was about sharing teamwork, a stark contrast to promoting family among workers only: "Our team does exciting things and we'd like to share some of that excitement with you."[120]

Boeing also went to great lengths to define itself as a global company. Some argued that despite Boeing's efforts to "go global," the company would always be local, an enterprise steeped in rigid regional traditionalism that went against Boeing's efforts to develop a global image. Indeed, in 2007 the aviation writer John Newhouse had described the company as "provincial."[121] The irony of course is that more than five years after Boeing leaders had attempted to globalize the company and moved their headquarters, they were accused of being "provincial."

Although Boeing moved its headquarters to reflect a more global image, the company still faced enormous changes beyond the central geographic one. Firms at this time were more focused on finance, and the company workforce was increasingly dispersed across different locations. Despite these changes, the decline of familialism at Boeing or other corporations was not inevitable. Sanford Jacoby notes that some businesses, such as Kodak, 3M, and Hewlett-Packard, continued to have "cohesive industrial communities based on comprehensive benefits, employee involvement, and stable, albeit not permanent, jobs" despite heavy layoffs. For Kodak in particular, the new emphasis on globalization did not alter conceptions of family; Kodak has remained a "nonunion stronghold," and even with layoffs and "geographic decentralization," Kodak "still calls itself an industrial 'family.' It spends huge amounts on training, career planning, and fringe benefits, including the wage dividend."[122] At Boeing, and many other firms, the situation is markedly different.[123] Unlike Kodak, Boeing is a union stronghold, and the development of a familial atmosphere via management strategy no longer exists. This does not mean, however, that all aspects of the Boeing "family" are gone but that the focus, emphasis, and priorities of corporate culture have shifted.

While Seattle's economy has often been linked to the fortunes of Boeing, and increasingly of Microsoft, Weyerhauser, Amazon, Costco, and Starbucks, it has also featured a long history of labor organizing. Although the legacy of racial labor politics in Seattle and the Pacific Northwest is well documented, the protests against the World Trade Organization (WTO) meeting held in Seattle in 1999 thrust the city and its labor politics onto the world stage. Anne Slater, an organizer for Seattle Radical Women, one of the groups that participated in the protests, noted that the WTO protests also radicalized Seattle workers by making labor activists aware of how to organize more effectively for change at corporations like Boeing; she pointed to job actions like the SPEEA strike as "reverberations of the WTO and . . . people sensing the power we can actually have."[124] Another WTO protester noted that Boeing workers might no longer be complicit in the processes of capitalism that perpetuated the patriarchy in Boeing's corporate culture over the course of the postwar period. In his view, the long history of labor activism in Seattle could override the company's hiring practices and economic clout: "You have a long tradition of trade unionism, of forest activism defending our old growth forests, etc. People don't say Left Coast for nothing."[125] This is not to say, however, that workers have necessarily gained more power. Despite the sorrow and strong emotion many workers feel at being left vulnerable by the new workplace order that has emerged, many workers also marvel at the barriers that have been broken down at Boeing. Amy Laly, who had come to the United States from India in 1966 and worked for Boeing for nearly twenty-five years, noted in 2007 that the breakdown of Boeing's corporate culture was a positive development that signaled a major shift in employment discrimination. She observed that "Boeing still has a long way to go. But I have seen a sea change at Boeing and that is good. Maybe I am older and self assured. Women still get paid less than men doing the same work."[126] Although Laly remarked upon the changes that had opened up opportunities to women, her reflection on her age and the presence of a generational gap is testimony to the hurdle that Boeing's corporate culture represented to those who desired change in the dynamics of workplace organization. It is also testimony, however, to the possibility for workplace cultures to shift and thus allow for greater diversity and equal employment opportunities, a reality that corporations like Boeing would be wise to accept as the twenty-first century progresses.[127]

Gendered Inequalities

By the end of the twentieth century, Boeing's old corporate culture had been dismantled. The collapse of the familial metaphor under the strains of neoliberalism revealed the urgency of the situation, workers' diminished power, and their increasingly antagonistic relations with Boeing. But while men, especially engineers, looked to the past with a nostalgia for their once exalted place in the company hierarchy, women looked to the future; the past had not offered them the sort of empowerment men had enjoyed, since women had always been aware that they were discriminated against. The sense of urgency among both men and women energized union efforts. During contract negotiations in 2002, Bob Thayer, head of the IAM Aerospace Department, argued that "Boeing may be running away to Mexico and China, but we're not running anywhere. We will fight in court, in negotiations, in Congress and on the picket lines. We are making a stand right here, for the future of our kids and our communities. This is a fight for survival."[128]

However, workers did not experience the feelings of loss and anxiety in the same way, which is especially evident in women's experiences within the union. In April 2002 the District Lodge 751 Women's Committee cochairs, Gloria Millsaps and Susan Palmer, sent a letter to Dick Schneider, the aerospace coordinator, asking him to consider the role of gender in contract negotiations. They argued, "We feel it is most necessary and long overdue to strongly encourage our negotiators to respect all of our members by adding the words 'she' instead of just 'he' and 'her' instead of just 'him.'" They reminded the union, "We are all in this together."[129] Millsaps and Palmer's letter reflects not only the strengthening of union organizing at Boeing since the 1990s but also the very real ways in which union efforts, and Boeing's past, have been shaped by gender. It also serves as a reminder that the push for stable work and equal employment opportunities must occur within unions as well.

Conclusion

Corporate Capitalism in the Twenty-First Century

In 2011 Boeing announced that the company would produce its second line of 787 Dreamliners in North Charleston, South Carolina, rather than in the Puget Sound area. The announcement set off a firestorm of political wrangling. After union complaints, the National Labor Relations Board investigated and charged the company with relocating work to South Carolina in retaliation for labor agitation. In response, South Carolina governor Nikki Haley wrote an op-ed piece for the *Wall Street Journal* in which she praised the company for choosing South Carolina. She noted that the state had a "long tradition of distinguished and employee-friendly corporations," primarily due to its status as a "right to work state," where employees have a choice about joining the union. In Washington, Boeing employees had to join the International Association of Machinists and Aerospace Workers. Haley opined, "In choosing to manufacture in my state, Boeing was exercising its right as a free enterprise in a free nation to conduct business wherever it believed would best serve both the bottom line and the employees of its company. This is not a novel or complicated idea. It's called capitalism."[1] Haley's version of twenty-first-century capitalism, however, was quite different from the union's idea of capitalism.

While Haley (and many Republicans highlighting the economic role of corporations during the 2012 presidential election campaigns) praised Boeing's relocation as a sound business strategy that would benefit Boeing, the U.S. economy, and the American people, union leaders and others disagreed. They condemned the move as symbolic of the effort to concentrate power in the hands of Boeing leaders, and in corporations like Boeing, at the expense of the workers. Tom Wroblewski, president of District Lodge 751, observed that Boeing's move symbolized the company's divestment from Seattle and the familial obligations of an earlier time: "Instead of investing in a profitable shared future here in Puget Sound, with the people who have spent generations making Boeing a world leader, the smart guys in Chicago have doubled-down on the failed 787 business model, placing a multi-billion-dollar bet on a process that's a proven loser. Some people never learn."[2]

As Wroblewski's comments reveal, the company's decision to go with South Carolina for the next 787 was not the sort of teamwork that Boeing employees had been hoping for. Instead, the move signified all that had gone wrong with Boeing's corporate culture since the mid-1990s. The move also seemed to dismiss the dynamics of the Boeing "family," which had been built on the loyalty of Puget Sound workers to the company. As one former worker noted, the move "shows lack of loyalty to their roots."[3] After Lodge 751 received a contract promising more work in the Puget Sound region, its complaint was withdrawn and the NLRB dropped its charges. The issue, however, did not go away. Instead, debates over Boeing jobs, union politics, globalization, and neoliberal capitalism continued.

Even more attention was focused on the weakened position of Boeing workers during SPEEA contract negotiations in the summer of 2012. At the time of the merger with McDonnell Douglas in 1997, engineers reported feeling less concerned about job security than did shop-floor production workers. By 2003, however, both engineers and production workers shared the same level of fear over job security.[4] In 2012 the same issues and insecurities made contract negotiations contentious. SPEEA engineers wanted higher wages to bring their pay closer to competitive industry rates. They also wanted to achieve a sense that the company was investing in a future, and workforce, in the Pacific Northwest. *Seattle Times* columnist Jon Talton agreed with the engineers, arguing that Boeing's strategy amounted to "redistributing income from the middle class to the very rich while rubbing the union's face in it." Talton, like Wroblewski, argued that Boeing was neglecting its labor history and regional identity, particularly with respect to engineers. He claimed Boeing leaders were simply making bad decisions, observing that "smart management would want to invest in this culture, especially the people, rather than low-balling them. 'No nerds, no birds,' indeed. The American middle-class has been hollowed out by this kind of action across corporate America." He went on to describe the prevailing corporate climate as a "looter/taker mentality, with outrageous CEO pay, bad mergers, industry consolidation and a Wal-Mart attitude toward workers much at odds with the capitalism that made America great and exceptional."[5]

SPEEA members also believed that company leaders and managers were not recognizing workers' significance to the company. One SPEEA member, Roy Goforth, stated, "These are the most offensive and disrespectful negotiations I've ever been a part of. It appears they don't have any intention to reach a deal."[6] In these negotiations the issue of respect took center stage, much as it had in the 2000 SPEEA strike. The 2013 and 2014 negotiations over the 777X made it clear that the debate over Boeing's place in Seattle and the quality of the relationship between company leaders and workers has not ended, though it is apparent that the neoliberal context and the increasingly frequent company decisions to move work elsewhere have diminished expectations that Boeing will remain a top employer in region. In its February 2014 issue, for example, *Seattle* magazine featured an article on a hiring boom in the Seattle area but notably left Boeing off the list of "26 companies to watch for steady growth—and local job opportunities with great benefits." Boeing did receive coverage, but only to point out how drastically the company had changed from the familial ordering the company began with: "In the past, Boeing has been a big player in the region's job opportunity mix, with a famously boom-bust impact. Today, the role is anything but straightforward. While aerospace product and parts manufacturing companies employed more than 95,000 workers in the Seattle-Tacoma-Bellevue area in 2013, last year, Boeing shed nearly 4,000 Washington state jobs."[7]

The role that Boeing will play in the Pacific Northwest seems more tenuous than ever in the turmoil of global corporate capitalism. One of the challenges in writing recent history is accepting that the story is not finished. Renee C. Romano observes that historians who write recent history must "write histories that do not in fact aim for or achieve closure. If our pasts are 'not dead yet,' we can't pretend that they are by tying up our stories with a lovely narrative bow."[8] Certainly the story of Boeing and the company's labor politics will continue to dominate news headlines in the Pacific Northwest and, it appears, to contribute to national political debates as people examine not only workers' relationship to increased corporate power but also a neoliberal capitalist context that relies on and exacerbates inequalities. While Boeing's future may not be entirely clear, we can learn a great deal about corporate power from the company's long history as well as the company leaders' more recent decisions.

The story of the demise of the Boeing "family" reveals that Boeing's corporate culture, and corporate capitalism more broadly, is an obstacle to diversity, equal employment opportunities, and empowerment for all workers. When Boeing leaders were confronted with a more diversified workforce, they tried to uphold workplace order and economic stability by maintaining a gender division of labor. The heterosexual norms on which Boeing's familial culture was based provided the stability that company leaders and some workers wanted, particularly in times of crisis when it seemed that economic uncertainties of the global market needed a stabilizing force. Under the shifts of neoliberal capitalism all workers have lost power and are vulnerable in new ways. For women, who have been concentrated in the lowest-paying jobs and positioned lower in capitalist hierarchies, the effects are magnified. As Mimi Abramovitz argues, "The gender division of labour continues to assign women near-exclusive responsibility for care work—even when they work outside the home. The employment of women has increased their economic independence but reduced the time available to women for care work in the home." She further argues that the dismantling of the welfare state in the name of corporate capitalism will lead to social and economic instabilities, as well as instabilities within real families. She poses the critical question, "How long can corporate capitalism manage without the programmes that keep the current and future workforce healthy, educated, and productive, and that mediate the disruptive impact of too much class, race, and gender inequality?"[9]

The story of Boeing's workplace dynamics reveals the processes of capitalist empowerment of corporations in the twenty-first century at the expense of all workers and to the particular detriment of women. While the shift to "teamwork" might rhetorically seem to equalize opportunities between men and women, in the end it reflects corporate management of employees much the same way that the familial metaphor did, although with the decreasing support of the welfare state or corporate welfare programs. Despite the demise of the family metaphor and the new emphasis on global teamwork, all workers are more vulnerable to employment insecurities. Inequalities have not been eradicated even while rhetorically the teamwork metaphor may appear to level the playing field and open up opportunities. Business leaders no longer appear to be held accountable by workers for the loss of jobs nor do they seem bound by familial obligations to look out for the welfare of workers in the same way.

Debates over loyalty, of employees to the company and of the company to Puget Sound workers, suggest that Boeing is not likely to be completely disentangled from the Puget Sound region anytime soon despite the company's attempts to globalize. The historian William G. Robbins argues that global shifts have strained regional identity in the Pacific Northwest more broadly: "Since World War II, the revolutionary forces of an increasingly aggressive global economy have threatened to undermine regional culture and what had once been deep-rooted local traditions. Postwar affluence, the growing mobility of the professional classes, and the accelerating movement of capital around the globe have posed ever-greater challenges to the efficacy and meaning of regionalism."[10] Williams goes on to describe "placeless" and "faceless business people" who move through the Pacific Northwest and "who are weakening place as a central experience in everyday life."[11] Certainly the tensions between a regional versus a global identity underlie the fears expressed in debates over Boeing's decisions to open a plant in South Carolina and move company headquarters to Chicago, as well as in contract negotiations with SPEEA and IAM. Yet the very resistance that workers, both men and women, have expressed to completely abolishing Boeing's regional identity or erasing its historical identity as a product of the Pacific Northwest reveals the stakes, and power, that workers have in this process. It also suggests that aspects of the Boeing "family" will continue to endure despite Boeing's status as a global leader in airplane and aerospace production and as workers try to regain access to stable jobs.

The place of women within the new global Boeing team remains somewhat unclear, although recent developments show that some positive changes have been made. A 2007 issue of *Boeing Frontiers* examined the place of women engineers in the company. The article presents the successes and challenges of diversifying Boeing's ranks. John Tracey, a senior vice president for engineering, pointed out that a diversified engineering base had made the company more competitive and, in his view, remained the key to maintaining a competitive edge: "Engineering is our lifeblood. It is at the heart of everything we do. We need to find ways to fill the engineering pipeline and then draw from the best of the best. By increasing the diversity of our work force, we can better meet our growth requirements and also meet them in a way that enhances our ability to provide more creative and competitive solutions."[12] Mike Denton, vice president of engineering for Boeing Commercial Airplanes, similarly noted that diversity is a requirement in the twenty-first century: "In the future, white males will be a minority in the work force. We have to attract and retain women and minority engineers to get the talent we need to succeed."[13] Shelley Lavender, a program manager for navy aircraft, observed that Boeing had been working on building a "culture of inclusion." This culture, Lavender argued, had resulted in women feeling valued, a change she predicted "will retain everyone."[14] The teamwork metaphor provides room for a new recognition of diversity. As Deborah Limb, a director for Boeing's commercial division, observed, the workplace "should be a dynamic teamwork, bringing people from different cultures and backgrounds and achieving something more than any one of them could do alone."[15] However, as the author of the *Boeing Frontiers* article pointed out, the biggest obstacle to diversifying Boeing may be getting over the company's image as a place that is hostile to diversity. The author concluded, "Now the challenge is to spread the word that Boeing is a great place to work—for all employees."[16]

Boeing's history and culture, both real and imagined, still hold significant power. In 2004 Boeing's workforce still predominantly comprised males; women constituted only 25 percent of the workforce.[17] In 2012 women represented only 19.5 percent of the SPEEA membership. On the national level only one in five engineers is a woman. As the business writer Steve Wilhelm has noted, "Women are even more scarce in manufacturing's corner offices, where they fill one in 10 executive seats."[18] High numbers of women continue to report unequal treatment and sexual and gender discrimination. The American Association of University Women reported that in 2011 the Equal Employment Opportunity Commission received almost thirty thousand complaints of sex discrimination. Also sobering is the fact that the wage gap between men and women has hardly moved in a decade, going from an eighty-cent average (for every dollar men make) to an eighty-two-cent average for women.[19]

Equality for diverse sexual identities, in addition to gender, remains a battleground. This tension is particularly evident in the battles over pension benefits after Washington State's same-sex marriage law went into effect in December 2012. In November, during contract negotiations with SPEEA, Boeing announced it would have to "study" same-sex partner survivor pension benefits to decide if it would grant them. Of particular concern, company officials said, was funding the pensions. The fact that SPEEA raised the issue of survivor benefits for same-sex partners illustrates a widened recognition of sexual discrimination within the union ranks since the 1990s. Regardless of state law, however, the federal Defense of Marriage Act and other federal laws regulating retirement and pension benefits mean that Boeing does not have to follow state laws in recognizing same-sex spouses. A Boeing spokesperson stated, "This is obviously a new law, and we'll take a closer look to see how it impacts us across the board." In response, a SPEEA representative observed that Boeing was "using a loophole" to withhold benefits.[20] The satirical talk-show host Stephen Colbert quipped that Boeing's response was a "refreshing denial of human dignity," and, more to the point, he called it a "blatant devaluing of gay partners."[21] By January 2013 Boeing had changed its position, particularly after an online petition supporting the extension of pension benefits to same-sex couples garnered seventy-nine thousand signatures; company leaders and union representatives agreed that pension survivor benefits would cover "all spouses, as defined under either State or Federal law whichever defines the same sex person as a spouse."[22]

For employees to achieve workplace equality corporations and unions need to realize the power of work cultures to tolerate and promote inequalities and to stifle what both women and men imagine is possible. Alice

Kessler-Harris has argued that to fully open equal employment opportunity we must recognize "not only the ways in which traditional habits of mind have become embedded in our legislative, judicial, and policy-making apparatus but the difficulties of redefining social policies in the light of persistent gendered tensions surrounding them."[23] She further points out that "informal as well as formal rules constrain options."[24] The power of corporate culture to either support or dissuade equal employment opportunity needs to be taken more seriously. In their 2010 study of workplace relations at Boeing since 1997, Edward Greenberg, Leon Grunberg, Sarah Moore, and Patricia Sikora conclude, "While much of the overt forms of discrimination are nearly a thing of the past, more subtle forms of discrimination persist, contributing to a glass ceiling at higher levels of management." They also argue that "gains in areas of gender equality have come more slowly and are still in the midst of being realized."[25] It is my hope that this study contributes to this growing awareness by addressing the inequalities embedded within American capitalism. With awareness of the problem, workers can strengthen not only their own rights in the workplace but also their future economic outlook.

NOTES

PREFACE

1. Noble, *Religion of Technology*, 223.
2. Noble, *Religion of Technology*, 225.
3. See, for example, Newhouse, *Boeing versus Airbus*, esp. 4; Bilstein, *American Aerospace Industry*, 214, 219; Bauer, *Boeing in Peace and War*, e.g., 3, 21–28, 46–51, 147; Bauer, *Boeing*, e.g., 20–23, 81, 91, 131. Led by Alfred Chandler, author of *The Invisible Hand*, business historians have credited technology and technological efficiency with driving change in workplace organization. See also Clark Davis's essay on sources in his book *Company Men*, 280–85, where he explains the significance of responses to Chandler's work for the historiography of corporate cultures and business history studies.
4. As several scholars have noted, workers were not passive in the construction of corporate culture. See, for example, Sangster, "Softball Solution," 170–72. Aiwha Ong's analysis of Malaysian women argues that within corporate structures women exert agency and shape their own identities. Ong, *Spirits of Resistance and Capitalist Discipline*, 4. In her analysis of Caribbean offshore informatics workers, Carla Freeman argues that Afro Barbadian women's identity formation reveals a negotiation of power and expresses "both international corporate and local cultures." Freeman, *High Tech and High Heels in the Global Economy*, 226. See also Kunda, *Engineering Culture*.
5. Just a few of these include Benson, *Counter Cultures*; Kwolek-Folland, *Engendering Business*; Freeman, *High Tech and High Heels*; Tinsman, *Partners in Conflict*; and Pierce, *Gender Trials*. This study benefits from a growing attention to studies of masculinity and men's gender roles in recent years, in particular, Baron, *Work Engendered*; Bederman, *Manliness and Civilization*; Breazeale, "In Spite of Women"; C. Davis, *Company Men*; Halberstam, *Female Masculinity*, 1–44; Kocka, *White Collar Workers in America*; Kunda, *Engineering Culture*; Lewchuck, "Men and Monotony"; and Zunz, *Making America Corporate*.

6. Armitage, "Tied to Other Lives," 17.
7. The historian Karen Blair points out that only a handful of topics have been covered (none of them dealing with the postwar period) and argues that much more research needs to be done, especially in regard to women's participation in the workforce. Blair, "State of Research on Pacific Northwest Women," 48, 51, 54. For recent scholarship on the Pacific Northwest and regional identity, see Blair, *Women in Pacific Northwest History*; P. Harrison, *Open Spaces*; Robbins, *Great Northwest*; and Schwantes, *Pacific Northwest*.
8. S. Johnson, "Nail This to Your Door," esp. 606.
9. S. Johnson, "Nail This to Your Door," 615, 617.
10. Jacobs, "Western History," 298, 303.
11. For a good overview of debates on western women's history, see Jacobs, "Getting Out of a Rut," esp. 589, 591, for a discussion of women's work in the West. See also Jacobs, "Western History"; and S. Johnson, "Nail This to Your Door."
12. Warner, *Fear of a Queer Planet*, xxi. As Warner further explains, heteronormativity is embedded in social structures, institutions, and understandings and often viewed as natural, and it is distinct from heterosexuality, which is organized by framing homosexuality as its parallel. Heteronormativity defines sexuality as "not only heterosexual but normalized and functional" (ix).
13. Katz, "Invention of Heterosexuality," 7.
14. Hennessy, *Profit and Pleasure*, 54. She further notes, "This history is most often rendered opaque by appeals to the obviousness of their irrelevance to one another. Much of queer theory now continues this tradition; the very possibility of linking the changing organizations of sexuality to capitalism remains all but unspeakable" (54).
15. Ingraham, "Heterosexual Imaginary," 276.
16. See Freedman, *No Turning Back*, 166–67.
17. Greenwald and Pettigrew, "With Malice toward None and Charity for Some," 2.
18. T. M. Sell points out that "the history of The Boeing Company is regaled in varying detail in a hangarful of sanitized recitations, from Boeing public relations director Harold Mansfield's *Vision* to Robert Serling's company-sponsored *Legend and Legacy*. . . . Even less benign examinations, such as John Newhouse's *The Sporty Game*, have not really understood the company." Sell, *Wings of Power*, 12.
19. Some studies that provide important insight into this process, especially with regard to gender, include C. Davis, *Company Men*; Marchand, *Creating the Corporate Soul*; Kwolek-Folland, "Gender, Self, and Work in the Life Insurance Industry"; Kwolek-Folland, *Engendering Business*; and Mandell, *Corporation as Family*.
20. The historian Jacob Vander Meulen notes that several obstacles stand in the way of undertaking a comprehensive look at the American aerospace industry, including the complexity of the industry as well as limited access to archival research in

private firms. Vander Meulen, review of *American Aerospace Industry* by Bilstein, 590.

21. The term "military-industrial complex" was first used during Pres. Dwight Eisenhower's 1961 farewell speech to describe the relationship between the arms and weapon industry and the military establishment. As Roger Bilstein points out, however, the military-industrial complex has roots in the Truman administration, which began a program of increased government investment in defense spending for the purpose of national security amid Cold War concerns. Bilstein, *American Aerospace Industry*, 101.

22. With regard to the sexual division of labor, many scholars have shown how government and industry worked together to promote women's wartime work in aircraft plants, shipyards, and other wartime industries as temporary, thus retaining patriarchal definitions of workers as male breadwinners. Some crucial works include K. Anderson, *Wartime Women*; Hartmann, *Home Front and Beyond*; Honey, *Creating Rosie the Riveter*; Kesselman, *Fleeting Opportunities*; Milkman, *Gender at Work*; Meyer, *Creating G.I. Jane*; and Rupp, *Mobilizing Women for War*.

23. Folbre, *Invisible Heart*, 157.

24. Freedman, *No Turning Back*, 168.

INTRODUCTION

1. Jeffrey Johnson, "Machinists' Vote on Boeing Union Contract Defended the Middle Class," *Seattle Times*, November 17, 2014, http://seattletimes.com/html/opinion/2022269425_jeffjohnsonopedboeingunion18xml.html.

2. Harvey, *Brief History of Neoliberalism*, 2.

3. Marchand, *Creating the Corporate Soul*, 107.

4. Marchand, *Creating the Corporate Soul*, 103–14; Kwolek-Folland, "Gender, Self, and Work in the Life Insurance Industry," 168–90; Kwolek-Folland, *Engendering Business*; Mandell, *Corporation as Family*.

5. See, for example, Cloud, "Null Persona"; Hall et al., *Like a Family*; Mandell, *Corporation as Family*; and Marchand, *Creating the Corporate Soul*.

6. Marchand, *Creating the Corporate Soul*, 114.

7. Hall et al., *Like a Family*, 152. The authors point out how the family metaphor used by workers in a mill town in the Piedmont of South Carolina in the 1920s shaped relations among employees; in their view, family and community meant "conflict as well as reciprocity" and exclusion and repression as well as sustenance (xvii, 152).

8. See Folbre, *Invisible Heart*, 9.

9. See Weeks, *Problem with Work*, 137. Folbre also argues that women's unpaid labor in the home, including reproduction and caretaking, has sustained capitalist accumulation. Work within the family came to be defined as unproductive, despite the

primacy of reproduction and caretaking in processes of capitalist accumulation. Folbre, *Greed, Lust & Gender*, 252.

10. Hennessy, *Profit and Pleasure*, 23. For a useful summary of the debates between materialist and Marxist feminist views on capitalism and patriarchy, see Hennessy, *Profit and Pleasure*, 27–29.

11. See, for example, Linda Kerber's comments in Kerber et al., "Beyond Roles, Beyond Spheres," 566, 581; Warner, introduction to *Fear of a Queer Planet*; Canaday, "Building a Straight State"; Hennessy, *Profit and Pleasure*, 9, 54; and May, *Homeward Bound*.

12. See, for example, the essays in Meyerowitz, *Not June Cleaver*; Coontz, *Way We Never Were*, esp. 113–15; and Folbre, *Invisible Heart*.

13. Freedman, *No Turning Back*, 166–67.

14. Folbre, *Greed, Lust & Gender*, 128.

15. Weeks, *Problem with Work*, 143.

16. Folbre, *Invisible Heart*, 98–103.

17. Hennessy, *Profit and Pleasure*, 25. Hennessy further notes that women are now and have historically been defined in relation to men as "subordinate other, as (sexual) property, and as exploited laborer)," to the degree that "his control over social resources, his clear thinking, strength, and sexual prowess depend on her being less able, less rational, and never virile" (25).

18. As Hennessy argues, "Like capitalism, patriarchy is a politically urgent concept because it allows us to analyze and explain social hierarchies by which gender, sexuality, and their racial articulations are organized." Hennessy, *Profit and Pleasure*, 23.

19. Coontz, *Way We Never Were*, 145. As she argues, "In the final analysis, the entire notion of the state undermining some primordial family privacy is a myth, because the nuclear family has never existed as an autonomous, private unit except where it was the synthetic creation of outside forces" (145).

20. As Coontz argues, "Self-reliance is one of the most cherished American values, although there is some ambiguity about what the smallest self-reliant unit is. For some it is the rugged individualist; for most it is the self-sufficient family of the past, in which female nurturing sustained male independence vis-à-vis the outside world. While some people believe that the gender roles within this traditional family were unfair, and others that they were beneficial, most Americans agree that prior to federal 'interference' in the 1930s, the self-reliant family was the standard social unit of our society. Dependence used to be cared for within the 'natural family economy,' and even today the healthiest families 'stand on their own two feet.'" Coontz, *Way We Never Were*, 69.

21. C. Davis, *Company Men*, 10.

22. Fine, "Shopfloor Cultures," 1.

23. Fine, "Shopfloor Cultures," 2.

24. Greenwald and Pettigrew, "With Malice toward None and Charity for Some," 1.

25. Coontz, *Way We Never Were*, 115. As Coontz argues, "Using family as a model for public life produces an unrealistic, even destructive, definition of community" (115).
26. Cloud, "Null Persona," 186.
27. Freedman, *No Turning Back*, 166.
28. Harvey, *Spaces of Capital*, 240.
29. Hall et al., *Like a Family*, 145, 151.
30. Folbre, *Invisible Heart*, 19.
31. See, for example, Baron, *Work Engendered*; Boris, *Home to Work*; Cloud, "Rhetoric of 'Family Values,'" esp. 391–93; Hennessy, *Profit and Pleasure*, 15, 65, 232; Harvey, *Spaces of Capital*, 238; Hong, *Ruptures of American Capital*; Kwolek-Folland, *Engendering Business*; Milkman, *Gender at Work*; and Ramsay and Parker, "Gender, Bureaucracy, and Organizational Culture," 256–57.
32. Weeks, *Problem with Work*, 140–43 (quote, 141). Weeks poses a useful question for thinking about the deeper implications of social reproduction in a neoliberal context: "What happens when social reproduction is understood as the production of the forms of social cooperation on which accumulation depends, or alternatively, as the rest of life beyond work that capital seeks continually to harness to its times, spaces, rhythms, purposes, and values?" Weeks calls for a "biopolitical model of social reproduction" that fully addresses the neoliberal economic transformations of the recent past and changes the "work society" in which the neoliberal state enforces the primacy of work as a "basic obligation of citizenship" rather than an "economic necessity" (7–8).
33. Hennessy, *Profit and Pleasure*, 23.
34. Cloud, "Null Persona," 191.
35. Gibson-Graham, *End of Capitalism*, 182–83; Folbre, *Invisible Heart*, 4–5.
36. See Gibson-Graham, *End of Capitalism*; and Bergeron, "Political Economy Discourses of Globalization and Feminist Politics," 983, 996.
37. Ingraham, "Heterosexual Imaginary," 277.
38. Fine, "Shopfloor Cultures," 15.
39. Freedman, *No Turning Back*, 167.
40. Ramsay and Parker, "Gender, Bureaucracy, and Organizational Culture," 258.
41. Weeks, *Problem with Work*, 9.
42. "Seventeen Candles on Birthday Cake of Boeing Company," *Boeing News*, July 1933, 2, Boeing Historical Archives, Bellevue WA (hereafter cited as BHA). Once Westervelt moved to the East Coast, William Boeing incorporated the business in 1916 under the name Pacific Aero Products Company, which changed a year later to the Boeing Airplane Company. Boeing Historical Services, *Brief History of the Boeing Company*, 6.
43. Priscilla Kirk, interview by Esther H. Mumford, June 18, 1975, transcript, 16, Washington State Oral/Aural History Program, Accession No. BL-KNG 75-9em,

Washington State Archives, Olympia WA, on microfiche at the Center for Pacific Northwest Studies, Bellingham WA (hereafter cited as CPNS).

44. Boeing Historical Services, *Brief History of the Boeing Company*, 7; Bauer, *Boeing*, 22, 23.

45. Bilstein, *American Aerospace Industry*, 72–73.

46. Wilkinson, "Engineering Brain Drain?," 37.

47. E. N. Gott to C. A. Berlin, October 18, 1918, box 21 (copy in "Women at Boeing" box), BHA.

48. Wilkinson, "Engineering Brain Drain?," 37; Bauer, *Boeing*, 30–31; "Seventeen Candles on Birthday Cake of Boeing Company," *Boeing News*, July 1933, 2; "All in the Family," *Boeing News*, January 1939, 2.

49. Employment at the Seattle plant peaked at 31,750 in 1945. "Payroll Headcount," 1945, Annual Payroll Reports, box 5473, BHA.

50. "Payroll Headcount," 1948, Annual Payroll Reports, box 5473, BHA.

51. Mork, "Boeing Engineers, Their Union, and an Employment Crisis," 11, 15–17; "Annual Report 1954: Report to Stockholders, Year Ended December 31, 1954" (March 5, 1956), 22, file 2, box 1, Boeing Commercial Aircraft Marketing Documentation Collection, Smithsonian National Air and Space Museum Archives, Paul E. Garber Facility, Suitland, MD (hereafter cited as BCAMDC).

52. Noble, *Religion of Technology*, 224.

53. Noble, *Religion of Technology*, 224.

54. The urban growth fueled by military and defense spending, which achieved even greater heights during the Cold War, changed the relationship between western cities, industry, and the federal government. The western economy came to rely on and compete for federal funds through defense contracts while at the same time promoting individualism and local control over western resources. See McGirr, *Suburban Warriors*, 25–26, 37–38.

55. Frank Shrontz quoted in "Wilson Will Turn CEO Post over to Shrontz April 28," *Boeing News*, February 27, 1986, 1.

56. As the historian Richard Kirkendall notes, it was the funding provided by military contracts, as well as the lobbying efforts from air force and city of Seattle leaders, that made Boeing the dominant producer of commercial aircraft. Cold War fears allowed air force leaders to obtain money for bombers, and Seattle officials worked hard to draw that money into the city by obtaining federal contracts for Boeing. The security of military funding allowed Boeing leaders to gamble on commercial jets; they could afford to take bigger risks in funding commercial aircraft endeavors because their military contracts were fixed. The upshot of these efforts was that by the 1970s Boeing had achieved recognition as the "world leader" in commercial airline production. Kirkendall, "Boeing Company and the Military-Metropolitan-Industrial Complex," 148–49.

57. Serling, *Legend and Legacy*, 273-74. The SST project ended in 1971 after protests that ranged from environmental concerns about the effects of sonic booms to budgetary concerns about the cost of the program and the burden on taxpayers. The project was supposed to be the U.S. response to the French- and British-designed Concorde, although the plane was never built because, as archivists and writers employed by Boeing characterize it, the project "fell victim to adverse political pressures." Fush, *Year by Year*, 101.

58. "Boeing . . . Its People, Programs, and Products," August 1974, 11, copy in file 10, box 8, BCAMDC.

59. Thomas J. Bacher, director of international business, Boeing Commercial Airplane Company, "The Economics of the Civil Aircraft Industry," speech delivered in Singapore, September 24-25, 1981, at the Role of South East Asia in World Airline and Aerospace Development conference, 5, copy in file 7, box 13, BCAMDC. One Boeing manager observed, "Suddenly, in 1968, two-thirds of the market simply went away." J. E. Steiner, vice president-general manager, 707/727/737 Division, Boeing Company—Commercial Airline Group, "Problems and Challenges: A Path to the Future," speech delivered January 11, 1972, at the Pan American Management Club of New York, 1, copy in file 1, box 14, BCAMDC.

60. Although employment levels began to drop in October and November 1969, things got particularly bad in December 1969. One Boeing commercial division manager noted, "It was a bad Christmas for many." He recalled, "It was not until the Fall of 1969 that we realized that action beyond any we had taken in our Company's history would be necessary for survival." As the manager described it, "We studied the washrooms to make unnecessary plumbing facilities unavailable, and therefore, not subject to cleaning. We were quite ruthless in attempting to find the bottom, and in this particular case, quit scrubbing the lavatory floors until a good case of fungus appeared, and we decided that, in this one function, we had apparently found the bottom." Steiner, "Problems and Challenges," 6.

61. Boeing Historical Services, *Brief History of the Boeing Company*, 64-65.

62. "Boeing . . . Its People, Programs, and Products," August 1974, 11.

63. Greg Lange, "Billboard Reading 'Will the Last Person Leaving SEATTLE—Turn Out the Lights' Appears near Sea-Tac International Airport on April 16, 1971," HistoryLink.org Essay 1287, June 8, 1999, http://www.historylink.org/index.cfm?DisplayPage=output.cfm&file_id=1287.

64. Bacher, "Economics of the Civil Aircraft Industry," 6.

65. Steiner, "Problems and Challenges," 2. Some retirees argued that they had been forced out by age. In January 1974, for example, George Tweney wrote to Sen. Henry Jackson to ask for help. Tweney explained the direct impact of the economic downturn on his life and complained, "I was forced into early retirement by the shenanigans of The Boeing Company, where, if I could have worked just five more

years, I would have had a respectable pension." He went on to state his sense of powerlessness in the face of the power of Boeing: "If I could think of any way to meet a big corporation on equal terms, I would feel that I had some claim on the basis of having been forced into retirement because of age—and I am not the only early Boeing retiree that feels this way." George H. Tweney to Sen. Henry M. Jackson, January 25, 1974, box 9, George H. Tweney Papers, Accession No. 4558-002, University of Washington Libraries, Special Collections, Seattle WA (hereafter cited as UWLSC).

66. As Boeing involvement in the Apollo space program decreased and military contracts waned after the end of American involvement in Vietnam, company executives increasingly shifted their focus to the commercial aircraft market and the development of Boeing Commercial Aircraft Company (BCAC). Fush, *Year by Year*, 119; Boeing Historical Services, *Brief History of the Boeing Company*, 64-65. However, the company experienced a sharp decrease in sales of commercial jetliners due to rising fuel and oil prices after the Arab oil embargo of 1973. Fush, *Year by Year*, 119.

67. Of those engineers who remained, 60 percent belonged to SPEEA, or the Society of Professional Engineering Employees in Aerospace. Mork, "Boeing Engineers, Their Union, and an Employment Crisis," 2, 6.

68. By the 1960s some students had come to view engineering as too normative and strict. See, for example, William L. Carson to Mr. Swan, December 26, 1964, 1, folder: "Technical Note," box 17, Tweney Papers, Accession No. 4558-3. See also chap. 4 for a discussion of views about engineering in the 1960s.

69. Mork, "Boeing Engineers, Their Union, and an Employment Crisis," 34.

70. Mork, "Boeing Engineers, Their Union, and an Employment Crisis," 28-29.

71. The increasing bureaucracy and the transitional nature of Boeing's divisions was characteristic of the development of firms in the United States in the post-World War II period, particularly in the 1970s. These characteristics mark the growth of firms not only in the military-industrial complex but also in industry and business more broadly. As Steven High notes in his analysis of mill and factory workers in the Great Lakes region from 1969 to 1984, by the 1970s "the formalization of labour-management relations, combined with a growing number of corporate mergers and acquisitions, had further depersonalized the workplace." High, *Industrial Sunset*, 51.

72. The rhetoric of Boeing as a symbol of American capitalism succeeding without government intervention was less about a celebration of capitalism than about Boeing's competition with Europe-based Airbus, Boeing's major competitor in aircraft manufacturing in recent years. In 2003 a Washington State newspaper, the *Olympian*, summarized the history of the tensions: "Boeing advocates say Airbus benefits from major subsidies. Boeing critics say Boeing gets millions—or billions—of dollars in subsidies in the guise of defense contracts, infrastructure

improvements and tax breaks." Chris Clough, "Despite Cuts, Boeing Stays Vital to Economy," *Olympian*, September 21, 2003, 1. In the 1980s, when Airbus began to obtain more airplane contracts, Boeing leaders and government officials began to view their competition as particularly threatening. The aviation writer John Newhouse argues that, "given Airbus's apparent reliance on direct government support, American companies used to tell themselves that this oddly configured new player would be slow-moving and unable to match the standards of, say, Boeing. This line helped to breed complacency in Seattle. Boeing people didn't look beyond, or contest, their own dogma. Even now, one can hear Airbus described dismissively by some current and former Boeing staff as 'just socialism.'" Newhouse, *Boeing versus Airbus*, 9–10.

73. Barbara Minor, "Women in Engineering—for 330, It's the Place to Be," *Boeing News*, August 22, 1974, 2.

74. Susan Smith, "Women at Boeing: Their Numbers Are Thin in Top Company Positions," *Seattle Post-Intelligencer* (hereafter cited as *Seattle P-I*), June 19, 1989, A1.

75. Susan Smith, "Engineer: Emphasis on Skills," *Seattle P-I*, June 19, 1989, C4.

76. "Boeing Employees Are Featured in Film on 'Affirming the Future,'" *Boeing News*, May 13, 1988, 1.

77. Cloud, *We Are the Union*, 77.

78. Gimenez, "Dialectics of Waged and Unwaged Work," 30.

79. Greenberg et al., *Turbulence*, 128, 143.

80. Newhouse, *Boeing versus Airbus*, 29.

81. The telecommunications and entertainment industries have done better employment-wise. Microsoft and Intel, for example, added 140,000 new jobs. Moore and Lewis, *Foundations of Corporate Empire*, 273.

82. Ho, *Liquidated*, 127–28. See also Ott, *When Wall Street Met Main Street*.

83. B. Harrison and Bluestone, *Great U-Turn*, 113.

84. Folbre, *Invisible Heart*, 193.

85. Ho, *Liquidated*, 183.

86. Ho, *Liquidated*, 183; Ott, *When Wall Street Met Main Street*, 7–8.

87. Frank Shrontz, letter to Boeing employees, June 2, 1986, printed in *Boeing News*, June 6, 1986, 1.

88. Sam Howe Verhovek with Laurence Zuckerman, "Boeing, Jolting Seattle, Will Move Headquarters," *New York Times*, March 22, 2001, https://www.nytimes.com/2001/03/22/us/boeing-jolting-seattle-will-move-headquarters.html.

89. Condit stated, "We're continuing to transform our company.... Our new corporate architecture—with a leaner headquarters located separately from our major business units—is a fundamental element of our business strategy." Boeing Company, "Boeing Chooses Chicago as Center of New Corporate Architecture," news release, May 10, 2001, http://www.boeing.com/news/releases/2001/q2/news_release_010510a.html.

90. Ted C. Fishman, "Love-Struck Locales Woo Corporations," *USA Today*, April 25, 2001, 13A.

91. Jennifer Scott Cimperman, "Corporate HQ, Planet Earth: Main-Office Location Less Vital as Companies Push Global Image," *Cleveland Plain Dealer*, February 3, 2004, C1. See also Harvey, *Brief History of Neoliberalism*, 24–26.

92. Chicago and Illinois went to great lengths to snag Boeing; they offered Boeing an incentive package worth $61 million over twenty years. The package included perks such as reimbursement for moving expenses. David Roeder and Fran Speilman, "Boeing Kind of Town: Aircraft Giant Chooses City for Its New HQ," *Chicago Sun-Times*, May 11, 2001, 1.

93. Madigan quoted in Fishman, "Love-Struck Locales Woo Corporations," 13A.

94. For Boeing leaders, the company logo—centered very visibly on the side of a high-rise building in the heart of Chicago's vibrant and gentrified downtown business community—projected a global image, as well as material access to transnational networks. Chicago boasts a heavy concentration of capital; as a nexus of money and power, it provided Boeing with ample opportunities to enter a larger field of finance. Chicago's status as a global city that would enrich Boeing's resources and image is illustrative of what Saskia Sassen characterizes as a "transnational urban system," in which corporations have created networks linking cities all over the world in an effort to strengthen their financial markets. Sassen, *Cities in a World Economy*, xiii, 181. Chicago's heavy capital concentration leads Janet Abu-Lughod to define Chicago as a global city, which she characterizes as "those urban concentrations or nodes through which a disproportionate fraction of national and international interactions flow." Abu-Lughod, *New York, Chicago, Los Angeles*, 400. See also Cronon, *Nature's Metropolis*. Chicago also lays claim to a number of large corporate headquarters, such as McDonald's, Motorola, and Sears. See Kyung M. Song, "The Man Who Moved Boeing to Chicago Comes Back Home," *Seattle Times*, June 28, 2002, A1.

95. As the aviation writer John Newhouse has also pointed out, the "new Boeing" began a decade earlier in response to concerns about Boeing's future, particularly after its merger with McDonnell Douglas in 1997 and after Boeing leaders were embroiled in several very public scandals in the late 1990s and early 2000s. Newhouse, *Boeing versus Airbus*, 43, 202–16.

96. Fishman, "Love-Struck Locales Woo Corporations," 1.

97. Condit quoted in Roeder and Spielman, "Boeing Kind of Town," 2.

98. Fishman, "Love-Struck Locales Woo Corporations," 1.

99. See Cloud, *We Are the Union*, 36.

100. "Indians, Cowboys Greet Boeing 247," *Boeing News*, June 1934, 1.

101. Deloria, *Indians in Unexpected Places*, 230.

102. Bauer, *Boeing in Peace and War*, 5.

103. Carlos Schwantes argues that through the 1980s a "hinterland status" applied to the Pacific Northwest, with extractive industries such as mining and timber defining the region's image and economy. Schwantes, *Pacific Northwest*, 15.

104. Washington State Historical Society, *New Washington*, 240.

105. Bureau of Business Research, University of Washington, "The Impact of World War II Subcontracting by the Boeing Airplane Company upon Pacific Northwest Manufacturing," [n.d.], 9. Although there is no publication date, this report was probably published around 1954 or 1955 given that it was received at the University of Washington Library in 1955 and includes statistics up to 1953.

106. For an excellent study on plant relocations and labor control, see Cowie, *Capital Moves*.

107. "Boeing Has Landed," *Boston Globe*, September 6, 2001, C2; Song, "Man Who Moved Boeing to Chicago Comes Back Home," A1.

108. Locke quoted in Verhovek and Zuckerman, "Boeing, Jolting Seattle, Will Move Headquarters."

109. Quoted in Song, "Man Who Moved Boeing to Chicago Comes Back Home," A1.

110. Cranz quoted in Verhovek and Zuckerman, "Boeing, Jolting Seattle, Will Move Headquarters."

111. Blondin quoted in Verhovek and Zuckerman, "Boeing, Jolting Seattle, Will Move Headquarters."

112. Warner and Condit quoted in David Bowermaster, "'It's Just a Different Company': Transplanted Boeing Looks beyond Seattle," *Seattle Times*, September 6, 2001, C1.

113. O'Toole quoted in Verhovek and Zuckerman, "Boeing, Jolting Seattle, Will Move Headquarters."

114. Harvey, *Brief History of Neoliberalism*, 23, 42. See also Cloud, "Rhetoric of 'Family Values.'"

115. Quoted in Cimperman, "Corporate HQ, Planet Earth," C1.

116. Ho, *Liquidated*, 95.

117. Newhouse, *Boeing versus Airbus*, 24.

118. As Gimenez points out, "The 'family wage' is no longer a realistic possibility for most workers." Gimenez, "Dialectics of Waged and Unwaged Work," 30.

119. Bill Saporito, "Why Boeing Is Going to War with Its Employees," *Time*, November 19, 2013, http://business.time.com/2013/11/19/why-boeing-is-going-to-war-with-its-employees/.

120. Ralph Nader to Jim McNerney, December 26, 2013, http://nader.org/2013/12/26/letter-boeings-boss-squeezing-workers-corporate-welfare/.

121. Quoted in Dominic Gates, "DONE DEAL: 51% of Machinists Accept Boeing Contract," *Seattle Times*, January 4, 2014, A1.

122. Stapleton quoted in Gates, "DONE DEAL," A4.

123. Neal Jacobson quoted in W. J. Hennigan and Maria L. La Ganga, "Boeing Vote a Blow to Southern California," *Los Angeles Times*, January 3, 2014, http://articles.latimes.com/2014/jan/03/business/la-fi-0104-boeing-union-vote-20140104.

124. Harvey, *Brief History of Neoliberalism*, 31.

125. Cloud, "Rhetoric of 'Family Values,'" 391.

1. FRATERNALISM AND THE *BOEING NEWS*

1. "Boeing News to Publish Shop Notes," *Boeing News*, March 1932, 4.

2. "Shop Notes," *Boeing News*, April 1932, 3.

3. "Personal Notes about Our Personnel" (hereafter cited as "Personal Notes"), *Boeing News*, December 1937, 10.

4. Moccio, *Live Wire*, 22–23.

5. Moccio, *Live Wire*, 18.

6. Marchand, *Creating the Corporate Soul*, 109–14.

7. Marchand, *Creating the Corporate Soul*, 114.

8. Mandell, *Corporation as Family*, 10.

9. "From the Observer's Cockpit," *Boeing News*, November 1931, 2.

10. Bauer, *Boeing*, 91.

11. Johnson quoted in Bauer, *Boeing in Peace and War*, 66.

12. Marchand, *Creating the Corporate Soul*, 109–11.

13. "Shop Workers Vote to Organize: Plan as Yet Undecided," *Boeing News*, February 1934, 1. For works that provide insight into the history of union organizing at Boeing, see McCann, *Blood in the Water*; Orenic, *On the Ground*; and Rodden, *Fighting Machinists*.

14. Cleveland, *Boeing Trivia*, 82.

15. Ott, *When Wall Street Met Main Street*, 166. As Ott points out, the idea of an "investor democracy" has "tended to marginalize questions about the distribution of economic wealth, security, and power" (225).

16. See, for examples, "From the Observer's Cockpit," in *Boeing News*, June 1932, 1; March 1932, 2; and December 1933, 4.

17. "All in the Family," *Boeing News*, February 1939, 2.

18. "Personal Notes: Assembly Shop," *Boeing News*, February 1934, 3.

19. Mansfield, *Vision*, 86–87.

20. "Depression? Far from It!," *Boeing News*, November 1931, 1.

21. Mansfield, *Vision*, 103.

22. Boeing Historical Services, *Brief History of the Boeing Company*, 7; Bauer, *Boeing*, 22.

23. Mansfield, *Vision*, 104.

24. "Company Adopts 5-Day Week Plan," *Boeing News*, June 1933, 1. "Depression? Far from It!," *Boeing News*, November 1931, 1.

25. "$3,000,000 Spent Locally by Boeing Company Last Year," *Boeing News*, February 1934, 2.

26. Mansfield, *Vision*, 108.
27. Fush, *Year by Year*, 33–37.
28. Mansfield, *Vision*, 119.
29. Fush, *Year by Year*, 33–37; "All in the Family," *Boeing News*, January 1939, 2.
30. Mansfield, *Vision*, 118.
31. Boeing Historical Services, *Brief History of the Boeing Company*, 17. Eugene Bauer points out that Boeing did return to the company as a consultant for a brief period during World War II. See Bauer, *Boeing in Peace and War*, 77–78.
32. "An Editorial," *Seattle Times*, February 22, 1934, reprinted in *Boeing News*, March 1934, 1.
33. For a discussion of paternalism and corporate references to family, see Marchand, *Creating the Corporate Soul*, 23–26, 103–16.
34. Mansfield, *Vision*, 109.
35. McCann, *Blood in the Water*, 20–25.
36. "Personal Notes: Machine Shop," *Boeing News*, March 1933, 3.
37. "Personal Notes: Finishing Shop," *Boeing News*, August 1934, 4.
38. "Personal Notes: Finishing Shop," *Boeing News*, September 1934, 3.
39. K. L. Calkins quoted in Bauer, *Boeing in Peace and War*, 81.
40. McCann, *Blood in the Water*, 20–25.
41. McCann, *Blood in the Water*, 23–24.
42. "Shop Workers Vote to Organize; Plan as Yet Undecided," *Boeing News*, February 1934, 1.
43. "Personal Notes: Machine Shop," *Boeing News*, February 1934, 4.
44. McCann notes that the company sought to initially create a company union. McCann, *Blood in the Water*, 24.
45. McCann, *Blood in the Water*, 23.
46. Rodden, *Fighting Machinists*, 153.
47. McCann, *Blood in the Water*, 23.
48. Taylor, "Swing the Door Wide," 28.
49. McCann, *Blood in the Water*, 25.
50. Gary Cotton, "Do You Know That," *Aero Mechanic*, December 28, 1939, 6, http://cdm 9015.cdmhost.com/cdm/search.
51. "We Are Born," *Aero Mechanic*, May 12, 1939, 2, http://cdm9015.cdmhost.com/cdm /search.
52. Wayne Bryant, "Shop News," *Aero Mechanic*, May 12, 1939, 3, http://cdm9015 .cdmhost.com/cdm/search.
53. Gerry Cotton, "The President's Column," *Aero Mechanic*, May 12, 1939, 3, http://cdm 9015.cdmhost.com/cdm/search.
54. Henning, *Green-Eyed Engineer*, 98. Since 1999 SPEEA has stood for Society of Professional Engineering Employees in Aerospace, but when the group formed it was called Seattle Professional Engineering Employees Association. See Ross

Reider's entry for "SPEEA Union (Society for Professional Engineering Employees in Aerospace)," HistoryLink File #2211, http://www.historylink.org/_content /printer_friendly/pf_output.cfm?file_id=2211.

55. Henning, *Green-Eyed Engineer*, 109.

56. "Shop Notes," *Boeing News*, April 1932, 3.

57. "Personal Notes," *Boeing News*, February 1934, 3.

58. "Personal Notes," *Boeing News*, April 1933, 3.

59. "Personal Notes," *Boeing News*, March 1933, 3.

60. "Personal Notes," *Boeing News*, December 1933, 3.

61. "Personal Notes," *Boeing News*, April 1933, 3.

62. "Personal Notes," *Boeing News*, August 1934, 3.

63. "Personal Notes," *Boeing News*, November 1939, 7.

64. "Shop Dial," *Aero Mechanic*, August 18, 1939, 7, http://cdm9015.cdmhost.com/cdm /search.

65. "All in the Family," *Boeing News*, January 1939, 2.

66. See, for example, "Personal Notes: Production Control," *Boeing News*, September 1939, 7; "Personal Notes: Production Planning and Purchasing Department," *Boeing News*, October 1939, 7; "Personal Notes: Inspection Department," *Boeing News*, February 1939, 7; and "Personal Notes: Fabric and Upholstery Shop," *Boeing News*, April 1939, 8.

67. "Personal Notes," *Boeing News*, December 1939, 12.

68. "Personal Notes," *Boeing News*, May 1940, 11.

69. "Personal Notes," *Boeing News*, April 1939, 11; "Personal Notes," *Boeing News*, April 1939, 7.

70. "All in the Family," *Boeing News*, May 1938, 4.

71. "All in the Family," *Boeing News*, March 1939, 2.

72. Anonymous, "An Appeal to Ourselves," *Boeing News*, April 1939, 5.

73. "Personal Notes," *Boeing News*, June 1932, 3.

74. Personal Notes," *Boeing News*, April 1939, 7. On marriage during the Depression, see Coontz, *Marriage, a History*, 218-20.

75. "Personal Notes," *Boeing News*, November 1939, 7.

76. "Personal Notes," *Boeing News*, June 1934, 3.

77. See Kyvig, *Daily Life in the United States*, 137.

78. "Personal Notes," *Boeing News*, November 1932, 4.

79. "Personal Notes," *Boeing News*, June 1933, 3.

80. "Personal Notes," *Boeing News*, October 1939, 7.

81. "Personal Notes," *Boeing News*, November 1939, 7.

82. "Personal Notes," *Boeing News*, January 1939, 8.

83. "Personal Notes," *Boeing News*, May 1940, 11.

84. "Personal Notes," *Boeing News*, November 1939, 11.

85. "Second Generation," *Boeing News*, November 1939, 12.

86. As Roland Marchand argues, "Some corporations persisted in their penchant for company-as-family rhetoric even when the nuances of that metaphor contradicted other aspects of their desired image." Marchand, *Creating the Corporate Soul*, 105.

87. "Personal Notes," *Boeing News*, May 1938, 7.

88. "Personal Notes," *Boeing News*, September 1932, 3.

89. Canaday, *Straight State*, 133. See also Gordon, *Pitied but Not Entitled*.

90. Canaday, *Straight State*, 133.

91. Kessler-Harris, *In Pursuit of Equity*, 204.

92. Ann Stone, "Our Brief History," *Aero Mechanic*, December 28, 1939, 13, http://cdm 9015.cdmhost.com/cdm/search.

93. "The Clipperettes Goal," *Aero Mechanic*, December 28, 1939, 13, http://cdm9015 .cdmhost.com/cdm/search.

94. "Personal Notes," *Boeing News*, February 1939, 8.

95. "Introducing," *Boeing News*, February 1933, 1.

96. "Personal Notes," *Boeing News*, November 1939, 8.

97. Brandes, *American Welfare Capitalism*, 82, 148; Gitelman, *Legacy of the Ludlow Massacre*; Murphy, *Mining Cultures*.

98. Sangster, "Softball Solution," 170–72.

99. Fones-Wolf, "Industrial Recreation." The demand for increased industrial output as a result of the war allowed for an expansion of welfare capitalism. Fones-Wolf argues that while a highly fluid workforce, high turnover rates, and absenteeism undermined the influence of welfare programs organized by the unions, these same alterations in the workforce motivated employers to increase recreational and welfare opportunities and services. She further argues that many workers began to be less attracted to unions because government agencies controlled wage rates. Fones-Wolf, "Industrial Recreation," 242–44. Sanford Jacoby argues that in the period after the 1930s welfare capitalism was "modernized," meaning that workers were demanding more privileges while companies were attempting to "routinize" paternalism by offering insurance policies, for example. Jacoby, *Modern Manors*, 5. Corporate welfare work continued through World War II and the postwar period, though its continuation into the postwar period is understudied. See Mandell, *Corporation as Family*, 5.

100. "Our New Personnel Department," *Boeing News*, September 1939, 6.

101. "Ice Skaters," *Boeing News*, November 1939, 5; "Basketball Takes Interest Spotlight," *Boeing News*, September 1939, 6.

102. "Personal Notes," *Boeing News*, January 1939, 8; "Canadians Challenged," *Boeing News*, February 1939, 6.

103. "Grand Prize," *Boeing News*, November 1939, 4.

104. See, for example, the wood shop entry in "Personal Notes," *Boeing News*, October 1939, 8; and "Personal Notes," *Boeing News*, February 1940, 7.

105. "Ice Skaters," *Boeing News*, November 1939, 5.
106. "Personal Notes," *Boeing News*, February 1939, 8.
107. "Personal Notes," *Boeing News*, February 1940, 7.
108. "Personal Notes," *Boeing News*, March 1939, 7.
109. "Introducing," *Boeing News*, January 1933, 1.
110. "Introducing," *Boeing News*, July 1934, 1.
111. "Shop Veterans of Years Placed on Honor Roll List," *Boeing News*, December 1933, 1. See also "Personal Notes: Machine Shop," *Boeing News*, November 1932, 3.
112. "Introducing," *Boeing News*, April 1932, 1.
113. One example was Walter W. Way, who joined the company in 1917, worked in the company's wood shop during the "furniture days," and became a shop-floor supervisor in the assembly department in 1923. "Introducing," *Boeing News*, June 1932, 1.
114. "Corrections for Records of Shop Foremen Listed," *Boeing News*, April 1932, 3.
115. "Shop Dial," *Aero Mechanic*, August 18, 1939, 7, http://cdm9015.cdmhost.com/cdm/search.
116. Boeing's ties to UW date back to the company's earliest years. In 1916 William Boeing met with UW faculty to discuss the possibility of the university offering an aeronautics course; they even discussed the possibility of obtaining federal funding for the course. Jack Hull to W. E. Boeing, May 7, 1916, file: UW, BHA.
117. This is evident in the case of Louis S. Marsh, who in the September 1933 issue of the *Boeing News* earned the spotlight for having been on Boeing's payroll the longest. Marsh had begun working at Boeing in 1917 doing drafting work and by 1933 had been promoted to assistant chief engineer. A friend had encouraged him to apply at Boeing. The article noted that his career choice was not inspired by his time at UW: "Mr. Marsh, now with the title of assistant chief engineer, can't recall any particular kind of compelling urge which led him to the aeronautical industry. As a matter of fact, he had no thought of airplanes when he was studying mechanical engineering at the University of Washington. He more or less 'happened' into the business, that's all." "Introducing," *Boeing News*, September 1933, 1.
118. "From the Observer's Cockpit," *Boeing News*, March 1932, 3.
119. "Personal Notes," *Boeing News*, January 1939, 7.
120. "Introducing," *Boeing News*, August 1934, 1–2. See also "Introducing," *Boeing News*, December 1931, 1.
121. "Morrison Joins Boeing; Minshall, Kylstra Promoted," *Boeing News*, January 1939, 6.
122. For the role of politics and other networks that supported Boeing, see Kirkendall, "Boeing Company and the Military-Metropolitan-Industrial Complex."
123. Boeing's relationship with UW was an important part of the company's advancements in airplane manufacturing and aerospace research, and it helped company leaders navigate the boom-and-bust cycles of the postwar period. In addition to providing a steady labor force, UW also provided research. In the 1950s, for example, Boeing company leaders, University of Washington professors, and

other Seattle-area business leaders collaborated to create the Bureau of Business Research (BBR) at the University of Washington. The first study the BBR undertook was an investigation of the role of Boeing's wartime subcontracting activities on manufacturing in the Pacific Northwest. The resulting report of the BBR's findings commented that the study was "an experiment in business-education cooperation in the investigation of business and economic problems." Bureau of Business Research, University of Washington, "The Impact of World War II Subcontracting by the Boeing Airplane Company upon Pacific Northwest Manufacturing."

124. "Personal Notes," *Boeing News*, September 1934, 3.

125. For example, Phil Johnson, Boeing Company president during World War II, studied mechanical engineering at UW. Company founder William E. Boeing recruited Johnson from UW, and Johnson started with a position in the drafting department and then rose through the ranks of the company. Claire Egtvedt, who served as company president and took the position of board chair in 1939, was a student at UW while Johnson was, and he also earned a degree in mechanical engineering. Both Egtvedt and Johnson were referred to William Boeing after he requested that UW recommend for employment students from the school's mechanical engineering program. E. Eastwood to W. E. Boeing, May 29, 1917, 1; Boeing Airplane Co. to Dean Arthur Priest, June 7, 1917, both in file: UW, BHA.

126. There were several periods of overlap between the *Boeing News* and *Boeing Magazine*; the *Boeing News* stopped publication for fifteen months from 1935 to 1936 and changed to a monthly format, and then back to a weekly format in 1944. A monthly edition was retained, however, with the name *Boeing Magazine*, and in 1946 *Boeing News* shifted to "the complete job of employee information" while *Boeing Magazine* became an "external publication." Magazine editors noted that they hoped the magazine would "provide its customers and its friends throughout the ever-expanding aviation field a constant flow of readable, valid and useful information on a variety of interesting subjects." "Metamorphosis," *Boeing Magazine*, February 1946, 1.

127. *Boeing Magazine*, February 1963, 11, BHA.

128. "Personal Notes," *Boeing News*, April 1939, 9.

129. "Second Generation," *Boeing News*, February 1940, 12.

130. *Boeing News*, December 1942, 2.

131. "Shop Dial," *Aero Mechanic*, September 28, 1939, 4, http://cdm9015.cdmhost.com/cdm/search.

132. "Shop Dial," *Aero Mechanic*, July 14, 1939, 7, http://cdm9015.cdmhost.com/cdm/search.

133. Wayne Bryant, "Ideals," *Aero Mechanic*, December 28, 1939, 5, http://cdm9015.cdmhost.com/cdm/search.

134. "Shop Dial," *Aero Mechanic*, May 28, 1942, 4, http://cdm9015.cdmhost.com/cdm/search.

2. MANPOWER V. WOMANPOWER DURING WWII

1. "Boeing Craftsmen," *Boeing News*, October 1939, 12.
2. Sato, "Gender and Work in the American Aircraft Industry during World War II," 149.
3. "Easy Does It," Boeing Aircraft Company advertisement, *Life*, May 17, 1943, 63.
4. Kossoudji and Dresser, "Working Class Rosies," 432.
5. Boeing Aircraft Company, *This Is Boeing*, [n.p., n.d.], 1, copy in file 32, box 1241, BHA.
6. Bilstein, *American Aerospace Industry*, 71–72.
7. Evans, *Born for Liberty*, 201–2.
8. Sell, *Wings of Power*, 18.
9. Bilstein, *American Aerospace Industry*, 75; Boeing Historical Services, *Brief History of Boeing*, 26.
10. Fush, *Year by Year*, 45–46.
11. Sell, *Wings of Power*, 18; Fush, *Year by Year*, 47–48; "Housewarming at Plant 2," *Boeing News*, November 1940, 3.
12. K. Anderson, *Wartime Women*, 155.
13. Fush, *Year by Year*, 33–37; Boeing Aircraft Company, "Payroll Headcount," 1941, Annual Payroll Reports, box 5473, BHA; "All in the Family," *Boeing News*, January 1939, 2.
14. "Housewarming at Plant 2," *Boeing News*, November 1940, 3.
15. See Taylor, *Forging of a Black Community*, 160.
16. Melvin Phillip Winston Sr. and Klara Mae Winston, interview by Ruth Starke, January 19, 2000, transcript, 21, file: Winston, box 1, Black Heritage Society Collection, Accession number 5686-001, UWLSC.
17. Boeing Aircraft Company, "Payroll Headcount," 1941, 1942, 1945.
18. According to Fush, *Year by Year*, 46, the number of employees peaked at 46,000. See also Boeing Aircraft Company, "Payroll Headcount," 1945, which states that the highest number was 45,008.
19. Sell, *Wings of Power*, 19.
20. *Seattle P-I*, December 30, 1940; *Seattle Times*, November 10, 1940.
21. *Seattle P-I*, December 30, 1940 (West quote); *Seattle Times*, November 10, 1940.
22. Kessler-Harris, *Out to Work*, 275.
23. "The Margin Now Is Womanpower," *Fortune*, February 1943, 100. I am indebted to Sara Evans for pointing out this quotation—she also cites it in her book *Born for Liberty*, 221.
24. "Victory Gardens," *Life*, May 3, 1943, 28.
25. Evans, *Born for Liberty*, 223; K. Anderson, "Last Hired, First Fired," 84; Kessler-Harris, *Out to Work*, 279.
26. Boeing Aircraft Company, Staff Committee Minutes, October 10, 1941, 2, file 23, box 3091, BHA; May 29, 1942, 2, file 53, box 3091, BHA (hereafter cited as Staff Committee Minutes, with appropriate date and location).

27. Staff Committee Minutes, September 26, 1941, 2, file 21, box 3091, BHA.
28. Staff Committee Minutes, October 31, 1941, 2, file 25, box 3091, BHA.
29. Boeing Historical Services, *Brief History of Boeing*, 26–27.
30. Boeing Aircraft Company, "Boeing's Role in the War: A Report for the Year 1943," [n.p., n.d.], 3, Library of Congress, Washington DC.
31. *Seattle P-I*, March 28, 1942.
32. Nelson quoted in McCann, *Blood in the Water*, 53.
33. Worker quoted in *Seattle Times*, October 28, 1942.
34. Betty Russell, interview by James Hillegas, November 20, 2003, transcript, 15, Bellingham Centennial Oral History Project Records, CPNS.
35. Russell interview, 15.
36. Russell interview, 16.
37. See Coontz, *Marriage, a History*, 220–22.
38. Staff Committee Minutes, May 29, 1942, 2, file 53, box 3091, BHA.
39. "Boypower," *Life*, May 17, 1943, 45.
40. Russell interview, 16.
41. Quoted in Anne Swensson, "Boeing Has Job to Fit Nearly Everyone—And Needs All It Can Get," *Seattle Times*, October 25, 1942. The significance of the body was becoming apparent to Boeing workers; prior to the war Boeing leaders had taken for granted that company workers would not only be skilled but would also have no physical disabilities. For more discussion on the significance of the body, see Canning, "Body as Method?," 174–75.
42. Staff Committee Minutes, September 25, 1942, 1–2, file 10, box 3092, BHA.
43. Boeing Aircraft Company, "Payroll Headcount," 1943.
44. Boeing Historical Services, *Brief History of Boeing*, 27; Bilstein, *American Aerospace Industry*, 75.
45. Bilstein, *American Aerospace Industry*, 74–78.
46. Mansfield, *Vision*, 213.
47. Boeing Aircraft Company, *This Is Boeing*, 7.
48. "Woman's Place Just Like in the Home," *Boeing News*, June 1942, 8–9.
49. Boeing pointed out that its production record surpassed that of other companies in that Boeing had the greatest production efficiency in combined utilization of staffing power and facilities. Boeing Aircraft Company, "Boeing's Role in the War," 1, 4–5. The original designs and manufacturing of both the B-17 and B-29 were Boeing's, though the company acted in cooperation with other major aircraft manufacturers to produce the planes for the war effort. Boeing provided engineering and manufacturing plans to other companies, including Douglas, Lockheed, Bell, Martin, and the Fisher Body Division of General Motors. Boeing noted that its cooperative agreement with these companies represented "a new industrial relationship without precedent and without parallel example in the present war effort" (15).

50. Quoted in *Seattle Times*, October 18, 1942.
51. Margaret "Peggy" Meeker to George Hooper, October 2, 1943, in Litoff and Smith, *Since You Went Away*, 177.
52. Margaret "Peggy" Meeker to George Hooper, June 15, 1944, in Litoff and Smith, *Since You Went Away*, 179.
53. Burks quoted in Coney, "Overcoming Barriers," 11.
54. Coney, "Overcoming Barriers," 65.
55. Worker quoted in McCann, *Blood in the Water*, 59–61.
56. Quoted in *Seattle Times*, October 22, 1942.
57. Quoted in *Seattle Times*, October 22, 1942.
58. Render quoted in Coney, "Overcoming Barriers," 14.
59. For a more detailed explanation of efforts to integrate the IAM and other unions, see K. Anderson, *Wartime Women*, 55–60; McCann, *Blood in the Water*, 46–49; and Taylor, *Forging of a Black Community*, 163–67.
60. May, "Expanding the Past," 226.
61. Archie Smith, interview by Esther Mumford, March 4, 1976, transcript, 44, Oral History Transcripts, Washington State Oral/Aural History Program, Washington State Archives, Accession No. BL-KNG-75-37em, copy available on microfiche at CPNS.
62. George Alvin Scott, interview by Esther H. Mumford, December 5, 1976, transcript, 47, Oral History Transcripts, Washington State Oral/Aural History Program, Washington State Archives, Accession No. BL-KNG 76-66e, copy available on microfiche at CPNS.
63. Taylor, "Swing the Door Wide," 28.
64. Staff Committee Minutes, October 10, 1941, 2, box 3091, BHA. For a more detailed discussion of the Fair Employment Practices Committee, see Reed, *Seedtime for the Modern Civil Rights Movement*.
65. *Seattle Times*, October 14, 1941.
66. *Northwest Enterprise* (Seattle), August 25, 1943.
67. Taylor, "Swing the Door Wide," 27; LeEtta S. King to Walter White, September 6, 1940, part 13, microfilm reel 2: NAACP and Labor, 1940-55, series A, General Office File, NAACP Papers, copy at University of Washington Libraries, Seattle WA.
68. *Northwest Enterprise* (Seattle), April 26, 1940.
69. McCann, *Blood in the Water*, 47, 86; Taylor, "Swing the Door Wide," 29. Marilynn Johnson discusses suspected communist infiltration in shipyard unions and the ways in which it weakened local control of unions. See M. Johnson, *Second Gold Rush*, 81.
70. King to White, September 6, 1940, NAACP Papers.
71. Thurgood Marshall to John E. Prim, October 30, 1940; Jack Steinberg to Personnel Manager, Boeing Aircraft Company, June 28, 1941; Paul Fredrickson to Jack Steinberg, July 10, 1941; Jack Steinberg to Mark Ethridge, August 23, 1941, all in

part 13, microfilm reel 2: NAACP and Labor, 1940–55, series A, General Office File, NAACP Papers.

72. Randolph quoted in *Seattle Times*, October 14, 1941.

73. Quoted in *Northwest Enterprise*, April 6, 1942.

74. Duncan quoted in "AMU No. 751 Fails to Heed Handwriting on the Wall," *Northwest Enterprise*, April 6, 1942, also quoted in part in McCann, *Blood in the Water*, 48.

75. M. Johnson, *Second Gold Rush*, 71–72, 80–81; Self, *American Babylon*, 54–55.

76. McCann, *Blood in the Water*, 87–88.

77. *Northwest Enterprise*, June 2, September 8, 1943.

78. McCann, *Blood in the Water*, 48, 87.

79. M. Johnson, *Second Gold Rush*, 71–72, 80–81; Self, *American Babylon*, 54–55.

80. M. Johnson, *Second Gold Rush*, 81.

81. *Northwest Enterprise*, June 2, September 8, 1943.

82. *Northwest Enterprise*, June 2, 1943.

83. *Northwest Enterprise*, October 13, 1943.

84. *Northwest Enterprise*, January 5, 1944; McCann, *Blood in the Water*, 47–49.

85. Staff Committee Minutes, April 17, 1942, 2, box 3091, BHA.

86. See, for example, *Boeing News*, July 19, 1945.

87. K. Anderson, "Last Hired, First Fired," 84.

88. Taylor, *Forging of a Black Community*, 164; Staff Committee Minutes, July 15, 1943, box 3091, BHA.

89. Sato, "Gender and Work in the American Aircraft Industry during World War II," 151.

90. M. Johnson, *Second Gold Rush*, 81.

91. Coontz, *Marriage, a History*, 221.

92. Izetta Spearman Hatcher, interview by Islamah Rashid, April 28, 2001, 19, file: Hatcher, box 1, Black Heritage Society Oral History Project Transcripts, Accession number 5686-001, UWLSC. Quintard Taylor also chronicles the 1942 hiring of Spearman, though he spells her name differently; see Taylor, *Forging of a Black Community*, 164.

93. Elizabeth Dean Wells, interview by Esther H. Mumford, December 12, 1975, transcript, 29, Oral History Transcripts, Washington State Oral/Aural History Program, Washington State Archives, Accession No. BL-KNG 75-35em, copy available on microfiche at CPNS.

94. Boeing managers reported, "This shortage developed from factors beyond the control of the company, the chief factor being an established wage scale for shipyard work substantially above the established and frozen scale for aircraft work, in a limited labor area in which shipyards and aircraft building were the two main war industries, both competing for available manpower." In addition to competing with the shipyards for workers, Boeing was also competing with local businesses. Boeing Aircraft Company, "Boeing's Role in the War," 2.

95. However, D. K. MacDonald, president of the Seattle Chamber of Commerce, was concerned not only about Boeing's production but also about retaining local control: "It should be borne in mind . . . that the war department and the several other federal agencies working in conjunction with it have given Seattle management and labor an opportunity to work out their own salvation. If they don't do it, the government will step in. It is far better to chart our own course than to have it blue-printed for us by Washington, whose officials have limited knowledge of local conditions, and whose sole purpose is to recruit manpower for Flying Fortresses, no matter what the cost to private business." Quoted in *Seattle Star*, July 16, 1943.

96. The company reported, "From May to September the ever-increasing efficiency was just able to offset employee losses and further acceleration of delivery schedules was interrupted during this period." Boeing Aircraft Company, "Boeing's Role in the War," 2.

97. *Seattle P-I*, Sunday Part Two, July 25, 1943.

98. *Seattle Star*, July 16, 1943.

99. Boeing Aircraft Company, "Boeing's Role in the War," 2.

100. Boeing Aircraft Company, "Boeing's Role in the War," 8, 16.

101. *Seattle Times*, July 28, 1943.

102. Sato, "Gender and Work in the American Aircraft Industry during World War II," 160.

103. Staff Committee Minutes, January 7, 1943, 2, file 24, box 3092, BHA.

104. Staff Committee Minutes, December 17, 1942, 4, file 21, box 3092, BHA.

105. Staff Committee Minutes, February 4, 1943, 3, file 27, box 3092, BHA.

106. Staff Committee Minutes, December 17, 1942, 4-5, file 21, box 3092, BHA.

107. The seven Work Projects Administration nurseries and three private nurseries in Seattle handled only 350 children, while the Seattle Civilian War Commission reported fifteen hundred requests for child care. K. Anderson, *Wartime Women*, 125, 127.

108. Boeing Aircraft Company, *Boeing Family Day*, pamphlet in news clips: Boeing Manpower Campaign, Summer 1943, BHA (hereafter cited as *Boeing Family Day*).

109. *Boeing Family Day*.

110. Coleman, *Rosie the Riveter*, 67.

111. "Flying Fortress Fashions," *Life*, May 17, 1943, 66.

112. "After Hours," Boeing Aircraft Company advertisement, news clips: Boeing Manpower Campaign, Summer 1943, BHA.

113. Cleveland, *Boeing Trivia*, 90, 98.

114. The notice also indicated to readers, "You are now all appointed as reporters for your Aero Mechanic Woman's Page." *Aero Mechanic*, May 7, 1942, 16, http://cdm9015 .cdmhost.com/index.php.

115. K. Anderson, *Wartime Women*, 45.

116. Boris, "'You Wouldn't Want One of 'Em Dancing with Your Wife,'" 87, 89 (quote).

117. Boris, "'You Wouldn't Want One of 'Em Dancing with Your Wife,'" 81, 84 (quote).
118. Taylor, *Forging of a Black Community*, 165.
119. Duncan quoted in *Northwest Enterprise*, April 3, 1942.
120. Taylor, *Forging of a Black Community*, 159–60.
121. Clem Gallerson Sr., interview by Gwen Howard, May 6, 2000, transcript, 12, file: Gallerson; Albert J. Smith Sr., interview by Avril Madison, February 5, 2000, transcript, 26, file: Smith; Fred E. Wingo, interview by Ruth Starke, December 15, 1999, transcript, 15, 19, file: Wingo, all in box 1, Black Heritage Society, Oral History Project Transcripts, Accession No. 5686-001, UWLSC.
122. Cloud, "Null Persona," 178. See also Hall et al., *Like a Family*.
123. Kimsey quoted in *Seattle P-I*, February 19, 2002.
124. Wingo interview, 16.
125. Staff Committee Minutes, July 15, 1943, 2, file 48, box 3092, BHA; Boeing Aircraft Company, "Payroll Headcount," 1943.
126. Staff Committee Minutes, July 29, 1943, 2, file 50, box 3092, BHA; July 15, 1943, 2, file 48, box 3092, BHA.
127. Staff Committee Minutes, July 29, 1943, 2, file 50, box 3092, BHA.
128. *Seattle Times*, July 25, 1943.
129. Hardy quoted in *Seattle P-I*, July 17, 1943.
130. "Sure! We Need Women—But We Need MEN Just as Much!" Boeing Aircraft Company advertisement, copy in news clips: Misc. Clips—1943-49, BHA.
131. Serling, *Legend and Legacy*, 57.
132. *Seattle Times*, July 28, 1943.
133. Staff Committee Minutes, February 24, 1944, 2, file 77, box 3092, BHA.
134. Staff Committee Minutes, March 30, 1944, 1, file 82, box 3092, BHA.
135. Boeing Aircraft Company, "Payroll Headcount," 1944; M. Johnson, *Second Gold Rush*, 81.
136. Staff Committee Minutes, September 25, 1942, 1–2, file 10, box 3092, BHA; February 24, 1944, 2, file 77, box 3092, BHA.
137. Staff Committee Minutes, February 24, 1944, 2, file 77, box 3092, BHA.
138. Staff Committee Minutes, March 16, 1944, 2, file 80, box 3092, BHA.
139. Staff Committee Minutes, March 16, 1944, 2, file 80, box 3092, BHA.
140. "Mrs. Miniver—USA," February 1943, Boeing Aircraft Company advertisement, news clips: B-17 . . . and Misc. Clips—1943-49, BHA.
141. Staff Committee Minutes, March 16, 1944, 2, file 80, box 3092, BHA.
142. "Married Men under 38," Boeing Aircraft Company advertisement, news clips: Boeing Manpower Campaign, Summer 1943, BHA.
143. "My Mom Works at Boeing!," Boeing Aircraft Company advertisement, news clips: Boeing Manpower Campaign, Summer 1943, BHA.
144. "You Too!," Boeing Aircraft Company advertisement, news clips: Boeing Manpower Campaign, Summer 1943, BHA.

145. Honey, *Creating Rosie the Riveter*, 6.

146. Rupp, *Mobilizing Women for War*, 96.

147. Mansfield, *Vision*, 214.

148. "Ladies in Weight-ing," *Boeing Magazine*, October 1942, 2.

149. "Jitterbugs Get Audience during Renton Lunch Time Show," *Boeing News*, August 2, 1945.

150. "Now You See It," *Boeing News*, February 1, 1945.

151. Boeing Historical Services, *Brief History of the Boeing Company*, 34.

152. Boeing Aircraft Company, "Payroll Headcount," 1948.

153. Leni LaMarche, interview by Cynthia Altick, December 9, 1982, transcript, 41, tape 595-B, Washington State Jewish Archives Project, Accession No. 3452, UWLSC.

154. K. Anderson, "Last Hired, First Fired," 84, 95–97; Kossoudji and Dresser, "Working Class Rosies," 443–44; Gluck, *Rosie the Riveter Revisited*, 7–9; Kesselman, *Fleeting Opportunities*, 22; Kessler-Harris, *Out to Work*, 276–79.

155. Hellen Nelson quoted in McCann, *Blood in the Water*, 58. For further discussion of the way women viewed their wartime work, see Kesselman, *Fleeting Opportunities*, esp. 4–11.

156. Kossoudji and Dresser, "Working Class Rosies," 433–34. See also Evans, *Born for Liberty*, 229–34; and Kessler-Harris, *Fleeting Opportunities*, 286–87.

157. Sato, "Gender and Work in the American Aircraft Industry during World War II," 168.

158. Most of the focus on Boeing in the postwar years has been on the relatively swift technological transition from World War II bombers to the jet aircraft and aerospace products of the Cold War era. Scholars, aviation and aerospace historians in particular, have characterized this transition as smooth and often inevitable. See, for example, Bauer, *Boeing in Peace and War*, 165–85; Bilstein, *American Aerospace Industry*, 80–84, esp. 81; and Serling, *Legend and Legacy*, 84–120.

159. The result was a line of products that were surprisingly oriented toward the domestic. Among the designs from the "Hidden Cave" were a mobile kitchen-bathroom unit that could be installed inside a house, a left-handed eggbeater, and a mousetrap. Cleveland, *Boeing Trivia*, 77–79.

160. Rodden, *Fighting Machinists*, 154.

161. Rodden, *Fighting Machinists*, 153.

162. Findlay and Hevly, *Atomic Frontier Days*, 178–79.

163. On August 10, 1945, the *Seattle Times* declared Boeing B-17s and B-29s to be the "pride of 'industry and labor,'" as quoted in Findlay and Hevly, *Atomic Frontier Days*, 146–47. See also Findlay, *Magic Lands*; and Kirkendall, "Boeing Company and the Military-Metropolitan-Industrial Complex," 149.

164. McGirr, *Suburban Warriors*, 25–26, 37–38; Findlay, *Magic Lands*, 219.

165. Their concern for Boeing began immediately after World War II ended, when Boeing stopped producing bombers, laid off workers by the thousands, and moved

production of the B-47 to the company's plant in Wichita, Kansas, after the federal
government raised concerns about the heavy concentration of defense plants on
the West Coast. Rumors began to circulate that Boeing would move all production
to Wichita. The mayor of Seattle, along with business leaders and union officials,
lobbied Congress to keep Boeing in Seattle and protect Boeing jobs. Kirkendall,
"Boeing Company and the Military-Metropolitan-Industrial Complex," 137–39,
142–49; Taylor, *Forging of a Black Community*, 160–61, 175; Sell, *Wings of Power*,
19–22; Findlay and Hevly, *Atomic Frontier Days*, 152–55.

166. Kirkendall, building on an earlier proposal by Roger Lotchin, uses the term to
reflect the complexity of the myriad relationships of business, military, education,
and urban space in the postwar period and, in the particular case of Boeing, the
significance of the U.S. Air Force. Kirkendall, "Boeing Company and the Military-
Metropolitan-Industrial Complex," 137, 148–49.

167. United States Arms Control and Disarmament Agency (hereafter cited as USACDA),
"A Case Study of the Effects of the Dyna-Soar Contract Cancellation upon Employ-
ees of the Boeing Company in Seattle, Washington," July 1965, 23, available at the
Library of Congress, Washington DC.

168. Fishman et al., "Reemployment Experiences of Defense Workers," 23.

169. Fishman et al., "Reemployment Experiences of Defense Workers," 4.

170. Boeing's 1955 annual report, for example, noted, "The government has requested
industry to accept a larger share of the research and development burden and
to finance more of the required facilities. . . . The company is preparing to make
the largest capital expenditures in its history toward this end. The security of the
nation demands that we do so." Boeing Airplane Company, "Annual Report 1955:
Report to Stockholders, Year Ended December 31, 1955," March 5, 1956, 24, file 3,
box 1, BCAMDC.

171. Boeing's employment levels began to decline in 1958, and they "bottomed out"
in April 1960, when the Bomarc missile contract was canceled and the company
announced layoffs. By 1961 military production had increased as Boeing obtained
a $300 million contract for a Saturn booster rocket. But by 1964 things began to
look particularly bleak for Boeing when the $480 million Dyna-Soar contract was
canceled and work began to decline on the Minuteman contract. Employment
once again decreased. By February 1964 employment was at the lowest level since
August 1960, and by April of 1964 it had dropped even further, with employment
levels that had sunk to levels matching those of October 1956. USACDA, "Effects
of the Dyna-Soar Contract Cancellation," 32–38.

172. USACDA, "Effects of the Dyna-Soar Contract Cancellation," 20.

173. John Findlay notes in *Magic Lands* that "the Boeing Airplane Company was a prime
reason local leaders felt that a 'Festival of the West' was needed" (219). The fair
included buildings and rides that advertised Boeing's aerospace technology and
a company-sponsored employment booth on the fairgrounds (228).

174. Anonymous city official quoted in Rick Anderson, "What's behind Seattle Bombings?," *Seattle P-I*, May 4, 1970.
175. Cuordileone, *Manhood and American Political Culture in the Cold War*, 237. See also Dean, *Imperial Brotherhood*; and D. Johnson, *Lavender Scare*.
176. Chet Chatfield, "Women at Boeing on Equal Footing with Men," *Boeing News*, March 22, 1951.
177. *Boeing Magazine*, September 1953.
178. Broussard, "Rejected Applicant," 7.
179. The study found that "three out of every four applicants were male. Generally, the applicant applied for work in November, had neither been employed by Boeing before, nor did he have relatives working at B.A.C. [Boeing Airplane Company]. Far more likely to be a member of the white race, his birth place was North Dakota rather than any other single state or foreign country. Married, with no dependents, the applicant[']s age was between twenty-one and twenty-five, with a high school education and no previous military service. . . . Taken separately, the women applicants showed substantially the same modal characteristics as the men. In proportion to the number of female applicants, fewer were married, a far larger number had been formerly employed at Boeing and had relatives there, while only a fraction had had military service. As was to be expected, the work histories of the two groups varied considerably. . . . The small number of non-whites in the sample (6%) while differing materially from the average white applicant, did so in the direction of what is known about the general population. Their education was usually at the primary school level, their occupations most commonly unskilled, their income lower, mobility higher and the number of their dependents larger. The makeup of this population was 82% negro, 9% Japanese, 6% Filipino, 2% Chinese, 1% Hawaiian, and 1% East Indian." Broussard, "Rejected Applicant," 36–37.
180. Albert Smith interview, 45.
181. Sampson C. Valley, interview by Esther H. Mumford, May 23, 1975, transcript, 18, Oral History Transcripts, Washington State Oral/Aural History Program, Washington State Archives, Accession No. BL-KNG-75-6em, copy available on microfiche at CPNS.
182. Edward Hart Foulks, interview by Esther H. Mumford, November 4, 1975, transcript, 28, Oral History Transcripts, Washington State Oral/Aural History Program, Washington State Archives, Accession No. BL-NG 75-30em, copy available on microfiche at CPNS.
183. "Boeing had a policy, that on certain days they would hire so many minority. . . . There were certain days if you applied it wouldn't make any difference how many people they needed, you weren't going to get hired, they did have a quota system on certain days, and I just happened to hit it right." Foulks interview, 28–29.
184. Foulks interview, 28.

185. Boeing Airplane Company, "Annual Report 1954: Report to Stockholders, Year Ended December 31, 1954," 22, file 1, box 1, BCAMDC.
186. In 1962, for example, the company hosted the "Boeing Advanced Aircraft, Missile, Space and Technology Forum." *Boeing Magazine*, February 1963, 11.
187. As Sell notes, by the 1950s Boeing "had a top-drawer engineering school at the University of Washington; it had the beginnings of generations of workers whose children and grandchildren were going to grow up and work at Boeing." Sell, *Wings of Power*, 24–25.
188. Boeing Management Association, company album dated October 1965, 8, copy in file: "Boeing Management Album," box 19, Tweney Papers, Accession No. 4558-3.
189. Betty Szyperski quoted in Phyllis K. Collier, "Boeing Women and How They're Managing," *Seattle P-I*, November 2, 1980, 5.
190. Zakir Parpia, interview by Amy Bhatt, November 15, 2007, transcript, 28, South Asian Oral History Project, Accession No. 5415-001, UWLSC, copy at http://content .lib.washington.edu/cdm4/document.php?CISOROOT=/saohc&CISOPTR=40 &REC=10.
191. For more on how the Immigration and Nationality Act was related to Cold War concerns, see Borstelmann, *Cold War and the Color Line*, 194–95. For more on ideas about Asian Americans constituting "the model minority" after this wave of immigration and in affirmative action debates, see Parpia interview, 28; and MacLean, *Freedom Is Not Enough*, 258–59.
192. Many Filipino immigrants were able to apply for citizenship in the 1940s, and several describe pursuing citizenship for the opportunity to work at Boeing; see, for example, the information provided by eighteen-year Boeing employee Mariano Laigo, interview by Carolina D. Koslosky, transcript, 18–20, Accession No. FIL 75-10ckB; as well as Mr. and Mrs. Vincent Medoza, interview by Cynthia C. Mejia, transcript, 10, Accession No. FIL-KNG 76-40cm; Leonard Lagmay, transcript, Accession No. FIL-KNG 76-45dc; Genevieve Laigo transcript, 13, Accession No. FIL 75-10ck, all in Oral History Transcripts, Washington State Oral/Aural History Program, copies on microfiche at CPNS.
193. "Distribution List," July 9, 1967, attachment to Kito Kaneta to Brock Adams, letter dated July 10, 1967; Appendix I, July 9, 1967, attachment to Kito Kaneta to Federal Fair Employment Practices Commission and Brock Adams, letter dated July 10, 1967, all in file 1, box 4, Brock Adams Papers, Accession No. 1096,-2,-3,-4, UWLSC.
194. "Distribution List," July 9, 1967, attachment to Kaneta to Adams, July 10, 1967.
195. Kaneta to Adams, July 10, 1967, 1.

3. WOMEN'S PLACE IN EOE

1. Mark Jaroslaw (Boeing Archives Department), "*The Women of Boeing* Project," memo, August 22, 1989, file: Women of Boeing, box: Women, BHA.

2. Dave Olsen [*sic*] to Bob Delappe, Subject: "Debriefing on investigation for a monograph 'Women at Boeing' for our historical records," October 5, 1989, 1, file: Women of Boeing, box: Women, BHA.

3. Dave Olson, Mark Jaroslaw, and Ryan DeMares, "An Historical Abstract: The Women of Boeing, Working Partners for Four Generations," 1, file: Paris Thoughts, Box: Women, BHA.

4. Jaroslaw, "*The Women of Boeing* Project," August 22, 1989, 1.

5. Subject AA, summary of interview, transcript, 1, interview by Boeing Historical Archives Department, Spring 1989, file: Women of Boeing, box: Women, Women of Boeing Collection, BHA. (Interviews will hereafter be cited as "Subject," with appropriate letter and page number). All interviews took place in the spring of 1989 and were conducted by staff of the Boeing Historical Archives. Throughout the chapter, the emphases in the text and the words in parentheses are taken verbatim from the oral history interview transcripts. The words in brackets are words that I have added; it is not clear what the words in parentheses are in relation to the oral history interview—that is, whether they were added by the person transcribing the interview or whether they were spoken by the person being interviewed. In an effort to be accurate I have included all text directly as recorded in the oral history interview transcripts; my words in brackets usually offer a clarification or correct an obvious error.

6. Olson to Delappe, October 5, 1989, 1.

7. The "glass ceiling" is a phrase coined to reflect women's inability to reach top management positions or advance in corporate positions. Joyce Fletcher's definition is particularly useful. She argues that, in order to really understand the glass ceiling, it is necessary to look at the power dynamics that operate in the workplace. She argues that there is a "more complicated dynamic" at play than men not wanting to share power with women. Fletcher posits that it is often not overt or intentional but hidden in power dynamics that make it seem as though there are no alternative choices and that current, and dominant, ways of thinking seem unchangeable. See Fletcher, *Disappearing Acts*, 11, 16, 17.

8. Fletcher, *Disappearing Acts*, 16.

9. Greenwald and Pettigrew, "With Malice toward None and Charity for Some," 3.

10. Kessler-Harris, *In Pursuit of Equity*, 5–6. See also Boris, *Home to Work*; and Boydston, *Home and Work*.

11. Kessler-Harris, *In Pursuit of Equity*, 290.

12. Kessler-Harris, *In Pursuit of Equity*, 291.

13. Subject F, 2.

14. Subject F, 4.

15. Bailey, "'She Can Bring Home the Bacon,'" 109.

16. Zaretsky, *No Direction Home*, 12.

17. Bailey, "'She Can Bring Home the Bacon,'" 119.

18. Cowie, "'Vigorously Left, Right, and Center,'" 83.
19. Moccio, *Live Wire*, 18, 102–3.
20. Mark Jaroslaw, "The Women of Boeing: Working Partners for Four Generations," monograph chapter draft, file: Paris Thoughts, box: Women, BHA.
21. See Kessler-Harris, *In Pursuit of Equity*, 233–38.
22. Kessler-Harris, *Out to Work*, 314.
23. Barry, *Femininity in Flight*, 153. For a good discussion of Title VII, see Barry, *Femininity in Flight*, 144–73.
24. Evans, *Tidal Wave*, 137.
25. Kessler-Harris, *Out to Work*, 314–15; MacLean, *Freedom Is Not Enough*, 302.
26. MacLean, *Freedom Is Not Enough*, 302.
27. Kessler-Harris, *Out to Work*, 315.
28. Cowie, *Stayin' Alive*, 239, 240.
29. For a discussion of the difficulties women faced in trying to have the EEOC enforce its policies, see MacLean, *Freedom Is Not Enough*, esp. 70–71, 111, 123–27, 301–2.
30. MacLean, *Freedom Is Not Enough*, 112–13, 176–77.
31. MacLean, *Freedom Is Not Enough*, 219–24.
32. Stacey, *Brave New Families*, 259–60.
33. Stacey, *Brave New Families*, 260. Stacey notes, "The insecure and undemocratic character of postmodern family life fuels nostalgia for the fading modern family, now recast as the 'traditional' family. Capitalizing on this nostalgia, a vigorous, antifeminist 'profamily' movement was able to score impressive political victories in the 1980s. It successfully, if incorrectly, identified feminism as the primary cause of the demise of the modern family, rather than the mopping-up operation for postindustrial transformations that were long underway" (259).
34. Stacey, *Brave New Families*, 260.
35. Evans, *Tidal Wave*, 219.
36. See, for example, an internal company report by a Boeing EEO officer that mentions compliance: Janet Anderson, "Career Development Programs for Minorities and Females," March 1989, 2, box: Women, BHA.
37. Boeing Company, "Is Boeing an Equal Opportunity Employer?," brochure, file: Equal Rights/Affirmative Action, Equal Rights and Affirmative Action Manuscript Collection, BHA.
38. J. Anderson, "Career Development Programs for Minorities and Females," 1.
39. Sylvia Damon, "Boeing Beware!," 1970, 51, copy in box: Women, BHA.
40. See, for example, Puget Sound Women's Peace Camp, "Unity Statement," 1, file 16, box 1, Gay and Lesbian Miscellaneous Manuscripts Collection, CPNS. Another version of this statement is in *We Are Ordinary Women*.
41. "The Puget Sound Women's Peace Camp: Feminist Revolutionary Force for Change," in *We Are Ordinary Women*, 16.
42. "Unity Statement," in *We Are Ordinary Women*, 34.

43. Diana Siemens, "The Price of Working at Boeing," in *We Are Ordinary Women*, 110.
44. Wanda (no last name provided), in *We Are Ordinary Women*, 59.
45. Subject F, 4.
46. Subject F, 4.
47. Kessler-Harris, *In Pursuit of Equity*, 291.
48. Susan Smith, "Women at Boeing," A1.
49. Evans, *Tidal Wave*, 111.
50. Jaroslaw, "Women of Boeing," monograph chapter draft, 2.
51. Susan Smith, "Women at Boeing," A1.
52. J. Anderson, "Career Development Programs for Minorities and Females," 1.
53. J. Anderson, "Career Development Programs for Minorities and Females," 10.
54. Boeing Company, "Women in Industry: A National and Company Perspective on Professional Advancement," 1, file: Paris Thoughts, box: Women, BHA (hereafter cited as "Women in Industry").
55. "Women in Industry," 11, 12.
56. "Women in Industry," 1–2.
57. "Women in Industry," 9.
58. Subject I, 2.
59. Olson to Delappe, October 5, 1989, 1.
60. Subject F, 4.
61. There are a couple different versions of this report in the "Women" box at Boeing Historical Archives. One version is in the file folder marked "Paris Thoughts." The internal report appears to have gone through several drafts, and the historical record provides at least two drafts of the report. One draft contains more criticism of Boeing's past and present attitude toward women. The other is a more polished summary of past negative experiences.
62. Subject J, 2.
63. Subject B, 3.
64. Subject J, 1.
65. Subject I, 2.
66. Subject I, 1.
67. Subject F, 3.
68. "Boeing Employees Are Featured in Film on 'Affirming the Future,'" *Boeing News*, May 13, 1988, 1.
69. "Boeing Employees Are Featured in Film on 'Affirming the Future,'" *Boeing News*, May 13, 1988, 1.
70. Lorenia Smith quoted in "Boeing Employees Are Featured in Film on 'Affirming the Future,'" *Boeing News*, May 13, 1988, 1.
71. "Boeing Strikers Show Mettle, Solidarity on Picket Lines," *The Machinist*, November 1989, 1, accessed in file 11, box 1, Jackie Boschok Papers, Accession No. 5688-001, UWLSC.

72. Tom Baker, "Aeronotes," *Aero Mechanic*, December 1, 1989, 2, http://cdm 9015.cdmhost.com/cdm/search/searchterm/November%201989/mode/all/order /datea/page/2.

73. Tom Baker, "Aeronotes: 'No Money, No Airplanes,'" *Aero Mechanic*, November 11, 1989, 2, http://cdm9015.cdmhost.com/cdm/search/searchterm/November%201989 /mode/all/order/datea/page/2.

74. Dan Hunter quoted in Baker, "Aeronotes," November 11, 1989, 2.

75. Flor Angela Davila, "The Boeing Strike—Machinists' Resolve Runs in the Family— Two Generations Get Together to Face an October at Boeing," *Seattle Times*, October 13, 1995, http://community.seattletimes.nwsource.com/archive/?date =19951013&slug=2146662.

76. Timothy Egan, "Boeing Strike Halts Work on $80 Billion in Planes," *New York Times*, October 5, 1989, http://www.nytimes.com/1989/10/05/us/boeing-strike-halts -work-on-80-billion-in-planes.html.

77. Holly Martin quoted in "Boeing Strikers Show Mettle, Solidarity on Picket Lines," 1.

78. McCann, *Blood in the Water*, 181.

79. Brainard quoted in "Roundtable: Women in Engineering, Consulting Fields Break- ing New Ground, Increasing Their Numbers and Impact," *Woman Inc. Magazine*, January 23, 1989, 8–9.

80. Brainard quoted in "Roundtable," 8.

81. Phyllis K. Collier, "Boeing Women and How They're Managing," *Seattle P-I*, November 2, 1980, 5.

82. Subject E, 1.

83. Subject AA, 2.

84. Subject B, 1.

85. Subject C, 1.

86. Subject F, 2.

87. Subject I, 1.

88. Subject B, 1.

89. Subject K, 1.

90. Subject B, 2.

91. J. Anderson, "Career Development Programs for Minorities and Females," 2.

92. J. Anderson, "Career Development Programs for Minorities and Females," 3.

93. J. Anderson, "Career Development Programs for Minorities and Females," 3.

94. "Industry Must Note Changing Work Force," *Boeing News*, May 13, 1988.

95. Unidentified subject (some transcripts missing; see note on page 2 of report) quoted in Jaroslaw, "Women of Boeing Project" memo, August 22, 1989, part two, 10, under category titled, "The perception that Boeing is unequal in its treatment of employees."

96. Arneil, "Gender, Diversity, and Organizational Change," 53, 60. As Arneil's study shows, while the Girl Scouts embraced change and diversity, and attracted members

as a result, the Boy Scouts did not, and that organization came to be viewed as outdated, thus losing members. She argues that because the Boy Scouts had defined their organization narrowly, with a hierarchical organization and identity built around white heteronormativity, the organization "had little room to maneuver within its own narrowly conceived organizational identity" (59).

97. Maier, "Gender Equity, Organizational Transformation and Challenger," 944.
98. Maier, "Gender Equity, Organizational Transformation and Challenger," 945.
99. Subject J, 2.
100. Cleveland, *Boeing Trivia*, 52–53, 63.
101. Cleveland, *Boeing Trivia*, 71.
102. J. Anderson, "Career Development Programs for Minorities and Females," 3.
103. J. Anderson, "Career Development Programs for Minorities and Females," 9.
104. J. Anderson, "Career Development Programs for Minorities and Females," 4.
105. Subject K, 2.
106. Subject J, 1.
107. Subject F, 3.
108. Summary of interview, Subject E, 1.
109. Subject B, 4.
110. Subject K, 1.
111. Subject AA, 3.
112. Subject C, 4.
113. Subject E, 1.
114. Subject C, 2.
115. Subject I, 1.
116. Subject B, 2.
117. Subject K, 1.
118. Subject K, 3.
119. Subject C, 3.
120. Subject AA, 3.
121. Subject C, 2.
122. Subject E, 2.
123. "Women in Industry," 13.
124. Subject K, 2.
125. J. Anderson, "Career Development Programs for Minorities and Females," 5.
126. See, for example, the case file on Boeing employment discrimination charges in Human Rights Department Case File, Record Group: Human Rights Department, 1975–88, ID: 3805-01, Seattle Municipal Archives, Seattle WA.
127. Unnamed complainant, "Notes from case file," 5, Employment Complaint, Case No. SHR81PE236, Human Rights Department Case File, Record Series, 3805-01, Seattle Municipal Archives, Seattle WA (hereafter cited as Employment Complaint,

with appropriate case and page numbers). The names of complainants have been
withheld at the request of the Seattle Municipal Archives.

128. Employment Complaint, Case No. SHR81PE060, 1.
129. Employment Complaint, Case No. SHR81PE044, 2.
130. Subject C, 2.
131. James and Wooten, "Diversity Crises," 1116.

4. JANE DOE V. BOEING COMPANY

1. Jane Doe's real name has been withheld, as she requested anonymity in all legal
documentation. She had initially sought media coverage prior to her termination
and approached the *Seattle Times*, which did a story on her. Doe subsequently
backed away from press attention, however, choosing instead to push for anonymity, which the court granted to her in June 1986. Verbatim Report of Proceedings,
vol. 1, *Jane Doe v. Boeing Company*, January 29, 1990, 4–5, accessed at Peterson,
Young and Putra (law firm), Seattle WA (hereafter cited as PYP); Motion to Proceed
Anonymously, *Jane Doe v. Boeing Company*, June 6, 1986; Order Granting Motion
to Proceed Anonymously, *Jane Doe v. Boeing Company*, June 6, 1986, copies of
both in Add-on File #S-11174, King County Judicial Administration Records and
Research Division, Seattle WA (hereafter cited as King County Judicial Records).

2. Testimony of Jane Doe, Verbatim Report of Proceedings, vol. 3, *Jane Doe v. Boe-
ing Company*, January 31, 1990, 403, accessed at PYP; Testimony of Edwin Frank
Carlson, Verbatim Report of Proceedings, vol. 4, *Jane Doe v. Boeing Company*,
February 1, 1990, 545, accessed at PYP.

3. Testimony of Jane Doe, 404–5.

4. Deposition of Sherrill R. Marquiss, *Jane Doe v. Boeing Company*, December 6, 1989,
57, copy in Add-on Film File #S-11090, King County Judicial Records; Testimony
of Sherrill R. Marquiss, Verbatim Report of Proceedings, vol. 1, *Jane Doe v. Boeing
Company*, January 29, 1990, 52, accessed at PYP; Testimony of Geoffrey Stamper,
Verbatim Report of Proceedings, vol. 1, *Jane Doe v. Boeing Company*, January 29,
1990, 35, accessed at PYP.

5. McRuer, *Crip Theory*, 9.

6. L. Davis, "Constructing Normalcy," 13.

7. "Boeing Lays Off Person Because of Positive HTLV-III Test," in *Seattle Gay News*,
October 4, 1985, 1; "Human Rights Ruling Doesn't Stop Boeing Employee Discrimination," *Seattle Gay News*, March 6, 1987, 1.

8. "Focus: The Beagles," *Voice Northwest*, June 16, 1989, 6.

9. See, for example: Gluckman and Reed, *Homo Economics*; Hunt, *Laboring for Rights*;
Krupat and McCreery, *Out at Work*; and Raeburn, *Changing Corporate America
from Inside Out*.

10. "Knocking on the Corporate Closet Door," *GSBA News* 4, no. 6 (July 1985): 1.

11. "Knocking on the Corporate Closet Door," 1. It is also important to keep in mind, as Meyerowitz notes, that by the 1990s the transgender movement had "convinced major gay rights groups, such as the National Gay and Lesbian Task Force, to include the rights of transgendered people in their political efforts." Meyerowitz, *How Sex Changed*, 283.

12. See her analysis of the term "homonormative" and understandings of transgender identities and history in Stryker, "Transgender History, Homonormativity, and Disciplinarity," 145.

13. Deposition of Jane Doe, *Jane Doe v. Boeing Company*, December 14, 1989, 90–91, accessed in Add-on Film File #s-11090, King County Judicial Records.

14. Testimony of Geoffrey Stamper, January 29, 1990, 17–18; Deposition of Jane Doe, 87–91. Geoffrey Stamper also testified that between 1982 and 1990 there were approximately eight transsexual employees at Boeing, with about six still employed at Boeing as of 1990. Testimony of Geoffrey Stamper, Verbatim Report of Proceedings, vol. 4, *Jane Doe v. Boeing Company*, February 1, 1990, 479–80, accessed at PYP.

15. Deposition of Jane Doe, 90–91.

16. Deposition of Jane Doe, 50.

17. Deposition of Jane Doe, 90–91.

18. Testimony of Geoffrey Stamper, January 29, 1990, 17.

19. Deposition of Jane Doe, 55.

20. Deposition of Jane Doe, 55–82.

21. Testimony of Jane Doe, 410; Declaration of Jane Doe, *Jane Doe v. Boeing Company*, February 23, 1988, 3, accessed in Add-on Film File #s-14583, King County Judicial Records; Meyerowitz, *How Sex Changed*, 255; Harry Benjamin International Gender Dysphoria Association, *Standards of Care: The Hormonal and Surgical Sex Reassignment of Gender Dysphoric Persons*, 1, frame 2061, copy in Film File #s-11090, King County Judicial Records.

22. Declaration of Jane Doe, 3.

23. Burch and Sutherland, "Who's Not Yet Here?," 128.

24. See Levi and Klein, "Pursuing Protection," 80–83; Butler, "Undiagnosing Gender," 274–98; Currah, "Gender Pluralisms under the Transgender Umbrella," 12–13; and Butler, *Undoing Gender*, 7.

25. Halberstam, *Female Masculinity*, 165–66.

26. Meyerowitz, *How Sex Changed*, 12–13.

27. Testimony of Jane Doe, 470.

28. Deposition of Jane Doe, 217–18, 219.

29. Testimony of Jane Doe, 385–86.

30. Declaration of Jane Doe, 3.

31. Testimony of Jane Doe, 395–96.

32. Testimony of Edwin Frank Carlson, 549.
33. Ramsay and Parker, "Gender, Bureaucracy, and Organizational Culture," 265–66.
34. Ramsay and Parker, "Gender, Bureaucracy, and Organizational Culture," 267–68.
35. Meyerowitz, *How Sex Changed*, 241–53; Spade, "Compliance Is Gendered," 227–28, 232–33.
36. Cole and Cate, "Compulsory Gender and Transgender Existence," 285.
37. Cole and Cate, "Compulsory Gender and Transgender Existence," 284.
38. Testimony of Geoffrey Stamper, January 29, 1990, 16–17.
39. Deposition of [Wayne] Barry Noel, *Jane Doe v. Boeing Company*, December 6, 1989, 12, copy in Add-on Film File #s-11090, King County Judicial Records. The court testimony shows Noel's name as Wayne Barry Noel, but the cover page for the deposition says Barry Noel. He testified that he goes by the name Barry.
40. Deposition of [Wayne] Barry Noel, 16–17, 53.
41. Whittle, "Where Did We Go Wrong?," 199–200.
42. Deposition of Jane Doe, 99; *Jane Doe v. Boeing Company*, 121 Wn.2d 8 P.2d 531 (1993).
43. Declaration of Jane Doe, 2.
44. Testimony of Timothy J. Smith, MD, Verbatim Report of Proceedings, vol. 2, *Jane Doe v. Boeing Company*, January 30, 1990, 164, accessed at PYP; Testimony of Jane Doe, 362–63.
45. Testimony of Sherrill Marquiss, 63.
46. This transition in name and sex is striking because transgender people have struggled, and continue to struggle, to change identification records, particularly with regard to sex. Identification records remain tied to medical evidence; states that allow people to change sex identity on birth certificates require evidence of sexual reassignment surgery. At this historical moment when Jane Doe was trying to navigate the system, however, legal precedents were sparse, which meant that some individuals managed to change their identification documents with little obstruction. See Meyerowitz, *How Sex Changed*, 241–53; and Spade, "Compliance Is Gendered," 227–28, 232–33.
47. "Statement of Subject," Department of Defense interview by Special Agent Joyce Foderaro, July 12, 1985, 3, copy in Add-on Film File #s-11175, King County Judicial Records.
48. "Discipline Meeting Reconvened with [Jane Doe]," October 25, 1985, 1, Exhibit 41, in Deposition upon Oral Examination of Geoff Stamper, *Jane Doe v. Boeing Company*, December 5, 1989, accessed at PYP.
49. Testimony of Sherrill Marquiss, 51.
50. Testimony of Geoffrey Stamper, January 29, 1990, 32–33. See also Testimony of Jane Doe, 390; and Testimony of Sherrill Marquiss, 54.
51. Deposition of Jane Doe, 18–24, 27–29; Deposition of Sherrill Marquiss, 45–46; Deposition of Barry Noel, 28–33.

52. See Currah, Juang, and Minter, *Transgender Rights*, xvii.

53. Testimony of Wayne Barry Noel, Verbatim Report of Proceedings, vol. 2, *Jane Doe v. Boeing Company*, January 30, 1990, 205, accessed at PYP.

54. Deposition of Jane Doe, 28.

55. Deposition of Jane Doe, 97. Doe's struggles with regard to clothing are typical of other transgender people in places such as schools and workplaces, where gender norms are highly regulated; in schools in particular transgender students have been subjected to rigid gender-based dress codes enforced at the discretion of school administrators. See, for example, the cases in Currah, "Gender Pluralisms under the Transgender Umbrella," 7–13.

56. Deposition of Jane Doe, 27.

57. Ramsay and Parker, "Gender, Bureaucracy, and Organizational Culture," 265–67; Wendell, "Toward a Feminist Theory of Disability," 266.

58. Testimony of Sherrill Marquiss, 63–64.

59. Testimony of Geoffrey Stamper, January 29, 1990, 29.

60. Testimony of Geoffrey Stamper, January 29, 1990, 40.

61. Deposition of Jane Doe, 89.

62. Testimony of Geoffrey Stamper, January 29, 1990, 27; Testimony of Sherrill Marquiss, 64; Sherry Marquiss to M. G. Stamper, with subject: "Complaint Regarding Use of Women's Restrooms by Jane Doe," September 25, 1985, 285, copy in Film File #S-11175, King County Judicial Records.

63. Testimony of Geoffrey Stamper, January 29, 1990, 33; Corrective Action Memo, October 25, 1985, 1, signed by Robert Masters, November 7, 1985, accessed in Jane Doe case file, PYP.

64. Typed notes on Elaine DeLappe telephone call (author unknown, see Deposition of Geoffrey Stamper, 53–55), dated October 16, 1985, Exhibit 39 in Deposition of Geoffrey Stamper, *Jane Doe v. Boeing Company*, December 5, 1989, accessed in Jane Doe case file, PYP.

65. See Jacoby, *Modern Manors*, 261.

66. These characteristics mark the growth of firms not only in the military-industrial complex but also in industry and business more broadly. As Steven High notes in his analysis of mill and factory workers in the Great Lakes region from 1969 to 1984, by the 1970s "the formalization of labour-management relations, combined with a growing number of corporate mergers and acquisitions, had further depersonalized the workplace." High, *Industrial Sunset*, 51. John Newhouse points out that by the 1990s customers and workers were critiquing Boeing for being bogged down in bureaucracy. Newhouse, *Boeing versus Airbus*, 13–14.

67. Jacoby, *Modern Manors*, 263.

68. Harvey, *Brief History of Neoliberalism*, 24–26, 33.

69. Harvey, *Brief History of Neoliberalism*, 31.

70. Ross, *No-Collar*, 34–41; Hennessy, *Profit and Pleasure*, 13–14.

71. Frank Shrontz quoted in "Objectives in Adherence to Corporate Creed," *Boeing News*, March 20, 1986, 2.

72. "Referral Program Keeps It All in the Family," *Boeing News*, August 15, 1985, 1.

73. Employment figure from "Stable Employment Forecast through 1986," *Boeing News*, July 18, 1986, 1.

74. Ingrid C. Knorr, "Discipline Meeting Reconvened with [Jane Doe]," meeting notes/memo, October 25, 1985, 1, Exhibit 41 in Deposition of Geoffrey Stamper.

75. Testimony of Sherrill Marquiss, 57; Deposition of Jane Doe, 145.

76. Testimony of Jane Doe, 389.

77. Testimony of Jane Doe, 382–83.

78. Deposition of Jane Doe, 14.

79. Testimony of Sherrill Marquiss, 106.

80. Moore and Lewis, *Foundations of Corporate Empire*, 269; Bergeron, "Political Economy Discourses of Globalization and Feminist Politics," 996.

81. Robert Masters, "Meeting with Jeff [*sic*] Stamper," October 15, 1985, Exhibit 15 in Deposition of Robert Masters, *Jane Doe v. Boeing Company*, October 2, 1989.

82. Ingrid C. Knorr, "Discipline Meeting Reconvened with [Jane Doe," meeting notes/ memo, October 25, 1985, p. 2, Exhibit 41 in Deposition of Geoff Stamper.

83. Testimony of Jane Doe, 427.

84. Deposition of Jane Doe, 20.

85. Ramsay and Parker, "Gender, Bureaucracy, and Organizational Culture," 266.

86. Robert Masters, "Meeting tuesday [*sic*]," notes dated October 22, 1985, Exhibit 11 in Deposition of Robert Masters.

87. Knorr meeting notes/memo, 1.

88. Deposition of Jane Doe, 27. Doe's decision to pursue litigation against Boeing by arguing that the "diagnosis" of gender dysphoria as a "handicap" can be viewed not only as recognition of transsexual identities but also as a sign of the limitations of surrounding institutions and culture that rely on gender diagnoses.

89. Ramsay and Parker, "Gender, Bureaucracy, and Organizational Culture," 266.

90. Associated Press, "Necklace Costs Sex-Changer Job," *Spokane Chronicle*, December 12, 1985, C9.

91. Testimony of Jane Doe, 395; Deposition of Jane Doe, 75–79.

92. Gender dysphoria and gender identity disorder were formal diagnoses established by the medical profession in the early 1970s to refer to a "range of crossgender identifications that might ultimately lead to surgery." Meyerowitz, *How Sex Changed*, 254.

93. Associated Press, "Man Fired for Dressing Like a Woman Files Suit," *Spokane Spokesman-Review*, June 7, 1986, A8.

94. Meyerowitz, *How Sex Changed*, 247–48.

95. Meyerowitz, *How Sex Changed*, 274.
96. See, for example, Gluckman and Reed, *Homo Economics*; Hunt, *Laboring for Rights*; Krupat and McCreery, *Out at Work*; and Raeburn, *Changing Corporate America from Inside Out*.
97. Meyerowitz, *How Sex Changed*, 283.
98. Levi and Klein, "Pursuing Protection," 74, 90.
99. *Jane Doe v. Boeing Company*, 121 Wn.2d 8 P.2d 531 (1993).
100. Jack Hopkins, "Sex Change Worker's Appeal Upheld," *Seattle P-I*, February 11, 1992, sec. B.
101. Hon. Frederick T. Rasmussen, Judge Pro Tem, Court's Oral Decision, *Jane Doe v. Boeing Company*, Superior Court of the State of Washington, February 2, 1990, 2, accessed at PYP (hereafter cited as Court's Oral Decision).
102. Court's Oral Decision, 8. As Susan Burch and Ian Sutherland point out, "handicap" is a term fraught with controversy. See Burch and Sutherland, "Who's Not Yet Here?," 128, 137, 141.
103. Court's Oral Decision, 6.
104. Court's Oral Decision, 6–7.
105. Burch and Sutherland, "Who's Not Yet Here?," 129.
106. Court's Oral Decision, 10.
107. Court's Oral Decision, 10
108. Court's Oral Decision, 12.
109. Burch and Sutherland, "Who's Not Yet Here?," 139.
110. Declaration of Jane Doe, 3.
111. Kelby Fletcher in Testimony of Jane Doe, 350–51.
112. Hopkins, "Sex Change Worker's Appeal Upheld," 2.
113. Court's Oral Decision, 34.
114. Anonymous Boeing worker, "Critique of Boeing's Workplace Restrictions against Me," [n.d.], 3, accessed in Jane Doe file at PYP. Letters and correspondence written by this individual are marked "confidential"; the name has been withheld to respect this person's privacy.
115. Wendell, "Toward a Feminist Theory of Disability," 261.
116. See Boeing's company profile on the Human Rights Campaign website, http://w3 .hrc.org/.
117. Debra Rosenberg, "(Rethinking) Gender," *Newsweek*, May 21, 2007, 56.
118. Hennessy, *Profit and Pleasure*, 13–14.
119. Ross, *No-Collar*, 34–41.
120. Hong, *Ruptures of American Capital*, 108–15.
121. "Community Resource List," *Seattle Gay News*, January 5, 1990, 41; "Focus: The Beagles," *Voice Northwest*, June 16, 1989, 6.
122. "Focus: The Beagles," 6.

123. Jenny Kurzweil, "Shattering the Glass Closet," *Science Career Magazine*, December 5, 2008, http://sciencecareers.sciencemag.org/career_magazine/previous_issues /articles/2008_12_05/science.opms.r0800063.

124. Joe [last name omitted to preserve privacy] quoted in Cloud, *We Are the Union*, 78.

125. Connie Summers, "Administration of the Boeing Transgender Guidelines," March 2009, http://www.slideshare.net/hrcworkplace/boeing-co-hrc-innovation -award-2009-presentation-1210978.

126. Boeing began to implement guidelines for transgender employees in 2004, well after the end of the Doe case. Connie Summers, a diversity and inclusion manager at Boeing, described transgender transitions since the 1980s as a "hidden process." Summers, "Administration of the Boeing Transgender Guidelines," 3.

127. Summers, "Administration of the Boeing Transgender Guidelines," 5.

128. Marilynn Laird, telephone interview by author, January 4, 2014.

129. Marilynn Laird, email to author, January 13, 2014.

130. Laird interview.

131. See Irving, "Normalized Transgressions"; Valentine, *Imagining Transgender*, 16.

132. Bartlett, "Only Girls Wear Barrettes," 2542.

133. Laird email.

5. EMPLOYING TEAMWORK

1. Cloud, *We Are the Union*, 99.

2. Cloud, *We Are the Union*, 82.

3. See Cloud, *We Are the Union*, 83–99.

4. Cloud, *We Are the Union*, 99.

5. Cloud, *We Are the Union*, 117.

6. *Beck v. The Boeing Company*, "Summary of Settlement," 1, accessed in file 3, box 3, Boschok Papers.

7. Shirleen Holt, "Company to Pay, Change Practices to End Gender Case," *Seattle Times*, July 17, 2004, Business and Technology section, http://seattletimes.com/html /businesstechnology/2001982052_boeingsettle17.html.

8. *Beck v. The Boeing Company*, "Notice of Proposed Class Action Settlement and Fairness Hearing," accessed in file 3, box 3, Boschok Papers.

9. Shirleen Holt and David Bowermaster, "Trial Nears on Class-Action Suit Accusing Boeing of Gender Bias," *Seattle Times*, May 14, 2004, Business and Technology section, http://seattletimes.com/html/businesstechnology/2001928571_boeing14 .html.

10. Originally the suit was to be national in scope, but a judge ordered it to be broken up by states. Holt and Bowermaster, "Trial Nears on Class-Action Suit." In 2001 the court ruled that the class in the class-action suit was as follows: "Women employed at Boeing's facilities in the Puget Sound area of the State of Washington

at any time since February 25, 1997, seeking punitive damages for gender discrimination in compensation and IAM hourly overtime, and injunctive relief for gender discrimination in compensation, promotion, and IAM hourly overtime assignments." *Beck v. The Boeing Company*, "Summary of Settlement," 1.

11. Boeing Company, news release, July 16, 2004, http://www.boeing.com/news/releases/2004/q3/nr_040716a.html.

12. Holt and Bowermaster, "Trial Nears on Class-Action Suit."

13. Anderson quoted in Mike James, "White Collar Strike," *NewsHour with Jim Lehrer*, March 22, 2000, transcript, http://www.pbs.org/newshour/bb/business/jan-june00/boeing_3-22.html.

14. Cole quoted in James, "White Collar Strike."

15. Abramovitz, "Women, Social Reproduction and the Neo-Liberal Assault on the U.S. Welfare State."

16. Holt and Bowermaster, "Trial Nears on Class-Action Suit."

17. Barry, *Femininity in Flight*, chap. 6, esp. 145–53. The EEOC found itself so burdened with complaints of sex discrimination that it began to focus exclusively on class-action cases, which, as Kathleen Barry, Nancy MacLean, and Alice Kessler-Harris point out, weakened the effectiveness of the laws. Kessler-Harris, *Out to Work*, 314–15; MacLean, *Freedom Is Not Enough*, 302.

18. "751 Women's Conference: IAM WOMEN Hear Us Roar," *751 Aero Mechanic*, May 2000, 6, accessed in file 10, box 1, Boschok Papers.

19. Cloud, *We Are the Union*, 79; see also 73–79.

20. For more on intersectionality as a way to conceptualize feminism and women's empowerment, see Nash, "On Difficulty."

21. "The Slow Death of Boeing Man," *Economist*, March 16, 2000, from the print edition, accessed at http://www.economist.com/node/331030.

22. Tyrone Beason, "Never Done," *PacificNW* (in the *Seattle Times*), August 12, 2012, 12.

23. Harvey, *Brief History of Neoliberalism*, 33; Ross, *No-Collar*, 19–20.

24. See, for example, Chuck Goslin's description of Grumman in Beers, *Blue Sky Dream*, 212.

25. Ross, *No-Collar*, 34–37.

26. Hennessy, *Profit and Pleasure*, 13–14.

27. Work was reconfigured so that periods of unemployment are seen as a standard feature or norm of American capitalism, a feature the striking engineers had observed; see Ross, *No-Collar*, 8, 34–41. Corporate managers began to focus on individuality, informal work environments, and flexible work arrangements, though these characteristics did not result in less oversight, regimentation, or exploitation; see Ross, *No-Collar*, 18–19.

28. Beason, "Never Done," 10.

29. Quoted in Beason, "Never Done," 13.

30. Cloud, *We Are the Union*, 33.
31. Sanford Jacoby argues, "Far less attention was paid to the huge loss of thousands of blue-collar jobs in the late 1970s and early 1980s, a contraction that put a permanent dent in the labor market for blue-collar workers. Only in the 1990s, when professionals and managers were the ones at risk, did the politically influential middle class begin to feel threatened and the media take notice. This is not to deny the significance of the changes that occurred at firms like IBM and AT&T, but reports of the demise of career jobs have been exaggerated." Jacoby, *Modern Manors*, 260–61.
32. Jacoby, *Modern Manors*, 260.
33. "Slow Death of Boeing Man."
34. "Slow Death of Boeing Man."
35. Bergeron, "Political Economy Discourses of Globalization and Feminist Politics," 996. The phrase "globalized, turbo-charged capitalism" comes from Moore and Lewis, *Foundations of Corporate Empire*, 269.
36. Boeing Company, "Breaking Down Barriers in Aerospace Is 'Good for All of Us,'" Says Boeing," news release, June 15, 1997, http://www.boeing.com/news/releases /1997/news.release.970615a.html.
37. Newhouse, *Boeing versus Airbus*, 4.
38. Stanley Holmes, "Coverup at Boeing?," *BusinessWeek*, June 28, 2004, http://www .businessweek.com/magazine/content/04_26/b3889088.htm.
39. Noble, *America by Design*, 311–12.
40. Michelle Dunlop, "SPEEA's Influence Has Grown since 2000 Strike," *HeraldNet* (*Everett Herald* online), September 23, 2010, Business section, http://www.heraldnet .com/article/20100923/BIZ/709239947.
41. "Slow Death of Boeing Man."
42. Ron Wanttaja, "The Boeing Strike: A Report from the Trenches," *AVweb*, February 12, 2000, http://www.avweb.com/news/atis/181947-1.html.
43. Rodino-Colocino, "Geek Jeremiads," 29.
44. Rodino-Colocino, "Geek Jeremiads," 37–38.
45. Mork, "Boeing Engineers, Their Union, and an Employment Crisis," 37.
46. Mork, "Boeing Engineers, Their Union, and an Employment Crisis," 11.
47. Wanttaja, "Boeing Strike."
48. "Slow Death of Boeing Man."
49. Newhouse describes Wilson as a "vivid, dominating, sure-handed leader" and notes that, after Wilson left, Boeing started to decline. Newhouse, *Boeing versus Airbus*, 5.
50. According to George Kau, quoted in Serling, *Legend and Legacy*, 449.
51. Jusela quoted in Serling, *Legend and Legacy*, 444.
52. Shrontz quoted in Serling, *Legend and Legacy*, 446.
53. See Cloud, *We Are the Union*, 36–37.

54. Cloud, *We Are the Union*, 36.

55. Condit quoted in James, "White Collar Strike."

56. James, "White Collar Strike."

57. "Slow Death of Boeing Man."

58. Quoted in Mark A. Moshay, "SPEEA Strike Was One Day at a Time—for 40 Days," *SPEEA Newsletter*, March 3, 2001, accessed at http://www.speea.org/publications /files/archivenews/News_2001/News_03-03-01.html#story1.

59. Condit quoted in James, "White Collar Strike."

60. Ross Reider, "SPEEA Union," March 20, 2000, HistoryLink.org Essay 2211, http:// www.historylink.org/index.cfm?DisplayPage=output.cfm&File_Id=2211.

61. Cloud, *We Are the Union*, 37.

62. Wanttaja, "Boeing Strike." See also Cloud, *We Are the Union*, 36–37.

63. Stanley Holmes, "Mcdonnell Douglas—Boeing's Big Gulp," *Seattle Times*, August 3, 1997, http://community.seattletimes.nwsource.com/archive/?date=19970803&slug =2552924.

64. Quoted in James, "White Collar Strike."

65. Boeing Company, "Boeing and SPEEA Reach Strike Settlement Agreement," press release, March 17, 2000, http://www.boeing.com/news/releases/2000/news _release_000317b.html.

66. In 1986, for example, Lodge 751 obtained a full union-shop agreement. McCann, *Blood in the Water*, 189.

67. Wanttaja, "Boeing Strike."

68. Levi quoted in Dunlop, "SPEEA's Influence Has Grown since 2000 Strike."

69. "Boeing Machinists Back Historic White-Collar Strike," *IAM Journal*, May–June 2000, 19, accessed in file 15, box 1, Boschok Papers.

70. Wanttaja, "Boeing Strike."

71. Sergeant quoted in Kyung M. Song, "Boeing's 'Brains' Showing Brawn," *Seattle Times*, February 10, 2000, http://community.seattletimes.nwsource.com/archive/?date =20000210&slug=4004087.

72. Wanttaja, "Boeing Strike."

73. Mulally quoted in Boeing Company news release, March 5, 2000, http://www.boeing .com/news/releases/2000/news_release_000305a.html.

74. Wanttaja, "Boeing Strike."

75. Levi quoted in Dunlop, "SPEEA's Influence Has Grown since 2000 Strike."

76. District Lodge 751 represented 26,500 Puget Sound–area Boeing employees in 2001. "IAM Launches Massive Organizing Drive at Boeing's Disenfranchised," *IAM Journal*, Summer 2001, accessed in file 15, box 1, Boschok Papers. SPEEA membership stood at around 26,000. "Boeing Machinists Strike Back Historic White-Collar Strike," 19.

77. Quotes from "IAM Launches Massive Organizing Drive at Boeing's Disen franchised."

78. Rodino-Colocino, "Geek Jeremiads," 37–38.

79. "751 Women's Conference," 6.

80. "Working Women 2000: Give Gore a Rousing Send-Off," *IAM Journal*, May–June 2000, file 15, box 1, Boschok Papers.

81. Stanley Holmes, "A Pattern of Discrimination at Boeing?," *BusinessWeek*, April 27, 2004, http://www.businessweek.com/bwdaily/dnflash/apr2004/nf20040426 _1818_db016.htm.

82. Boeing Company, "Boeing Settlement of Lawsuits Alleging Racial Discrimination Approved," news release, September 30, 1999, http://www.boeing.com/news /releases/1999/news_release_990930b.html.

83. *Beck v. The Boeing Company*, "Notice of Proposed Class Action Settlement and Fairness Hearing," file 3, box 3, Boschok Papers.

84. See Stanley Holmes, "A New Black Eye for Boeing?," *BusinessWeek*, April 26, 2004, http://www.businessweek.com/magazine/content/04_17/b3880112.htm; and Holmes, "Pattern of Discrimination at Boeing?"

85. Subject F, 2.

86. Subject K, 1.

87. Subject C, 2.

88. Subject K, 3.

89. Quoted in Holmes, "New Black Eye for Boeing?"

90. Anderson quoted in Holt and Bowermaster, "Trial Nears on Class-Action Suit."

91. Quoted in Holt and Bowermaster, "Trial Nears on Class-Action Suit."

92. Holmes, "Pattern of Discrimination at Boeing?"

93. Holt and Bowermaster, "Trial Nears on Class-Action Suit."

94. Marcella Fleming quoted in Holmes, "New Black Eye for Boeing?"

95. Quoted in Holmes, "New Black Eye for Boeing?"

96. Holt and Bowermaster, "Trial Nears on Class-Action Suit."

97. *Beck v. The Boeing Company*, "Summary of Settlement," 4, file 3, box 3, Boschok Papers.

98. Holt and Bowermaster, "Trial Nears on Class-Action Suit."

99. Marcella Fleming quoted in Holmes, "New Black Eye for Boeing?"

100. Holt and Bowermaster, "Trial Nears on Class-Action Suit."

101. Quoted in Holmes, "New Black Eye for Boeing?"

102. Holt and Bowermaster, "Trial Nears on Class-Action Suit."

103. Boeing paid $4.5 million to settle the Labor Department investigation. Holmes, "New Black Eye for Boeing?"

104. Holt and Bowermaster, "Trial Nears on Class-Action Suit."

105. *Beck v. The Boeing Company*, "Summary of Settlement," 4, 6.

106. "Boeing vigorously denied the allegations, but wrongfully withheld for years, according to the Court, documents pertinent to plaintiffs' claims. . . . Nearly a million pages of documents were produced, there were over 250 depositions,

and more than 90 motions were filed with the Court. Copies of the briefing and exhibits on the motions occupy approximately 31 feet of shelf space. The case settled only after the Court ordered Boeing to produce evidence the Court found Boeing should have provided to plaintiffs years earlier." *Beck v. The Boeing Company*, "Summary of Settlement," 1.

107. *Beck v. The Boeing Company*, "Summary of Settlement," 1.
108. Renae Merle, "Boeing Settle Sex-Bias Suit," *Washington Post*, July 17, 2004, E01, http://www.washingtonpost.com/wp-dyn/articles/a56624-2004jul16.html.
109. *Beck v. The Boeing Company*, "Summary of Settlement," 6.
110. Holmes, "Coverup at Boeing?"
111. Quoted in "Boeing to Pay $72.5 Million to Settle Sex-Discrimination Lawsuit," KOMO News, last updated August 31, 2006, http://www.komotv.com/news/archive /4169196.html.
112. Ken Mercer quoted in Shirleen Holt, "Boeing Wins Ethnic-Bias Case," *Seattle Times*, June 3, 2004, http://seattletimes.com/html/businesstechnology/2001945817 _boeingcase03.html.
113. Both quoted in Greenberg et al., *Turbulence*, 141.
114. As Roland Marchand notes, "The idea of family was also more compatible with the hierarchical image of the company. It conveyed a more paternalistic concern for the welfare of subordinates than did the notion of a team." Marchand, *Creating the Corporate Soul*, 107.
115. Verhovek, *Jet Age*, 201.
116. Christine Hauser, "Boeing Board Ousts Chief, Citing Relationship with Executive," *New York Times*, March 7, 2005, http://www.nytimes.com/2005/03/07/business /07cnd-boei.html.
117. Newhouse, *Boeing versus Airbus*, 210–11.
118. Newhouse, *Boeing versus Airbus*, 24.
119. Cloud, *We Are the Union*, 36.
120. "Boeing's Frontiers Magazine Gets Wider Audience," *Seattle Times*, March 9, 2012, http://seattletimes.com/html/businesstechnology/2017708240_boeingfrontiers 10.html.
121. Newhouse, *Boeing versus Airbus*, 15.
122. Jacoby, *Modern Manors*, 261.
123. See, for example, Andrew Ross's examination of Razorfish, a high-tech company based in New York, in Ross, *No-Collar*.
124. Anne Slater, interview by Gillian Murphy, December 12, 2000, 6, WTO History Project, copy in WTO Seattle Collection, Accession No. 5177-3, UWLSC (hereafter cited as WTO History Project), available at http://depts.washington.edu/wtohist/interviews /Slater.pdf.
125. Kevin Danaher, interview by Miguel Bocanegra, February 15, 2000, 6, WTO History Project, available at http://depts.washington.edu/wtohist/interviews/Danaher.pdf.

126. Amy Laly, interview by Amy Bhatt, September 20, 2007, transcript, 17, South Asian Oral History Project, Accession No. 5415-001, UWLSC, copy available at http://content.lib.washington.edu/cdm4/document.php?CISOROOT=/saohc &CISOPTR=59&REC=1.

127. Newhouse, for example, argues that "Boeing's homogeneity contrasts sharply with Airbus, a collection of forty or so nationalities and, one is told, no sense of hierarchy." Newhouse characterizes Boeing as possessing a "monoculture." Newhouse, *Boeing versus Airbus*, 16.

128. "Boeing 2002 Contract Negotiations: Jobs and Job Security," *IAM Journal*, Summer 2002, 10–11, accessed in file 6, box 1, Boschok Papers.

129. Gloria Millsaps and Susan Palmer, memo to Dick Schneider, April 23, 2002, file 15, box 9, Boschok Papers.

CONCLUSION

1. Nikki Haley, "Obama's Silence on Boeing Is Unacceptable," *Wall Street Journal*, April 29, 2011, http://online.wsj.com/articles/SB100014240527487037781045762872 90266016016.

2. Tom Wroblewski, "Report from the President: Members Are the Fundamental Operating Engine of Boeing," *751 Aero Mechanic*, November 2009, 2, accessed in file 1, box 1, Boschok Papers.

3. Laird email.

4. Greenberg et al., *Turbulence*, 11.

5. Jon Talton, "Boeing and the Race to the Bottom," *Seattle Times*, September 6, 2012, Business and Technology section, http://seattletimes.com/html/soundeconomywith jontalton/2019082417_boeing_and_the_race_to_the_bot.html.

6. Goforth quoted in Dominic Gates, "Bitter Tone in Boeing Talks with Engineers," *Seattle Times*, September 6, 2012, A1.

7. Jackie Micucci, "Now Hiring! Where the Jobs Are in Seattle," *Seattle*, February 2014, 75.

8. Romano, "Not Dead Yet," 36. Romano also notes, "I also have concerns about my inability to construct a historical narrative with any sense of finality, because the events I research are still ongoing and their effects are not yet clear" (24). See also 37–38 in "Not Dead Yet" for her discussion of recent histories that are distinguished by a "lack of closure."

9. Abramovitz, "Women, Social Reproduction and the Neo-Liberal Assault on the U.S. Welfare State," 41, 44.

10. Robbins, *Great Northwest*, 2.

11. Robbins, *Great Northwest*, 2, 5.

12. Tracey quoted in Wilkinson, "Engineering Brain Drain?," 32–33.

13. Denton quoted in Wilkinson, "Engineering Brain Drain?," 39.

14. Lavender quoted in Wilkinson, "Engineering Brain Drain?," 38.

15. Limb quoted in Wilkinson, "Engineering Brain Drain?," 39.
16. Wilkinson, "Engineering Brain Drain?," 39.
17. Shirleen Holt, "Bias Lawsuit Recalls Pain of Ex-Boeing Workers," *Seattle Times*, July 5, 2004, http://seattletimes.com/html/businesstechnology/2001972196_boeing women05.html.
18. Steve Wilhelm, "In a Man's World, 3 Women Run Boeing Jet Plants," June 22, 2012, *Puget Sound Business Journal*, http://www.bizjournals.com/seattle/news/2012 /06/22/in-a-mans-world-3-women-run-boeing.html?page=all.
19. Davidson, "Graduating to a Pay Gap."
20. Quoted in Lornet Turnbull, "Boeing Undecided about Pension Survivor Benefits for Gay Spouse," *Seattle Times*, November 25, 2012, http://seattletimes.com/html /localnews/2019765521_gaymarriageboeing.html.
21. Colbert quoted in Aubrey Cohen, "Colbert Lauds Boeing's 'Refreshing Denial of Human Dignity,'" *Seattle p-i*, November 30, 2012, http://www.seattlepi.com /business/boeing/article/Colbert-lauds-Boeing-s-refreshing-denial-of-4081406 .php.
22. Dominic Holden, "Boeing Agrees to Provide Equal Pension Benefits to Married Gay Couples," The Stranger, January 17, 2013, http://slog.thestranger.com/slog/archives /2013/01/17/boeing-agrees-to-provide-equal-pension-benefits-to-married-gay -couples.
23. Kessler-Harris, *In Pursuit of Equity*, 295–96.
24. Kessler-Harris, *In Pursuit of Equity*, 296.
25. Greenberg et al., *Turbulence*, 129.

BIBLIOGRAPHY

ARCHIVES AND MANUSCRIPTS
Boeing Historical Archives, Bellevue WA (BHA).
Anderson, Janet K. "Career Development Programs for Minorities and Females." Boeing Report, March 1989. Box: Women.
Annual Payroll Reports. Box 5473.
Boeing Aircraft Company. Advertisements. News clips: B-17, B-29, C-97, B-50, XB-47, 377 Stratocruiser and miscellany, Boeing Manpower Campaign (1943).
Boeing Aircraft Company. *Building with Boeing* [ca. 1945]. File 28, box 2971.
Boeing Aircraft Company. Equal Opportunity Manuscript Collection. File: "Jobs Now Program."
Boeing Aircraft Company. "Boeing's Role in the War: A Report for the Year 1943." [N.d.] Library of Congress, Washington DC.
Boeing Aircraft Company. Staff Committee Minutes, 1941–44.
Boeing Aircraft Company. *This Is Boeing.* File 32, box 1241.
Boeing Company. Employee Orientation Manuscript Collection. File: Employee Orientation.
Boeing Company. Equal Rights and Affirmative Action Manuscript Collection. File: Equal Rights/Affirmative Action.
Boeing Company. News releases. Available at http://www.boeing.com/news /releases.
Boeing Company. "Women in Industry: A National and Company Perspective on Professional Advancement." Report [ca. 1989]. File: Paris Thoughts. Box: Women.
Boeing Magazine (formerly *Boeing News*).
Boeing News. Also available at Library of Congress, Washington DC.
Oral History Interview Transcripts. Files: Women of Boeing and Paris Thoughts. Box: Women.

"Women of Boeing" project. Memos, correspondence, abstracts, and chapter
draft. Files: Women of Boeing and Paris Thoughts. Box: Women.

Boeing Commercial Aircraft Marketing Documentation Collection. Smithsonian National
Air and Space Museum Archives, Paul E. Garber Facility, Suitland, MD (BCAMDC).
Annual reports, speeches, and miscellaneous reports.

Bureau of Business Research, University of Washington. "The Impact of World War II
Subcontracting by the Boeing Airplane Company upon Pacific Northwest Manufacturing." [N.d.] Copy available at Library of Congress, Washington DC.

Center for Pacific Northwest Studies. Western Washington University, Bellingham
WA (CPNS).

Bellingham Centennial Oral History Project Records.

Gay and Lesbian Miscellaneous Manuscripts Collection.

Oral History Transcripts (microfiche copy), from Washington State Oral/Aural
History Program, Washington State Archives, Olympia WA.

Fishman, Leslie, Jay Allen, Byron Bunger, and Curt Eaton. "Reemployment Experiences
of Defense Workers: A Statistical Analysis of the Boeing, Martine, and Republic
Layoffs: ACDA/E-113." Prepared for the U.S. Arms Control and Disarmament
Agency. December 1968. Copy at University of Washington Libraries, Seattle WA.

Human Rights Department Case File. Record Group: Human Rights Department,
1975–88, ID: 3805-01. Seattle Municipal Archives, Seattle WA.

Jane Doe v. Boeing Company. 121 Wn.2d 8 P.2d 531 (1993).

Jane Doe v. Boeing Company. Case file, briefs, evidence, trial transcript, and deposition
transcripts. Peterson, Putra, and Young law firm (PYP), Seattle WA.

King County Judicial Administration, Records and Research Division, Seattle WA.

Harry Benjamin International Gender Dysphoria Association. *Standards of Care:
The Hormonal and Surgical Sex Reassignment of Gender Dysphoric Persons,*
frame 2061, 1. Add-on Film File #S-11090.

Jane Doe v. Boeing Company. Case file, briefs, evidence, trial transcript, and deposition transcripts. Microfilm Files #S-11174, #S-11090, and #S-14583.

NAACP Papers. Part 13: NAACP and Labor, 1940–55. Microfilm reel 2. Copy at University
of Washington Libraries, Seattle WA.

United States Arms Control and Disarmament Agency (USACDA). "A Case Study of
the Effects of the Dyna-Soar Contract Cancellation upon Employees of the Boeing
Company in Seattle, Washington." July 1965. Library of Congress, Washington DC.

University of Washington Libraries, Special Collections, Seattle WA (UWLSC).

Adams, Brock. Personal papers, letters, and political correspondence.

Black Heritage Society Oral History Project. Transcripts.

Boschok, Jackie. Personal papers, letters, and employment documents.

South Asian Oral History Project. Oral History Interview Transcripts.

Tweney, George H. Papers.

Washington State Jewish Archives Project.

WTO History Project. Oral History Interview Transcripts.

PUBLISHED SOURCES

Abramovitz, Mimi. "Women, Social Reproduction and the Neo-Liberal Assault on the U.S. Welfare State." In *The Legal Tender of Gender: Law, Welfare, and the Regulation of Women's Poverty*, edited by Dorothy Chunn and Shelley P. Gavigan, 15–46. Oxford: Hart Publishing, 2010. Available at http://www.hunter.cuny.edu/socwork/faculty /Abramovitz,%20%20social%20reprod%20&Neoliberalism%28%20onati%29 .pdf.

Abu-Lughod, Janet L. *New York, Chicago, Los Angeles: America's Global Cities*. Minneapolis: University of Minnesota Press, 1999.

Anderson, Karen. "Last Hired, First Fired: Black Women Workers during World War II." *Journal of American History* 69, no. 1 (June 1982): 82–97.

———. *Wartime Women: Sex Roles, Family Relations, and the Status of Women during World War II*. Westport CT: Greenwood Press, 1981.

Armitage, Susan. "Tied to Other Lives: Women in Pacific Northwest History." In *Women in Pacific Northwest History: An Anthology*, edited by Karen J. Blair, 5–24. Rev. ed. Seattle: University of Washington Press, 2001.

Arneil, Barbara. "Gender, Diversity, and Organizational Change: The Boy Scouts vs. Girl Scouts of America." *Perspectives on Politics* 8, no. 1 (March 2010): 53–68.

Bacevich, Andrew. *The Limits of Power: The End of American Exceptionalism*. New York: Metropolitan Books, 2008.

———. *The New American Militarism: How Americans Are Seduced by War*. Oxford: Oxford University Press, 2005.

———. *Washington Rules: America's Path to Permanent War*. New York: Metropolitan Books, 2010.

Bailey, Beth. "'She Can Bring Home the Bacon': Negotiating Gender in Seventies America." In *America in the Seventies*, edited by Beth Bailey and David Farber, 107–28. Lawrence: University Press of Kansas, 2004.

Baron, Ava, ed. *Work Engendered: Toward a New History of American Labor*. Ithaca NY: Cornell University Press, 1991.

Barry, Kathleen M. *Femininity in Flight: A History of Flight Attendants*. Durham: Duke University Press, 2007.

Bartlett, Katharine T. "Only Girls Wear Barrettes: Dress and Appearance Standards, Community Norms, and Workplace Equality." *Michigan Law Review* 92, no. 8 (August 1994): 2541–82.

Bauer, Eugene E. *Boeing in Peace and War*. Enumclaw WA: TABA Publishing, 2000.

———. *Boeing: The First Century*. Enumclaw WA: TABA Publishing, 1991.

Bederman, Gail. *Manliness and Civilization: A Cultural History of Gender and Race in the United States, 1880-1917.* Chicago: University of Chicago Press, 1995.

Beers, David. *Blue Sky Dream: A Memoir of America's Fall from Grace.* San Diego: Harcourt Brace, 1996.

Benson, Susan Porter. *Counter Cultures: Saleswomen, Managers, and Customers in American Department Stores, 1890-1940.* Urbana: University of Illinois Press, 1988.

Bergeron, Suzanne. "Political Economy Discourses of Globalization and Feminist Politics." *Signs* 26, no. 4 (Summer 2001): 983-1006.

Bilstein, Roger E. *The American Aerospace Industry: From Workshop to Global Enterprise.* New York: Twayne, 1996.

Blair, Karen. "The State of Research on Pacific Northwest Women." *Frontiers: A Journal of Women Studies* 22, no. 3 (2001): 48-56.

——, ed. *Women in Pacific Northwest History: An Anthology.* Rev. ed. Seattle: University of Washington Press, 2001.

Boeing Historical Services. *A Brief History of the Boeing Company.* Seattle: Boeing Historical Services, 1998.

Boris, Eileen. *Home to Work: Motherhood and Industrial Politics in the United States.* Cambridge: Cambridge University Press, 1994.

——. "'You Wouldn't Want One of 'Em Dancing with Your Wife': Racialized Bodies on the Job in World War II." *American Quarterly* 50, no. 1 (March 1998): 77-108.

Borstelmann, Thomas. *The Cold War and the Color Line: American Race Relations in the Global Arena.* Cambridge MA: Harvard University Press, 2001.

Boydston, Jeanne. *Home and Work: Housework, Wages, and the Ideology of Labor in the Early Republic.* Oxford: Oxford University Press, 1994.

Brandes, Stuart D. *American Welfare Capitalism, 1880-1940.* Chicago: University of Chicago Press, 1970.

Breazeale, Kenon. "In Spite of Women: *Esquire* Magazine and the Construction of the Male Consumer." *Signs* 20, no. 1 (Autumn 1994): 1-22.

Broussard, John A. "The Rejected Applicant: A Study of the Unsuccessful Factory Job Seeker." MA thesis, University of Washington, 1951.

Burch, Susan, and Ian Sutherland. "Who's Not Yet Here? American Disability History." *Radical History Review*, no. 94 (Winter 2006): 127-47.

Butler, Judith. "Undiagnosing Gender." In *Transgender Rights*, edited by Paisley Currah, Richard M. Juang, and Shannon Price Minter, 274-98. Minneapolis: University of Minnesota Press, 2006.

——. *Undoing Gender.* New York: Routledge, 2004.

Canaday, Margot. "Building a Straight State: Sexuality and Social Citizenship under the 1944 G.I. Bill." *Journal of American History* 90, no. 3 (December 2003): 935-56.

——. *The Straight State: Sexuality and Citizenship in Twentieth-Century America.* Princeton: Princeton University Press, 2009.

Canning, Kathleen. "The Body as Method? Reflections on the Place of the Body in Gender History." In *Gender History in Practice: Historical Perspectives on Bodies, Class, and Citizenship*, 168–89. Ithaca NY: Cornell University Press, 2006.

Chandler, Alfred. *The Invisible Hand: The Managerial Revolution in American Business*. Cambridge MA: Harvard University Press, 1977.

Cleveland, Carl M. *Boeing Trivia: Unique Characters, Amusing Anecdotes, and Rare Humor Mark Boeing History over the Years*. Seattle: CMC Books, 1989.

Cloud, Dana L. "The Null Persona: Race and the Rhetoric of Silence in the Uprising of '34." *Rhetoric & Public Affairs* 2, no. 2 (1999): 177–209.

———. "The Rhetoric of 'Family Values': Scapegoating, Utopia, and the Privatization of Social Responsibility." *Western Journal of Communication* 62, no. 4 (Fall 1998): 387–419.

———. *We Are the Union: Democratic Unionism and Dissent at Boeing*. Urbana: University of Illinois Press, 2011.

Cobble, Dorothy Sue. "Recapturing Working-Class Feminism: Union Women in the Postwar Era." In *Not June Cleaver: Women and Gender in Postwar America, 1945–1960*, edited by Joanne Meyerowitz, 84–102. Philadelphia: Temple University Press, 1994.

Cole, C. L., and Shannon L. C. Cate. "Compulsory Gender and Transgender Existence: Adrienne Rich's Queer Possibility." *Women's Studies Quarterly* 36 (Fall–Winter 2008): 279–87.

Coleman, Penny. *Rosie the Riveter: Women Working on the Home Front in World War II*. New York: Crown, 1995.

Coney, Cheryl M. "Overcoming Barriers: Black Women at Boeing." MA thesis, University of Washington Tacoma, 2013. http://digitalcommons.tacoma.uw.edu/cgi/view content.cgi?article=1015&context=ias_masters.

Coontz, Stephanie. *Marriage, a History: How Love Conquered Marriage*. Seattle: Penguin Books, 2005.

———. *The Way We Never Were: American Families and the Nostalgia Trap*. New York: Basic Books, 1992.

Cowie, Jefferson. *Capital Moves: RCA's Seventy-Year Quest for Cheap Labor*. New York: New Press, 1999.

———. *Stayin' Alive: The 1970s and the Last Days of the Working Class*. New York: New Press, 2010.

———. "'Vigorously Left, Right, and Center': The Crosscurrent of Working-Class America in the 1970s." In *America in the Seventies*, edited by Beth Bailey and David Farber, 75–106. Lawrence: University Press of Kansas, 2004.

Cronon, William. *Nature's Metropolis: Chicago and the Great West*. New York: Norton, 1992.

Cuordileone, K. A. *Manhood and American Political Culture in the Cold War*. New York: Routledge, 2005.

Currah, Paisley. "Gender Pluralisms under the Transgender Umbrella." In *Transgender Rights*, edited by Paisley Currah, Richard M. Juang, and Shannon Price Minter, 3-31. Minneapolis: University of Minnesota Press, 2006.

———, Richard M. Juang, and Shannon Price Minter, eds. *Transgender Rights*. Minneapolis: University of Minnesota Press, 2006.

Davidson, Renee. "Graduating to a Pay Gap." *Outlook: Magazine of the AAUW* 107, no. 1 (Winter 2013): 8-11.

Davis, Clark. *Company Men: White-Collar Life and Corporate Cultures in Los Angeles, 1892-1941*. Baltimore: Johns Hopkins University Press, 2000.

Davis, Lennard. "Constructing Normalcy: The Bell Curve, the Novel, and the Invention of the Disabled Body in the Nineteenth Century." In *The Disability Studies Reader*, edited by Lennard J. Davis, 3-16. New York: Routledge, 1997.

Dean, Robert D. *Imperial Brotherhood: Gender and the Making of Cold War Foreign Policy*. Amherst: University of Massachusetts Press, 2001.

Deloria, Philip J. *Indians in Unexpected Places*. Lawrence: University Press of Kansas, 2006.

Dowd Hall, Jacquelyn, James Leloudis, Robert Korstad, Mary Murphy, Lu Ann Jones, and Christopher B. Daly. *Like a Family: The Making of a Southern Cotton Mill World*. Chapel Hill: University of North Carolina Press, 1987.

Evans, Sara. *Born for Liberty: A History of Women in America*. New York: Free Press, 1989.

———. *Tidal Wave: How Women Changed America at Century's End*. New York: Free Press, 2003.

Findlay, John M. *Magic Lands: Western Cityscapes and American Culture after 1940*. Berkeley: University of California Press, 1992.

———, and Bruce Hevly. *Atomic Frontier Days: Hanford and the American West*. Seattle: Center for the Study of the Pacific Northwest in association with the University of Washington Press, 2011.

Fine, Gary Alan. "Shopfloor Cultures: The Idioculture of Production in Operational Meteorology." *Sociological Quarterly* 47, no. 1 (Winter 2006): 1-19.

Fletcher, Joyce. *Disappearing Acts: Gender, Power, and Relational Practice at Work*. Cambridge MA: MIT Press, 1999.

Folbre, Nancy. *Greed, Lust, and Gender: A History of Economic Ideas*. Oxford: Oxford University Press, 2009.

———. *The Invisible Heart: Economics and Family Values*. New York: New Press, 2001.

Fones-Wolf, Elizabeth. "Industrial Recreation, the Second World War, and the Revival of Welfare Capitalism, 1934-1960." *Business History Review* 60, no. 2 (1986): 232-57.

Foucault, Michel. *The History of Sexuality: An Introduction, Volume I*, translated by Robert Hurley. New York: Vintage Books, 1990.

Freedman, Estelle. *No Turning Back: The History of Feminism and the Future of Women*. New York: Ballantine Books, 2002.

Freeman, Carla. *High Tech and High Heels in the Global Economy: Women, Work, and Pink-Collar Identities in the Caribbean*. Durham: Duke University Press, 2000.

Fush, Lisa, ed. *Year By Year: 75 Years of Boeing History, 1916–1991*. Seattle: Boeing Historical Archives, November 1991.

Gelber, Steven. *Hobbies: Leisure and the Culture of Work in America*. New York: Columbia University Press, 1999.

Geisst, Charles R. *Wall Street: A History*. Oxford: Oxford University Press, 1997.

Gibson-Graham, J. K. *The End of Capitalism (as We Knew It): A Feminist Critique of Political Economy*. Malden MA: Blackwell, 1996.

Gimenez, Martha E. "The Dialectics of Waged and Unwaged Work: Waged Work, Domestic Labor and Household Survival in the United States." In *Work without Wages: Comparative Studies of Domestic Labor and Self-Employment*, edited by Jane L. Collins and Martha Gimenez, 25–45. Albany: State University of New York Press, 1990.

Gitelman, H. M. *Legacy of the Ludlow Massacre: A Chapter in American Industrial Relations*. Philadelphia: University of Pennsylvania Press, 1988.

Gluck, Sherna Berger. *Rosie the Riveter Revisited: Women, the War, and Social Change*. Boston: Twayne, 1987.

Gluckman, Amy, and Betsy Reed, eds. *Homo Economics: Capitalism, Community, and Lesbian and Gay Life*. New York: Routledge, 1997.

Gordon, Linda. *Pitied but Not Entitled: Single Mothers and the History of Welfare*. New York: Free Press, 1994.

Greenberg, Edward S., Leon Gunberg, Sarah Moore, and Patricia B. Sikora. *Turbulence: Boeing and the State of American Workers and Managers*. New Haven: Yale University Press, 2010.

Greenwald, Anthony G., and Thomas Pettigrew. "With Malice toward None and Charity for Some: Ingroup Favoritism Enables Discrimination." *American Psychologist* (2014). doi:10.1037/a0036056.

Grewal, Inderpal, and Caren Kaplan. "Global Identities: Theorizing Transnational Studies of Sexuality." GLQ 7, no. 4 (2001): 663–79.

Halberstam, Judith. *Female Masculinity*. Durham: Duke University Press, 1998.

Harrison, Bennett, and Barry Bluestone. *The Great U-Turn: Corporate Restructuring and the Polarizing of America*. New York: Basic Books, 1988.

Harrison, Penny, ed. *Open Spaces: Voices from the Northwest*. Seattle: University of Washington Press, 2011.

Hartmann, Susan. *The Home Front and Beyond: American Women in the 1940s*. Boston: Twayne, 1982.

———. "Women's Employment and the Domestic Ideal in the Early Cold War Years." In *Not June Cleaver: Women and Gender in Postwar America, 1945–1960*, edited by Joanne Meyerowitz, 84–102. Philadelphia: Temple University Press, 1994.

Harvey, David. *A Brief History of Neoliberalism*. Oxford: Oxford University Press, 2005.

———. *Spaces of Capital: Towards a Critical Geography*. New York: Routledge, 2001.

Hennessy, Rosemary. *Profit and Pleasure: Sexual Identities in Late Capitalism*. New York: Routledge, 2000.

Henning, Richard A. *The Green-Eyed Engineer.* N.p.: Emerald City Graphics, 1988.

Hevly, Bruce, and John M. Findlay, eds. *The Atomic West.* Seattle: University of Washington Press, 1998.

High, Steven. *Industrial Sunset: The Making of North America's Rust Belt, 1969-1984.* Toronto: University of Toronto Press, 2003.

Ho, Karen. *Liquidated: An Ethnography of Wall Street.* Durham: Duke University Press, 2009.

Honey, Maureen. *Creating Rosie the Riveter: Class, Gender, and Propaganda during World War II.* Amherst: University of Massachusetts Press, 1984.

Hong, Grace Kyunwon. *The Ruptures of American Capital: Women of Color Feminism and the Culture of Immigrant Labor.* Minneapolis: University of Minnesota Press, 2006.

Hunt, Gerald, ed. *Laboring for Rights: Unions and Sexual Diversity across Nations.* Philadelphia: Temple University Press, 1999.

Ingraham, Chrys. "The Heterosexual Imaginary: Feminist Sociology and Theories of Gender." In *Materialist Feminism: A Reader in Class, Difference, and Women's Lives,* edited by Rosemary Hennessy and Chrys Ingraham, 275-90. New York: Routledge, 1997.

Irving, Dan. "Normalized Transgressions: Legitimizing the Transsexual Body as Productive." *Radical History Review,* no. 100 (Winter 2008): 38-59.

Jacobs, Margaret. "Getting Out of a Rut: Decolonizing Western Women's History." *Pacific Historical Review* 79, no. 4 (2010): 585-604.

———. "Western History: What's Gender Got to Do with It?" *Western Historical Quarterly* 42 (Autumn 2011): 297-304.

Jacoby, Sanford M. *Modern Manors: Welfare Capitalism since the New Deal.* Princeton: Princeton University Press, 1997.

James, Erika Hayes, and Lynn Perry Wooten. "Diversity Crises: How Firms Manage Discrimination Lawsuits." *Academy of Management Journal* 49, no. 6 (December 2006): 1103-18.

Johnson, David K. *The Lavender Scare: The Cold War Persecution of Gays and Lesbians in the Federal Government.* Chicago: University of Chicago Press, 2003.

Johnson, Marilynn. *The Second Gold Rush: Oakland and the East Bay in World War II.* Berkeley: University of California Press, 1993.

Johnson, Susan Lee. "Nail This to Your Door: A Disputation on the Power, Efficacy, and Indulgent Delusion of Western Scholarship That Neglects the Challenge of Gender and Women's History." *Pacific Historical Review* 79, no. 4 (2010): 605-17.

Katz, Jonathan Ned. "The Invention of Heterosexuality." *Socialist Review* 20, no. 1 (1990): 7-33.

Kerber, Linda, Nancy F. Cott, Robert Gross, Lynn Hunt, Carroll Smith-Rosenberg, and Christine M. Stansell. "Beyond Roles, Beyond Spheres: Thinking about Gender in the Early Republic." *William and Mary Quarterly,* 3rd ser., 46, no. 3 (July 1989): 565-85.

Kesselman, Amy. *Fleeting Opportunities: Women Shipyard Workers in Portland and Vancouver during World War II and Reconversion.* Albany: State University of New York Press, 1990.

Kessler-Harris, Alice. *In Pursuit of Equity: Women, Men, and the Quest for Economic Citizenship in 20th-Century America.* New York: Oxford University Press, 2001.

———. *Out to Work: A History of Wage-Earning Women in the United States.* 20th anniversary ed. Oxford: Oxford University Press, 2003.

Kirkendall, Richard. "The Boeing Company and the Military-Metropolitan-Industrial Complex, 1945–1953." *Pacific Northwest Quarterly* 85, no. 4 (October 1994): 137–49.

Kocka, Jürgen. *White Collar Workers in America, 1890–1940: A Social Political History in International Perspective.* Beverly Hills CA: Sage, 1980.

Kossoudji, Sherrie A., and Laura J. Dresser. "Working Class Rosies: Women Industrial Workers during World War II." *Journal of Economic History* 52, no. 2 (1992): 431–46.

Krupat, Kitty, and Patrick McCreery, eds. *Out at Work: Building a Gay-Labor Alliance.* Minneapolis: University of Minnesota Press, 2001.

Kunda, Gideon. *Engineering Culture: Control and Commitment in a High-Tech Corporation.* Philadelphia: Temple University Press, 1992.

Kwolek-Folland, Angel. *Engendering Business: Men and Women in the Corporate Office, 1870–1930.* Baltimore: Johns Hopkins University Press, 1994.

———. "Gender, Self, and Work in the Life Insurance Industry, 1880–1930." In *Work Engendered: Toward a New History of American Labor,* edited by Ava Baron, 168–90. Ithaca NY: Cornell University Press, 1991.

Kyvig, David. *Daily Life in the United States, 1920–1940: How Americans Lived through the Roaring Twenties and the Great Depression.* Chicago: Ivan R. Dee, 2004.

Lange, Greg. "Billboard Reading 'Will the Last Person Leaving SEATTLE—Turn Out the Lights' Appears near Sea-Tac International Airport on April 16, 1971." HistoryLink.org Essay 1287, June 8, 1999. http://www.historylink.org/index.cfm ?DisplayPage=output.cfm&file_id=1287.

Levi, Jennifer L., and Bennett H. Klein. "Pursuing Protection." In *Transgender Rights,* edited by Paisley Currah, Richard M. Juang, and Shannon Price Minter, 74–92. Minneapolis: University of Minnesota Press, 2006.

Lewchuck, Wayne A. "Men and Monotony: Fraternalism as a Managerial Strategy at the Ford Motor Company." *Journal of Economic History* 53, no. 4 (December 1993): 824–56.

Litoff, Judy Barrett, and David C. Smith, eds. *Since You Went Away: World War II Letters from American Women on the Home Front.* Lawrence: University Press of Kansas, 1991.

MacLean, Nancy. *Freedom Is Not Enough: The Opening of the American Workplace.* New York: Russell Sage Foundation, 2006.

Maier, Mark. "Gender Equity, Organizational Transformation and Challenger." *Journal of Business Ethics* 16, no. 9 (June 1997): 943–62.

Mandell, Nikki. *The Corporation as Family: The Gendering of Corporate Welfare, 1890-1930*. Chapel Hill: University of North Carolina Press, 2002.

Mansfield, Harold. *Vision: A Saga of the Sky*. New York: Duell, Sloan, and Pearce, 1956.

Marchand, Roland. *Creating the Corporate Soul: The Rise of Public Relations and Corporate Imagery in American Big Business*. Berkeley: University of California Press, 1998.

May, Elaine Tyler. "Expanding the Past: Recent Scholarship on Women in Politics and Work." *Reviews in American History* 10, no. 4 (December 1982): 216-33.

——. *Homeward Bound: American Families in the Cold War Era*. New York: Basic Books, 1999.

McCann, John. *Blood in the Water: A History of District Lodge 751, International Association of Machinists and Aerospace Workers*. Seattle: District Lodge 751, IAM&AW, 1989.

McGirr, Lisa. *Suburban Warriors: The Origins of the New American Right*. Princeton: Princeton University Press, 2001.

McRuer, Robert. *Crip Theory: Cultural Signs of Queerness and Disability*. New York: New York University Press, 2006.

Meyer, Leisa. *Creating G.I. Jane: Sexuality and Power in the Women's Army Corps during World War II*. New York: Columbia University Press, 1996.

Meyer, Steve. "Rough Manhood: The Aggressive and Confrontational Shop Culture of U.S. Auto Workers during World War II." *Journal of Social History* 36, no. 1 (2002): 125-47.

Meyerowitz, Joanne. *How Sex Changed: A History of Transsexuality in the United States*. Cambridge MA: Harvard University Press, 2002.

——, ed. *Not June Cleaver: Women and Gender in Postwar America, 1945-1960*. Philadelphia: Temple University Press, 1994.

Milkman, Ruth. *Gender at Work: The Dynamics of Job Segregation by Sex during World War II*. Urbana: University of Illinois Press, 1987.

Moccio, Francine A. *Live Wire: Women and Brotherhood in the Electrical Industry*. Philadelphia: Temple University Press, 2009.

Moore, Karl, and David Lewis. *Foundations of Corporate Empire: Is History Repeating Itself?* London: Pearson Education, 2000.

Mork, Bruce. "Boeing Engineers, Their Union, and an Employment Crisis." MA thesis, University of Washington, 1972.

Murphy, Mary. *Mining Cultures: Men, Women, and Leisure in Butte, 1914-1941*. Urbana: University of Illinois Press, 1997.

Nash, Jennifer. "On Difficulty: Intersectionality as Feminist Labor." *Scholar & Feminist Online* 8, no. 3 (Summer 2010). http://sfonline.barnard.edu/polyphonic/nash_03 .htm.

Newhouse, John. *Boeing versus Airbus: The Inside Story of the Greatest International Competition in Business*. New York: Knopf, 2007.

Noble, David. *America by Design: Science, Technology, and the Rise of Corporate Capitalism*. Oxford: Oxford University Press, 1977.

———. *The Religion of Technology: The Divinity of Man and the Spirit of Invention.* New York: Penguin Books, 1997.

Ong, Aihwa. *Flexible Citizenship: The Cultural Logics of Transnationality.* Durham: Duke University Press, 1999.

———. *Spirits of Resistance and Capitalist Discipline: Factory Women in Malaysia.* Albany: State University of New York Press, 1987.

Orenic, Liesel Miller. *On the Ground: Labor Struggle in the American Airline Industry.* Urbana: University of Illinois Press, 2009.

Ott, Julia. *When Wall Street Met Main Street: Quest for an Investors' Democracy.* Cambridge MA: Harvard University Press, 2011.

Pierce, Jennifer. *Gender Trials: Emotional Lives in Contemporary Law Firms.* Berkeley: University of California Press, 1995.

Raeburn, Nicole C. *Changing Corporate America from Inside Out: Lesbian and Gay Workplace Rights.* Minneapolis: University of Minnesota Press, 2004.

Ramsay, Karen, and Martin Parker. "Gender, Bureaucracy, and Organizational Culture." In *Gender and Bureaucracy*, edited Mike Savage and Anne Witz, 253–76. Oxford: Blackwell/Sociological Review, 1992.

Raynolds, Laura. "New Plantations, New Workers: Gender and Production Politics in the Dominican Republic." *Gender and Society* 15, no. 1 (February 2001): 7–28.

Reed, Merl E. *Seedtime for the Modern Civil Rights Movement: The President's Committee on Fair Employment Practice, 1941–1946.* Baton Rouge: Louisiana State University Press, 1991.

Robbins, William G. *The Great Northwest: The Search for Regional Identity.* Corvallis: Oregon State University Press, 2001.

Robinson, Sally. *Marked Men: White Masculinity in Crisis.* New York: Columbia University Press, 2000.

Rodden, Robert G. *The Fighting Machinists: A Century of Struggle.* Washington DC: Kelly Press, 1984.

Rodino-Colocino, Michelle. "Geek Jeremiads: Speaking the Crisis of Job Loss by Opposing Offshored and H-1B Labor." *Communication and Critical/Cultural Studies* 9, no. 1 (March 2012): 22–46.

Roediger, David R. *The Wages of Whiteness: Race and the Making of the American Working Class.* London: Verso, 1991.

Romano, Renee C. "Not Dead Yet: My Identity Crisis as a Historian of the Recent Past." In *Doing Recent History: On Privacy, Copyright, Video Games, Institutional Review Boards, Activist Scholarship, and History That Talks Back*, edited by Claire Bond Potter and Renee C. Romano, 23–44. Athens: University of Georgia Press, 2012.

Ross, Andrew. *No-Collar: The Humane Workplace and Its Hidden Costs.* Philadelphia: Temple University Press, 2003.

Rung, Margaret C. *Servants of the State: Managing Diversity & Democracy in the Federal Workforce, 1933–1953.* Athens: University of Georgia Press, 2002.

Rupp, Leila J. *Mobilizing Women for War: German and American Propaganda*. Princeton: Princeton University Press, 1978.

Sangster, Joan. "The Softball Solution: Female Workers, Male Managers and the Operation of Paternalism at Westclox, 1923–60." *Labour/Le Travail* 32 (Fall 1993): 167–99.

Sassen, Saskia. *Cities in a World Economy*. 2nd ed. Thousand Oaks CA: Pine Forge Press, 2000.

———. *The Global City: New York, London, Tokyo*. Princeton: Princeton University Press, 1991.

Sato, Chitose. "Gender and Work in the American Aircraft Industry during World War II." *Japanese Journal of American Studies*, no. 11 (2000): 147–72.

Schwantes, Carlos. *The Pacific Northwest: An Interpretive History*. Lincoln: University of Nebraska Press, 2000.

Scott, Joan Wallach. *Gender and the Politics of History*. New York: Columbia University Press, 1999.

Self, Robert O. *American Babylon: Race and the Struggle for Postwar Oakland*. Princeton: Princeton University Press, 2003.

Sell, T. M. *Wings of Power: Boeing and the Politics of Growth in the Northwest*. Seattle: University of Washington Press, 2001.

Serling, Robert. *Legend and Legacy: The Story of Boeing and Its People*. New York: St. Martin's Press, 1992.

Smith, Vicki. *Managing in the Corporate Interest. Control and Resistance in an American Bank*. Berkeley: University of California Press, 1990.

Spade, Dean. "Compliance Is Gendered: Struggling for Gender Self-Determination in a Hostile Economy." In *Transgender Rights*, edited by Paisley Currah, Richard M. Juang, and Shannon Price Minter, 217–41. Minneapolis: University of Minnesota Press, 2006.

Spechler, Jay W. *Reasonable Accommodation: Profitable Compliance with the Americans with Disabilities Act*. Delray Beach FL: St. Lucie Press, 1996.

Stacey, Judith. *Brave New Families: Stories of Domestic Upheaval in Late Twentieth Century America*. New York: Basic Books, 1991.

Stryker, Susan. "Transgender History, Homonormativity, and Disciplinarity." *Radical History Review*, no. 100 (Winter 2008): 145–57.

———, and Stephen Whittle, eds. *The Transgender Studies Reader*. New York: Routledge, 2006.

Taylor, Quintard. *The Forging of a Black Community: Seattle's Central District from 1870 through the Civil Rights Era*. Seattle: University of Washington Press, 1994.

———. "Swing the Door Wide: World War II Wrought a Profound Transformation in Seattle's Black Community." *Columbia: The Magazine of Northwest History* 9, no. 2 (Summer 1995): 26–32.

Tinsman, Heidi. *Partners in Conflict: The Politics of Gender, Sexuality, and Labor in the Chilean Agrarian Reform, 1950–1973*. Durham: Duke University Press, 2002.

Valentine, David. *Imagining Transgender: An Ethnography of a Category.* Durham: Duke University Press, 2007.

———. "We're 'Not about Gender': The Uses of 'Transgender.'" In *Out in Theory: The Emergence of Lesbian and Gay Anthropology,* edited by Ellen Lewin and William Leap, 222–45. Urbana: University of Illinois Press, 2002.

Vander Meulen, Jacob. Review of *The American Aerospace Industry: From Workshop to Global Enterprise,* by Roger E. Bilstein. *Technology and Culture* 39, no. 3 (July 1998): 589–91.

Verhovek, Sam Howe. *Jet Age: The Comet, the 707, and the Race to Shrink the World.* New York: Penguin, 2010.

Warner, Michael, ed. *Fear of a Queer Planet: Queer Politics and Social Theory.* Minneapolis: University of Minnesota Press, 1993.

Washington State Historical Society. *The New Washington: A Guide to the Evergreen State.* Portland OR: Binford & Mort, 1950.

We Are Ordinary Women: A Chronicle of the Puget Sound Women's Peace Camp. Seattle: Seal Press, 1985.

Weeks, Kathi. *The Problem with Work: Feminism, Marxism, Antiwork Politics, and Postwork Imaginaries.* Durham: Duke University Press, 2011.

Wendell, Susan. "Toward a Feminist Theory of Disability." In *The Disability Studies Reader,* edited by Lennard J. Davis, 260–78. New York: Routledge, 1997.

Whittle, Stephen. "Where Did We Go Wrong? Feminism and Trans Theory—Two Teams on the Same Side?" In *The Transgender Studies Reader,* edited by Susan Stryker and Stephen Whittle, 194–202. New York: Routledge, 2006.

Wilkinson, Louise. "Engineering Brain Drain?" *Boeing Frontiers,* December 2007. http://www.boeing.com/news/frontiers/archive/2007/december/ts_sf08.pdf.

Zaretsky, Natasha. *No Direction Home: The American Family and the Fear of National Decline, 1968–1980.* Chapel Hill: University of North Carolina Press, 2007.

Zunz, Oliver. *Making America Corporate, 1870–1920.* Chicago: University of Chicago Press, 1990.

INDEX

workforce counts. *See* employment
 counts
workforce diversification. *See*
 diversification
workforce participation rates, 99
workforce stability, 2, 6–7, 32, 34–36, 41–
 43, 167, 177–78, 186
work permit system, 73–74
work week standard, 32
World's Fair of 1962, 89–90, 215–16n173
World Trade Organization (wto),
 180–81

World War I, Boeing during, 10–11
World War II: overview of Boeing
 during, xi, xv, 11–12, 54–55, 57–59;
 production and workforce growth
 during, 59–70, 75, 209n49, 212n96;
 recruitment during, 82–87
Wroblewski, Tom, 184

Yamashita, Laura, 174
Young, Russ, 147–48

Zaretsky, Natasha, 99